Human Resource Management 'With Chinese Characteristics'

Five years into World Trade Organization membership, how is China's system of people-management adapting to the changing world? This edited book provides an up-to-date, state-of-the-art overview of current theory and practice of human resource management, 'with Chinese characteristics'. The latter is a phrase used to refer to the specific cultural, institutional and social setting in which such management structures and processes are to be found in the 'Middle Kingdom'. As the People's Republic of China becomes inexorably linked to the international economy and increasingly faces the challenges of globalization, its enterprises and their managers have to adapt to pressures to conform to external human resources and employment norms, whilst at the same time conforming to internal labour laws and socio-political demands. The tension between these two sets of factors provides an arena in which human resource managers, as well as workers, have to cope, perform and survive. The papers included in this collection are all based on empirical on-site research by specialists in the field. They deal with such HRM-related topics are expatriates, family demands, human capital, joint ventures, labour disputes, organizational commitment, psychological contracts, social networks, work behaviour and the like. The authors of the papers covered in the book come from a variety of backgrounds and university affiliations in Canada, Finland, Hong Kong, Macau, People's Republic of China, South Korea, Taiwan, United Kingdom and United States of America.

Malcolm Warner is at the Judge Business School, University of Cambridge, Cambridge, UK.

Human Resource Management 'With Chinese Characteristics'

Facing the challenges of globalization

Edited by
Malcolm Warner

Routledge
Taylor & Francis Group

LONDON AND NEW YORK

First published 2009 by Routledge
2 Park Square, Milton Park, Abingdon, Oxon, OX14 4RN

Simultaneously published in the USA and Canada by Routledge
270 Madison Avenue, New York, NY 10016

Routledge is an imprint of the Taylor & Francis Group, an informa business

Typeset in Times 10/12pt by Alden Multimedia, Northampton, UK
Printed and bound in Great Britain by MPG Books Ltd, Bodmin, Cornwall

British Library Cataloguing in Publication Data
A catalogue record for this book is available from the British Library

ISBN 10: 0-415-45766-1
ISBN 13: 978-0-415-45766-8

CONTENTS

List of Contributors

James B. Avey is at the College of Business, Central Washington University, Washington, DC, USA.

Ingmar Björkman is at the HANKEN, Swedish School of Economics, Helsinki, Finland.

Pawan Budhwar is at the Aston Business School, Aston University, Birmingham, UK.

Jaepil Choi is at the Department of Management of Organizations, Hong Kong University of Science and Technology, Hong Kong SAR, People's Republic of China.

Chris W. L. Chu is at Aston Business School, Aston University, Birmingham, UK.

Helen De Cieri is at the Department of Management, Monash University, Victoria, Australia.

Rachel Clapp-Smith is at the College of Business Administration, University of Nebraska-Lincoln, Lincoln, NE, USA.

Brian Cooper is at the Department of Management, Monash University, Victoria, Australia.

Jos Gamble is at the School of Management, Royal Holloway, University of London, London, UK.

Qihai Huang is at the Business School, Manchester Metropolitan University, Manchester, UK.

Ji Li is at the School of Business, Hong Kong Baptist University, Hong Kong SAR, People's Republic of China.

Weixing Li is at the College of Business Administration, University of Nebraska-Lincoln, Lincoln, NE, USA.

Yi Li is at the Business School, Shanghai University, Shanghai, People's Republic of China.

Stacy Liao is at the School of Business, Hong Kong Baptist University, Hong Kong SAR, People's Republic of China.

Fred Luthans is at the College of Business Administration, University of Nebraska-Lincoln, Lincoln, NE, USA.

Gongming Qian is at the Faculty of Business Administration, The Chinese University of Hong Kong, Hong Kong SAR, People's Republic of China.

Maria Rotundo is at the Joseph L. Rotman School of Management, University of Toronto, Toronto, Ontario, Canada.

Steven X. Si is at the Bsuiness School, Shanghai University, Shanghai, People's Republic of China and Department of Management, Bloomsburg University of Pennsylvania, Pennsylvania, PA, USA.

Adam Smale is at the Faculty of Business Studies, University of Vaasa, Finland.

Jennie Sumelius is at the HANKEN, Swedish School of Economics, Helsinki, Finland.

S. Bruce Thomson is at the Department of Management, Monash University, Victoria, Australia.

Sheng Wang is at the Department of Management, University of Nevada, Las Vegas, NE, USA.

Yingyan Wang is at the Graduate School of Management, Kyoto University, Kyoto, Japan.

Zhong-Ming Wang is at the School of Management, Zhejiang University, Hangzhou, People's Republic of China.

Malcolm Warner is at the Judge Business School, University of Cambridge, Cambridge, UK.

Feng Wei is at the Cheung Kong Graduate School of Business, Beijing, People's Republic of China.

Jia Lin Xie is at the Joseph L. Rotman School of Management, University of Toronto, Toronto, Ontario, Canada.

Shuming Zhao is at the School of Business, Nanjing University, Nanjing, People's Republic of China.

Cherrie Jiuhua Zhu is at the Department of Management, Monash University, Victoria, Australia.

INTRODUCTION

Reassessing human resource management 'with Chinese characteristics': An overview

Malcolm Warner

Introduction

In a recent study Zhu, Warner and Rowley (2007) discussed the possibility of a system of human resource management (HRM) 'with Asian characteristics'. The investigation looked at the similarities and differences between Western and Asian systems and asked if there was a 'hybrid system' in the making. The People's Republic of China (PRC) (*Zhonghua renmín gongheguo*) may be offered as a successful example of such a genre, for, as a transitional socialist economy (Warner, Edwards, Polansky, Pucko and Zhu 2005), it is clear that its attempts to open its door in order to reform its economy and its system of people-management have broadly speaking 'paid off' (see Budhwar 2004; Zhu and Warner 2004a; Zhu et al. 2007). However, China's reformers did not merely replicate foreign models uncritically. Where they have implanted overseas economic management (*jingji guanli*) practices since the late 1970s, principally from the US, Japan and Europe (roughly in that order), they did so by incorporating them into the Chinese 'way of doing things'.

An evolutionary process was consequently set in motion in which organizations that were better fitted to survive in this new environment were to displace others that were less suited (see Hodgson 1997) – and to accomplish this according to the new Chinese 'rules of the game' (see Nolan 2003). In terms of how such changes take place, organizational theorists suggest that evolutionary variance may be intentional or blind; variations in new organizations or new organizational populations may occur; selection criteria may be set by market forces, competitive pressures, peer groups and so on (Aldrich and Ruef 2006, pp. 20–21). All the preceding factors are highly relevant occurences in the PRC. As China now had to face the challenges of globalization (*quanqiu hua*), it adapted its system to promote institutional and organizational characteristics appropriate to a greater reliance on markets (see Qian 2000).

The new paradigm underlying the economic reforms that ensued after 1978 was to be known as socialism 'with Chinese characteristics' (*juyou Zhongguo tese de shehuizhuyi*).[1] This particular terminology was employed in the post-Mao period in order to reconcile what might appear to be 'foreign' (even 'capitalist' and therefore 'non-socialist') practices, with indigenous Chinese institutions based on Chinese values, whether traditional or communist – and even appearing to resolve the apparent contradiction. Both the latter, being in their different ways based on 'collectivistic' values, would therefore perhaps then be more reconcilable with what appeared to be 'individualistic' ones.[2] The dilemma was, on the one hand, not to appear to be 'taking the capitalist road' (*zou zibenzhuyi daolu*), a term used to refer to 'counter-revolutionary' policies in Maoist ideology, yet on the other hand, not to be seen as eschewing change.[3]

As economic reform proceeds in a given country, it is likely that a matching innovation in its management system follows (see Child 1994). This generalization appears to fit the Chinese model, as it moved from a 'command economy' to a 'market socialist' one soon after the death of Mao Zedong in 1976 (see Naughton 1996). The resulting changes in the Chinese ruling elite just after brought about significant shifts in the institutional and organizational environments faced by enterprises (see Li and Walder 2001; Nolan 2003; Aldrich and Ruef 2006, pp. 169–170). The World Bank, membership of which China assumed in 1980 (World Bank 2004, p. 22), sought to optimize 'resource allocation' and 'factor productivity' in what was seen as an inefficient economy, with loss-making state-owned enterprises (SOEs) at its core (see Granick 1990; Zhang 1996; Naughton 1996, 2006). As a result China began moving, in less time than anyone might have imagined, from 'plan' to 'market'.

Management in the PRC at that key point in time was faced with a 'strategic choice' as to how best to cope with the process of modernization. The strategists, i.e. those advising the Party leadership, could: first, leave things unreformed; second, evolve new indigenous forms; third, straightforwardly adapt Western types of management; or fourth, adapt the latter more specifically to its own local environmental conditions, using Western knowledge to implement an evolutionary change process but within the context of Chinese values. They chose the fourth of these options; and in doing so, looked to their cultural roots. This last option, of adaptation, may be subsumed under the rubric of 'linking up with the international track' (*yu guoji jiegui*), a notion that formally emerged in the PRC in the late 1980s (Wang 2007, pp. 13ff) although its roots may be seen even earlier. Emulating the USSR in earlier times, 'let's be Soviet and modern' (*xiang sulian moshi xuexi, sixian xiandaihua*) had been a popular slogan in the 1950s. When Deng Xiaoping's policies were introduced soon after Mao's death, the term 'linking up with the international track' entered the language but mostly in the economic realm, particularly in the context of market reform initially. It was soon to be seen in the non-economic arena as well. In public discourse, it referred to Western notions to modernize the country in everything from education to HRM (*renli ziyuan guanli*). It soon became a popular idea in the latter domain in place of old-style personnel management (*renshi guanli*).[4] 'Linking up with the international track' may be seen as part and parcel of how the PRC has attempted to adapt to globalization but at the same time tried to emphasize 'Chinese characteristics', to be seen as retaining its own values and therefore 'squaring the circle'.

A possible explanatory schema

The theoretical dimensions of this evolutionary change-process may be set out as shown in Figure 1.

In a possible explanatory (if admittedly deterministic) schema to explain how the reform process unfolded causally, we sketch out a number of changes in terms of the 'core' variables in the system indicated in the left-hand column of Figure 1, as moderated by 'contextual' ones in the centre, leading to innovations in the human resources 'outcome' variables set on the right. To put it concretely, as the Chinese government adopts a new direction in strategy, a package of economic reforms is then implemented, which in its turn has consequences, directly and indirectly, for management, labour-markets, employment and HRM. The schema outlined in Figure 2 would link all these levels together and may be seen as endogenously driven in its most straightforward model. It is, however, possible to incorporate exogenous variables in more complex variations of the above, such as responding to the challenges of globalization and the demands of the international economy, as it is arguable that these are as important as endogenous ones. The up-shot, in shorthand, may be seen as uni-linear, in theory at least, in that it appears to drive the systemic relationships between the sets of variables in a single direction, namely from past failures to future gains. However, one can anticipate that the 'devil is in the detail' when we see what actually ensued.

As the PRC becomes inexorably linked to the international economy and increasingly faces the challenges of globalization, its enterprises and their managers have not only to adapt to external market pressures, international norms and so on, but at the same time to respond to internal institutional ones (see Guthrie 1999). The tension between these factors, external as well as internal, provides an arena in which managers, as well as workers, now have to cope, perform and survive. The resulting outcomes take on the form of innovative management, nascent labour-markets, new kinds of employment and the implementation of HRM (see Figures 1 and 2).

How did such a change process unfold over time? The stereotypical people-management model we take as the point of departure is the one which was set up by the Chinese Communist Party (CCP) (*Zhongguo gongchan dang*) within the 'command

Sets of variables		
Core	*Context*	*Outcomes*
Strategic	Culture	Management
Macro-economic	Institutions	Labour-market
Micro-economic	Politics	Employment
Organizational	Values	HRM

Figure 1.   A schema of market-driven human resources reform.

Figure 2.   Uni-directional schema of variables.

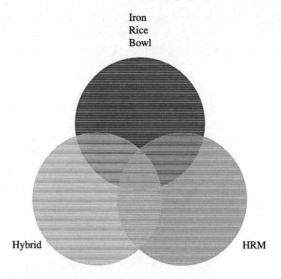

Figure 3.   Overlapping people-management characteristics.

economy' that emerged after the 'Liberation' (jiefang) in 1949 (see Schurman 1968). This model had a set of defined characteristics which have been well described in the literature (see Walder 1986) and which can be summed up in the term, the 'iron rice bowl' (*tie fan wan*) a form of 'life-time employment' status that workers enjoyed, much of which was derived from the Soviet model (see Kaple 1994) and analogous to yet different from the Japanese one (see Rowley, Benson and Warner 2004) as it was much more egalitarian than the latter. Although this model came with many variations, it was clearly recognizable as a stereotype, but its days, for better or worse, were numbered.

   The new point of arrival would have the features of a comprehensive HRM system that would be recognizable to an outside expert, as a strategic function carried out in an organization that facilitates the most effective deployment of people and human capital development (that is, employees) in order to achieve both its organizational and individual goals in a market context (see Cooke 2005, pp. 172ff). In short, the PRC was seemingly moving, from 'status' to 'contract'. The progression described above extends from one extreme point of a spectrum to another, that is, from one end at the point of origin being stereotypically 'collectivistic' in its 'iron rice bowl' form, to the other as potentially 'individualistic' at the HRM point of arrival – but with many intermediate, possibly overlapping positions in-between (see Figure 3). Sometimes, we know where this location is with some precision; other times, we know only the pace of change. Given the transitions noted above, the 'narrative' of Chinese human resource management (see Zhu 2005) may thus be seen as taking a recognizable path, from 'plan to market', from 'egalitarian to inegalitarian' and from 'status to contract', unintended consequences notwithstanding.

Economic background

In his attempt to throw off the incubus of the Maoist era, particularly the disorder and waste of the Cultural Revolution years, Deng Xiaoping had to be bold (see Zhang 1996). He soon, for example, institutionalized the 'Open Door' (kaifang) and 'Four Modernizations' (*sige xiandaihua*) policies in the years after 1978, a process that was to be an integral part of the 'modernization' programme and in turn set in train 'technology transfer', both 'hard' and 'soft'. The latter of these would involve, for example, management innovations and new ways of organizing enterprises, including preparing the ground for HRM experiments. Developing labour-markets (*laodongli shichang*), commodity labour (*shangpin laodong*) and HRM (*renli ziyuan guanli*) were to be integral to this demarche, all in order to optimize factor productivity – where the factor concerned was 'labour' (*laodong*). At the beginning, little was spelt out but there was openness to new ideas. If there was a strategy, it had been summed up in Chen Yun's phrase 'crossing the river by feeling for the stones' (*mo zhe shitou guohe*) (see Nolan 1994). Deng Xiaoping reputedly pointed out that, 'It's a good cat provided it catches mice and it doesn't matter at all whether the cat is black or white' (*wulun heimao baimao, zhuadao haozi jiushi haomao*), a phrase that still resonates today (see *China Daily* 2 August 2004, p. 1).

According to the Asian Development Bank, '[T]he People's Republic of China (PRC) has been one of the world's fastest-growing economies in the last two decades and posted another strong year in 2006, expanding by 10.7%. Per capita gross domestic product (GDP) was about US$2,000, and the number of rural poor living below the official poverty line fell to 21.5 million (2.3%) in 2006, from 250 million (30.7%) in 1978, when the Government began market-oriented economic reforms. However, a key challenge to the Government's aim of building a harmonious society is the widening gap between the rich and the poor; rural and urban; and the coastal, central, and western regions of the country' (Asian Development Bank 2007, p. 1). This account is high praise indeed (if the statistics are credible) though admittedly is delivered with a sting in the tail.

Even so, the pace of economic growth has been remarkable since the start of Dengist reforms (see Wu 2003; Perkins 2006; Naughton 2007), notwithstanding the effects of the 1989 Tiananmen Square protests (which soon led to sanctions), the 1997 Asian financial crisis (which slowed down the economy somewhat but much less than elsewhere in the region) and the 2003 SARS epidemic (which led to considerable uncertainty and an initial downturn) (see Rowley and Warner 2004a; Rawski 2006; Lee and Warner 2008). According to official Chinese government statistics, national income has been doubling every eight years. In 'purchasing-power parity' (PPP) terms, however, income per capita may be four or even five times higher than the official figure. There were those who thought the pace of growth would substantially slow down but it has not done so, although there have been, and still are, serious fears of 'over-heating'. The savings ratio remains impressive (around 50%) but, for better or worse, China now shows signs of becoming a 'consumer society' (see Gamble 2001; Croll 2006).

The State now runs less of the economy than it did in the past, however. The share of SOEs in total industrial output has fallen from 77.6% in 1978 to less than 30% now, a 'sea-change'. The so-called 'dinosaur' SOEs no longer dominate the economy, by either share of output or employment. But there are still some 170,000 SOEs with assets adding up to almost US$1 trillion, in fact more than in any other economy, and it is said that not a single stock-market listed former SOE has yet been fully 'privatized' (see Asia Development Bank 2006, p. 1).

Foreign direct investment (FDI) has continued to pour in and topped US$63 billion, in 2006, up 5% year-on-year. As an important indicator of its blending into economic globalization, China's foreign trade grew from US$100 billion to US$1 trillion in the 16 years up to 2005, while the ratio between foreign trade and GDP over the same period, which measures a country's foreign trade dependence, grew dramatically *pari passu*. Zhang Yuyan, a research fellow at the Chinese Academy of Social Sciences (CASS), notes that China's foreign trade dependence has advanced to 80%, which is considerably higher than that of other developed and developing countries. China has become the country with the highest foreign trade dependence in the world (*People's Daily* 12 September 2005, p. 2).

With the world's largest population (over 1.3 billion) and workforce (nearly 765 million), China has experienced demographic pressure; if mitigated by the 'one-child policy', the latter is now expected to be more liberally applied. At least 150 million people, perhaps more, have moved from the countryside into China's already over-crowded cities, namely the so-called 'migrant workers' (*mingong*) (see Solinger 1999; Lee and Warner 2007); but over 400 million, mainly peasants, have been raised from poverty-level. However, the rural sector now contributes less to the economy (with agriculture's share at around 12%, industry's at 48% and services' at 40%).

China's overall aggregate GDP now ranks sixth in the world after decades of rapid economic development although the World Bank has recently reduced its estimate of this aggregate by a considerable margin due to a new method of calculation. The country also has the world's second-largest foreign exchange reserves, about US$1.3 trillion. Real GDP growth as predicted exceeded 10.5% in 2007 but possibly slowing down to 9.6% in 2008. The government aims to continue to rebalance the economy, trying to make growth less dependent on exports and investment, correspondingly seeking to boost consumption; inflation has risen to nearly 5.5% in 2007 and may even double in 2008. The current-account surplus was nonetheless forecast to remain huge, equivalent to 10.7% of GDP in 2007 and 9.8% in 2008 (The Economist Intelligence Unit 2007, p. 2).

The PRC now joins the club of 'economic super-powers' (see Krug 2007). It had already entered WTO in late 2001 (see Lardy 2002; Bhalla and Qui 2004) and five years later was reaping the benefits: 'China's economic relations with the rest of the world are still in flux as a result of its WTO entry. Although problems have emerged, China has more in common with the rest of the world than it did before 2001. Both China and the global community benefit from international investment and trade, and the country now has a higher stake in keeping the multilateral trading system open' (Wang 2006, p. 1). An arguably over-valued currency continues to fuel US–China tensions, however. There have also been negative consequences arising from rapid growth in the economy, both in environmental costs, as well as in social impact.[5] Wage costs are rising but so is productivity; labour shortages are reported in boom sectors, particularly in Guangdong Province. Pollution has become a serious problem; corruption is widespread; income-inequality has grown. The standard of living and quality of life have improved for some but not for all, the old and women have not all gained (see Liu 2007). The Gini Coefficient has veered in the direction of greater inequality (up to around 0.45 from 0.25 in Mao's day; the lower the value of the coefficient, the more equally household income is distributed) and is probably becoming one of the most unequal in East Asia, which seems rather odd for a country officially characterizing itself 'socialist' (Khan and Riskin 2005; Si and Sato 2006; Shue and Wong 2007). Wage income also grew at a slower rate than overall income. This change was due to the worsening urban employment situation, because of economic restructuring and consequent downsizing. Unemployment (*shiye*) jumped to over 4.5% officially in the early 2000s (see Benson and Zhu 2005) but was probably a multiple of this in reality, around 9.5% (*The Economist* 21 July 2007a).[6] Half of the 24 million people who come into the job-market each year will not immediately be able to find work, in spite of the growth of the country's GDP, now expected to create about 10 million new jobs each year until 2010, although developments might be less predictable if there is a global recession on the horizon. Even so, as China becomes better off, its people-management system is likely to become even more complex and diversified as it adapts to the fast-changing market environment, even further towards what this writer has previously called HRM 'with Chinese characteristics' (see Warner 2005).

From personnel management to human resources

Under the old planned economy, the SOEs implemented a form of personnel management (*renshi guanli*) to organize their employees, which they had partly borrowed from their Soviet counterparts (see Schurman 1968; Kaple 1994; Warner 1995). The employment system, known as the 'iron rice bowl', as we have seen, had been the status quo from the early 1950s onwards in state firms (see Frazier 2002; Bian 2005; Bray 2005) and could even be seen as a paternalistic hangover from pre-communist times. The system as a whole was characterized by what were called the 'three old irons' (*jiu santi*), that is, the pillars of life-time employment (the 'iron rice bowl', tie fan wan), centrally administered wages (the 'iron wage', *tie gongzi*), and state-controlled appointment and promotion of managerial staff (the 'iron chair', *tie jiaoyi*) (see Ng and Warner 1998). Since market socialism was introduced in the 1980s, this enterprise-based system of 'lifetime employment' and 'cradle-to-grave' mini-welfare state (*xiao shehui*) has been eroded by various government initiatives: in 1986, for example, the authorities experimented with the introduction of labour contracts for new workers (see Korzec 1992; Zhu 2005). In 1992, the 'three personnel reforms' (*san gaige*) were initiated; this entailed the wider implementation of labour contracts, performance-linked rewards systems, and contributory social insurance (Warner 1995). In turn, access to health-care was to become more inequitable (see Wang, Zhang and Wang 2007). By this time, the system had already become a 'hybrid' one, mixing what remained of the old one with the newer features (see Figure 3).

Another step on the way to a more market-driven system was the promulgation of the Labour Law of 1994, implemented in 1995, which placed the emerging labour-market at its heart, legalizing individual contracts (*geren hetong*) and collective contracts (*jiti hetong*) and the like (Warner 1996). The All-China Federation of Trade Unions (ACFTU) (*Zhonghua quanguo zonggong hui*) was still the key player here, with its over 150 million members, 15 industrial unions and 1.2 million local branches (see Warner 1996; Warner and Ng 1999; Warner 2008). The implementation of such legislation led to what might be described as recognizable 'industrial relations' or what became known as 'labour relations' (*laodong guanxi*) in Chinese parlance (see Taylor, Chang and Li 2003). However, there is no 'right to strike' in the Chinese constitution. There have been many openly 'wild-cat' outbreaks and unofficial labour protests, most about unpaid wages and pensions, downsizing or factory closures (see Perry and Selden 2000). Officially recognized disputes can go to arbitration and many hundreds of thousands have done so since the 1994 Labour Law was enacted (see Thireau and Hua 2003; Cheng 2004); the new 2007 follow-up legislation will further help contain grievances; so, on paper at least, the system appears to be keeping the lid on the cauldron.[7]

More recently, the Labour Contract Law of 2007 took the previous legislation one step further (*The Economist* 28 July 2007c, p. 74; *People's Daily* 9 August 2007, p. 1). The new law, enacted by the Standing Committee of the National People's Congress, makes it mandatory for employers to provide written contracts to their workers, restricts the use of temporary labour and makes it more difficult to lay-off employees. The law, which will take effect in early 2008, also sets out to enhance the role of the Party-run trade unions, to boost workers' representative bodies and to facilitate 'collective bargaining' for wages and benefits, even litigation. At present, it is claimed that almost 50% of workers have 'collective contracts' with their employers.[8] These chaperoned contracts may possibly be regarded as a 'surrogate' for Western-type collective bargaining (see Warner and Ng 1999) but their critics allege that they are not based on 'freely' negotiated accords.[9] One of the major priorities of the ACFTU here is to encourage foreign-funded or multinational companies to unionize and sign agreements. To date, however, only about 26% of China's 150,000 or so overseas-funded firms have set up trade unions and only around 4 million new members signed up (*People's Daily*, 9 August 2006, p. 1). Many overseas multinational corporations remained hostile and had lobbied against an earlier draft of this law (mainly through their Chambers of Commerce in China, such as the American one, the Amcham), fearing that it would increase labour costs and reduce labour flexibility if firms were required to limit the use of temporary workers and seek approval from the trade unions before dismissing workers (see *Financial Times*, 2 May 2007, p. 1). Additionally, a new Mediation Law has been in the pipeline for implementation in early 2008 (*China Daily* 2007b, p. 1).

Pari passu, there was another piece of legislation passed recently which appeared to swing the balance away from employment protection in the Chinese enterprise. This initiative was the new Bankruptcy Law of 2007, which applies to all types of enterprises, including private firms, financial institutions and foreign-invested companies and SOEs, instituted in early June this year, of which *The Economist* noted: 'In the future, the claims of workers will take precedence only over unsecured creditors. Perhaps the new labour contract legislation was approved at about the same time, in order to assuage concerns in the Party ranks. Whether that creates social upheaval will depend on how many companies go bust (probably many); whether new jobs are available; and whether the government intervenes with emergency subsidies (it has in the past.)' (*The Economist*, 30 May 2007b, p. 97).

The philosophy behind the new labour legislation (*People's Daily*, 9 August 2007, p. 1) is known as the 'harmonious society' (*hexie shehui*), which is an attempt by the current Chinese dual-leadership of President Hu Jintao and Premier Wen Jibao to rectify perceived inequities in the economy and society. If taken seriously, it may in turn influence how Chinese enterprises of all kinds manage their human resources. The Party leaders have become increasingly aware of emergent social tensions arising from the less egalitarian income and wealth-distribution; so, it wants to maintain social harmony, appeasing the 'losers' somewhat, without penalizing the 'winners' too much.[10]

Contradictions had already built up, as the 'iron rice bowl' model rooted in the work-units (*danwei*) of the SOEs (see Lu and Perry 1997; Frazier 2002; Bian 2005; Bray 2005) has been and still is being phased out – and a more market-based version introduced incrementally, as we have already noted (see Warner 1995, 1997, 1999a, 2000, 2004, 2005, 2008). The new demarche was known as 'renli ziyuan guanli', literally meaning 'labour force resources management' with the same characters in the Chinese as in Japanese, as a synonym for what is, in effect, HRM. There were those who thought that:

> 'Personnel' was viewed as a word left over from the planned economy era, more a reminder of something related to administrative regulations … Maybe for the same reason, a report early released by the Development Research Centre (DRC) of the State Council indicates that most Chinese enterprises have renamed their 'personnel department' 'human resource department'. The wording change, though slight, has revealed that Chinese enterprises are undergoing changes in their personnel concept, according to experts. Ma Shuping, from the DRC's enterprise research section, has noted that, 'In comparison, "human resources" is of much more meaning than "personnel" and it clearly spells that people should be treated as a kind of resource, instead of simply as an administrative subject' (*People's Daily* 20 May 2004a, p. 1).

Sometimes, however, commentators had used this term loosely or misleadingly. Because of the evolutionary character of Chinese HRM, there has often been a lag in popular practice and it is only recently that there has been a more correct identification of what constitutes HRM in the Chinese context (Zhu and Warner 2004b). This phenomenon may be seen as a 'movable feast', as the evolution of management practices in China appears to be in almost continual flux, as seems to be the case in the rest of East Asia (see Rowley and Warner 2004b). The pace of economic growth continues and the degree of innovation seems unstoppable but this cannot be taken for granted. Investment in human capital, as well as HRM, as we shall see in the first study in this collection, has been extensive.[11] The matter is further complicated by the fact that the HRM system is now very much a hybrid one (see Rovai 2005) and that there is often a mixture of different management systems to be found in many enterprises. In this case, there is often an overlap between the old and new systems (see Figure 3). While Chinese enterprises are generally moving in the direction of the market-driven model, it is not however always a straightforward matter to pinpoint which particular system is predominant in a particular enterprise in a specific instance, as noted earlier.

As a generalization, HRM practices are among the last activities to be formalized in growing firms and there is a close relationship between the size of an organization (numbers employed) and its formalization and standardization of personnel functions (see Aldrich and Ruef 2006, p. 96). Many large Chinese enterprises, for example, have implemented what we would recognize as HRM systems. Where enterprises innovate, they normally do so by copying others' practices.[12] So, HRM is more frequently found in 'learning organizations', such as those more 'open' Sino-foreign enterprises or Multinational Corporations (MNCs).[13] It is in such firms we find new management practices have been initially transplanted, for example by the overseas partner when the Joint Venture (JV) was founded. Even in such cases, the kind of HRM to be found is often concerned with short-term issues like wages, welfare and promotion rather than long-term strategic ones. A recent monograph, for example, bemoans the lack of research that systematically explores in detail topics such as appraisal, compensation, planning and staffing (Zhu 2005, p. 34). Broadly speaking, it is mainly in larger business enterprises, whether they are former SOEs, JVs or Wholly Owned Foreign Enterprises (WOFEs), that we find the most definitive forms of strategic HRM in Chinese enterprises. There is less research on this corporate or strategic level of HRM than one would expect but this may be changing (see Braun and Warner 2002; Li 2003; Gadiesh, Di Paola, Caruso and Oi 2007; Yan, Child and Chong 2007) and some examples appear in this collection. A good deal of research in the field is nonetheless concerned with HR practices relating to workplace-level areas, such as life stress, organizational commitment, supervisor–employee bonds, psychological contracts and the like, as we shall see later.[14]

As the system stands, there are many state-owned and other enterprises which retain residues of the personnel management system associated with the 'iron rice bowl'. In a not inconsiderable number of SOEs or former state-sector firms, there are still those older workers who enjoy 'lifetime employment', for example. Many enterprises also have a legacy of pension obligations from the old days of the 'iron rice bowl', but in the same establishment, most employees (that is, those recruited after 1992) may have only short-term contracts and contributory social insurance. In a number of the reformed SOEs, we may find a little more or a little less of the new systems, depending on how far they have advanced towards implementing a suitable HRM configuration.[15] As one commentator observes, many elements in their HRM systems: 'have become outmoded and incompatible with the recent developments in the economic environment and the labour-markets' (Cooke 2005, p. 201). An illustration of such overlapping characteristics of people-management is set out in Figure 3.

In Chinese enterprises, other researchers have noted that there were at least three distinct forms of implementation in HRM: the first, minimal; second, transitional; and third, innovative (Benson and Zhu 1999). The minimal case would involve lip-service only to HRM practices. The transitional version would see a halfway house between the old and new systems. The innovative model would then involve moving to a recognizable HRM configuration. The majority of Chinese firms are likely to be positioned somewhere in the second case. Many of these could be SOEs which had acquired some HRM practices or they could be JVs which combine both old and new models.

In previous research, we found that HRM was associated with a number of factors such as the ownership of enterprises, their size and their location. The more they were foreign-owned, the more likely they were to have HRM embedded; the larger they were, the more likely they were to have HRM practices established; the more southern their location, the more HRM practices were to be found (Ding, Ge and Warner 2001; Ngo, Foley and Lau 2008).

Experts from the PRC State Council Development Research Centre observed recently that it had become a pressing issue for Chinese companies to set up HRM systems that can meet both corporate and human development needs, as the economy moves into the 'knowledge society'. One government researcher, Lin Zeyan, noted that: 'Any business wanting a promising future can't afford not to have a system that is both necessary for a company to reach its organizational goals and for an employee to realise his values and ideals' (*People's Daily* 8 November 2004b, p. 1). A year-long human resource study, carried out by the centre, found that in over 2100 Chinese firms more than 70% of the enterprises had not paid enough attention to the building of mechanisms to manage employees' careers. According to this analysis, during the 'transitional' period, many Chinese enterprises remain stuck with a traditional human resource management model that focuses on day-to-day affairs instead of actively figuring out ways to uncover employees' potential (2004b, p. 1).

It is thus clear that there is therefore a wide range of HRM implementation, ranging from none at all or the very minimum, to the other end, where we would find a recognizably Western or Japanese set of practices.[16] The precise frequency is not necessarily clear but it is likely this would probably correspond to the pattern of ownership of Chinese enterprises. Examples where HRM is predominant are likely to be found in WOFEs (see Goodall and Warner 1997; Ding et al. 2002). Each may have, in turn, implanted its national flavour of HRM within the parameters of the Chinese system, whether such practices be British, French, German, Japanese, US or others.

Since the economic reforms were launched, we have seen the proportion of SOEs fall from a plurality to a minority as noted earlier; correspondingly, the number of non-state-owned firms has risen (see Garnaut, Song, Tenev and Yao 2005). The latter consist of JVs, TVEs, WOFEs, joint-stock companies and privately owned domestic businesses.[17] Since the 'iron rice bowl' model was essentially associated with the state-owned sector, its reduction has more or less been mirrored by the decline of the latter. While HRM may now be found in large firms of many categories, both medium-sized and small firms, whether domestic or foreign-owned, still have more or less 'paternalistic' people-management regimes, particularly those with 'patriotic' investment from Hong Kong, Taiwan and the like, having no independent HRM function, or not even a personnel management department (see Zhu and Warner 2001; Ding, Ge and Warner 2004).

So, bearing in mind the possibility of organizational 'fit', a number of empirical propositions may be derived from the above:

1. The ownership configuration, we may hypothesize, will tend to mirror that of the economic structure.
2. The organizational configuration, we may hypothesize, will tend to mirror that of the ownership structure.
3. The HRM configuration, we may hypothesize, will tend to mirror that of the organizational structure.

Step by step, enterprises are evolving towards a new model. As a recent study, based on over 400 enterprises reveals: 'China plants with foreign equity structures are more likely to be pursuing HR best practices and are typically better able to turn practices into improved performance than their state-owned or private counterparts. In the 1980s, China began promoting self-management of state-owned enterprises and facilitated contact between Chinese and foreign-trading enterprises. Although many state-owned enterprises have been privatized, merged, or closed, many still exist and represent a drag on the Chinese economy. Privatized firms, even as they transform themselves into world-class competitors, often still carry state-owned stigma' (Wellins, Brandt, Taninecz and Tong 2005, p. 4).

An exemplification of the classic 'iron rice bowl' system in process of transformation may be seen in a long-standing 'show-case', former SOE, Capital Iron and Steel (Shougang) based in Beijing.[18] It was originally a 'cradle to grave' mini-welfare state (*xiao shehui*); its workers were the 'masters of the enterprise' (*zhurengong luantan*) (see Warner 1995; Nolan 1998; Steinfeld 1998). Today it has downsized to a fraction of what it once was, when it had 120,000 employees in Beijing alone in 1992, to 50,000 employees twenty years later and will cut this even further to 30,000 this year, as it tries to reduce pollution in the period before the 2008 Olympics. It will move out of the Beijing site altogether in 2010. However, it now has a HRM profile that has changed dramatically since the 1980s, with performance taking precedence over Party. By the mid-1990s, the changes were apparent (see Warner 1996). Its HRM department today deals with not only short-term issues but also longer-term priorities, such as downsizing. Shougang's Chairman, Zhu Jimin, commented: 'It's a problem we must solve for the sake of social stability and to meet our responsibilities, so that everyone can be taken care of and get a job' (Reuters, 9 March 2007, p. 1).

Further cases of HRM exemplification may also be found in other formerly state-owned enterprises that have become giant joint-stock companies. One such ex-SOE, formerly known as Legend (see Warner 1999a), now called Lenovo, has recently taken over the PC division of IBM[19] (see Ling and Avery 2006). A flagship of China's information technology industry, it renamed its 'personnel department' into a full 'human resource department' as early as in 1995. This raises problematic HR issues: 'Lenovo is a Chinese company, where a mandatory break for exercise at noon is part of the corporate culture. Expat Americans working with IBM have tended to describe the acquisition among themselves as a "Niagara Falls of tears". The cultural differences apart, this staff would have to draw Chinese salaries in the new company as Lenovo imposes "local hire" conditions on them in place of the dollar salaries they were drawing till now. This staff also cannot apply for IBM jobs since they are banned from doing so under the terms of the sell-off agreement' (Iyengar 2004, p.1). However, the company wants its employees to feel they belong: 'As a high-ranking official with Lenovo's human resources department says, "If an employee feels he or she is a screw in a foreign-funded enterprise, then Lenovo wants its employees to feel like its engine"' (Luo 2006, p. 2).

Another important example of 'late development', representing HRM implanted into a joint venture from its inception in the late 1990s, has been General Motors in Shanghai, a 'greenfield' site, with little legacy of older organizational forms.[20] Shanghai GM was set up on 12 June 1997 with a 50% investment each from Shanghai Automotive Industry Corporation (Group) locally and General Motors in Detroit (see Goodall and Warner 1997). Shanghai GM's location is in the Pudong Jinqiao Export Processing Zone and extends to an area of 800,000 square metres. Today, GM operates seven JVs and two WOFEs and has more than 20,000 employees in China. GM, along with its joint ventures, offers a wide range of vehicles and brands among foreign auto-makers in China. It relocated its Asia Pacific HQ, including corporate HR, to Shanghai from Singapore.

As the HRM model is most likely to be found in the newer forms of organization, we have to look there for its most explicit exemplification. The clearest example of this kind of organization may be found in large, high-tech WOFEs, like Motorola, which is the largest foreign investor in the PRC's electronics industry (see Farhoomand and Sethi 2005). Since coming to the PRC in 1987, it has made its commitment a long-term strategy. It had set up its Tianjin plant in 1992; by the end of 2006, it had over 9000 employees, enough for a very substantial HRM department. The company places a high premium on training its human resources. Motorola University China, so-called was established in 1988 to train and develop its employees.[21] It was founded in direct response to China's ongoing market-driven economy, and, by the early 1990s, it had reached an accord with the Chinese government to offer education initiatives in exchange for its business privileges. With centres in Guangzhou, Shanghai and Tianjin, the centre has developed many courses targeting senior and middle-level managers. Although in many ways China may be becoming more Westernized, the company's operating HR philosophy is to combine the best of local culture with the best of American culture whether from the company's suppliers, strategic partners, SOEs or customers. It seeks 'to help Chinese employees with the potential power of acting as a manager or even general manager to enhance his or her ability, such as promoting and cultivating Chinese employees, offering them opportunities of accepting training and attending international conferences, giving them chances of studying and practicing abroad' (Motorola 2007, p. 1).

At the extremity, we find MNCs like Wal-Mart (see Davies 2007) which has a corporate culture (*qiye wenhua*) allegedly like an egalitarian 'iron rice bowl' (*tie fan wan*) at least in the eyes of Chinese employees (2007 pp. 2-3) but which has been consistently hostile to trade unions, as was also the case with Motorola. Indeed, Wal-Mart did not recognize 'unions' until recently in China; they dubbed their workers as 'associates' (*tongren*) rather than co-workers (*tongshi*) let alone 'comrades' (*tongzhi*) (2007, p. 11). The MNC entered the Chinese market in 1996, now has 60 stores and employs 23,000 people in the PRC. For some years, given its HRM philosophy, it resisted unionization but last year relented under political pressure, offering recognition in all stores, as long as the union was affiliated with the ACFTU. The official statement was to the point: 'Should associates request formation of a union, Wal-Mart China would respect their wishes' (*People's Daily*, 9 August 2006, p. 1). Its HR managers have as their brief (with no mention of labour relations here): 'Develop and implement HR tactics and action plans in the store to support the stores in achieving the business objectives; Establish and maintain an effective communication system, to provide HR professional advices for the store management; Manage the HR function within the store, develop HR associates, increase the team productivity and service level; Maintain effective communication with Head Office HR policies and implement these HR programs in store' (Wal-Mart 2007, p. 1).

Irrespective of such considerations, many companies in China are struggling to hold on to their professional and support staff and face having to pay more generous rewards or excessive recruitment costs, according to a study in 2006. The China Employee Attraction and Retention Survey, carried out by Mercer Consulting, covered 114 businesses in Greater China, many of which are multinationals. About one-quarter (24%) were classified as high-tech. Others included consumer goods (19%), chemicals (14%), pharmaceuticals (11%), automotive (8%), and services (6%). The survey found that 54% of firms have seen an increase in turnover of professional staff since the previous year, while 42% have reported higher turnover of support staff employees. The report also shows that the average tenure for the age group most targeted by MNCs (25–35 year-olds) fell from an average of 3–5 years in 2004, to only 1–2 years in 2005. The survey found that a high proportion, 83%, of firms now offer healthcare and related insurance benefits, but only 41% provide health and fitness plans and as few as 24% offer flexible working. Even fewer, only 21%, have supplementary pension plans and 10% offer subsidized loans. The up-shot is that almost half these firms, 44% of them, are convinced that their employees are dissatisfied with the benefits offered and these are among the benchmark organizations to be found in China (HRM Guide 2006, p. 1).

According to a recent study, Chinese indigenous firms have outnumbered foreign-invested companies for the first time in the annual preferences of the nation's best employers among university students in 2007. ChinaHR.com, one of China's leading Web-based 'head-hunters', elicited responses from just under 50,000 graduates, in 656 mainland universities, from December 2006 until April 2007 about their attitudes vis à vis employment and employers. Among the top ten best employers, seven positions were taken by PRC home companies. The number of local firms accounted for half of the top 50 best employers. Until now foreign-invested enterprises have dominated the rankings since the annual survey began in 2003. Lenovo China, chosen as best-employer title in 2005, came out best once again, pursued by three other companies, China Mobile, Haier Group and Huawei Technologies Co Ltd, all local. P&G China, which was chosen as the highest-ranking FIE employer, dropped two positions this year to fifth. IBM China and Microsoft China are the other two foreign-invested firms in the top ten (Recruitment Advertising, 29 June 2007, p. 2).

The conclusions we can draw from the above (whether evidence from academic research papers, case-studies or consultants' surveys) reinforces what the review of research as noted in this overview earlier has suggested, that full-blown HRM is mostly associated with large-sized firms, whether 'red-chip' or 'blue-chip', –some of which are former SOEs (turned into joint-stock corporations), joint ventures (JVs), Town and Village Enterprises (TVEs) or Wholly Owned Foreign Enterprises (WOFEs); again, if they have over 2000 employees, they may have fully fledged HRM departments (Ding et al., 2001, 2004). In the former state-owned firms, such developments had taken root in the late 1990s. About 8% of plants of all categories of ownership (out of over 400 in the sample) studied by Wellins et al. (2005, p. 13) fell into the category of what they called 'Super-HRM' firms (i.e. cutting-edge practitioners): 'The China Super HR plants appear to operate differently than other facilities in China. Specifically, they are developing more skilled, higher-paid workers and are giving them the strategies and tools to improve. The impact from this effort, though, appears greater among Super HR JV/FEs, as described below. Approximately 11% of the JV/FEs were Super HR, compared to 8% of private and 6% of state-owned plants' (ibid.).

A combination of market forces and institutional constraints may thus lead to organizations converging in their forms and practices. As organizations face the same set of environmental conditions, isomorphism may force one unit in a population to resemble other units (DiMaggio and Powell 1983). In the latter process, HRM was to be emulated around the same time. It is highly likely that there was a common causal factor or set of factors operating here, as large-sized firms were exposed to the same set of influences vis à vis international practices, copying from either the Western or Japanese templates currently at hand in the profession, as well as pressure from the parent-firms or foreign partners, specifically where there were a large number of expatriates in the firms (see Björkman and Lu 2001).[22]

It is consequently often difficult to fully understand what is going on in China in terms of HRM because, as one recent Chinese-born expert concludes, there is 'an absence of debate among academics and practitioners in China as to what human resource management means in the Chinese context and in what ways, if any, it is different from the traditional personnel management approach. Instead there is a dangerous passion, or rather fashion, in which HRM as a Western imported concept is embraced uncritically as a progressive given. Considerable variations exist in the understanding, interpretation and configuration of HR concepts, a situation which one may justify has HRM with Chinese characteristics ... Most publications in China on human resource management are primarily introductory texts of Western HRM theories and practices with an unquestioned underlying assumption that they are advanced models to be learned by the Chinese organizations if they are to improve their performance ... While practitioners' journals on HRM tend to be simplistic and prescriptive, academics have yet to come up with more rigorous analyses, informed by empirical studies, on the appropriateness of theories in guiding practices in organizations' (Cooke 2005, pp. 205–206). It is hard to dissent from these observations, given what we have set out above in our account of how Chinese HRM has evolved over the last few decades and why we need more sophisticated analytical tools to fully understand how and why it has evolved in the particular forms we find it in today. Perhaps some of the studies summarized below may help us better comprehend what has been happening and direct towards deeper understanding. They cover a wide range of empirical studies, nearly all based in Chinese enterprises and studying workplace behaviour in depth. We hope that they may shed more light on HRM 'with Chinese characteristics' than others have done to date. Summaries of these 'state of the art' contributions to this symposium now follow.

Contributions

We begin here with a study by Shuming Zhao, based in the PRC, which deals with the relevance of human capital theory to the Chinese context. Since the author is one of the leading scholars in the People's Republic on HRM, he speaks with great experience of the Chinese scene at first hand. He argues that since the onset of Deng Xiaoping's economic reforms, Chinese economists and entrepreneurs have successfully obtained experience in applying human capital theory in the Chinese context. He argues that multiple and complex changes have taken place in the social and economic structure of China, and that the development of a knowledge-based economy is the major challenge confronting it. In recent years, research and application of human capital theory has received great attention from many Chinese scholars in different kinds of organizations, and the theory of human capital has provided, he continues, strong theoretical support to help the economic structures and corporations facing reform to establish a series of effective mechanisms for human capital investment and development to promote economic growth, as well as social and corporate development.

Based on research on the knowledge-based economy and other relevant investigations at home and abroad, the author discusses the application of human capital theory in PRC. First, he analyzes the present situation of the formation and development of human capital in China, including its rate of return and of the allocation, formation and investment of human capital. From the analyses on offer, the formation and development of human capital in China face many problems, such as the lower ROE of human capital investment compared with other countries; the disequilibrium between supply and demand of human capital and co-existence of labour shortages and labour lying idle; the restrictions that still exist in education choices, such that skilled human capital is determined not only by education but by experience. Second, he discusses the application of human capital theory from the point of view of government, enterprises and individuals. This part looks mainly at the successful measures adopted by these three entities in such areas as education investment, health services and public support, labour flows and allocation, labour-markets, training and incentive mechanisms of enterprises, human capital accounting and pricing, individual investment on human capital and so on. All the analyses are based on five basic hypotheses which he sets out, relating to what he dubs respectively: human-related 'complex men/women'; characteristics of the knowledge economy; Chinese transitional economy with its 'special characteristics'; Chinese enterprises in transformation with their 'special characteristics'; and knowledge economy with 'opportunities' for the economy, enterprises, and individuals.

The theory of human capital, he argues, enriches human ideology, as well as promoting the growth of society and the economy, leading to the comprehensive development of corporations and individuals. Compared with more mature studies in foreign countries, Chinese theoretical research in this field, he believes, is as yet in its early days. From the practical side of human capital theory in China, some policies and measures instituted on the basis of this theory still need elaborating, he concludes. For example, the country needs changes and improvements in national education investment policies, health and hygiene policies and human capital measurement. Last, there should be improvements in pricing, allocation and motivation in corporations devising optimized plans more suitable for indigenous applications of human capital in corporations.

The next contribution, by Luthans and colleagues, based in the US, looks at the value of Chinese workers' psychological capital. This noted scholar and associates argue that China's dramatic degree of change and its emergence as a leader in the global economy present many challenges. In particular, there are inevitable conflicts associated with the 'one country – two systems' and the toxic side-effects of rapid change, such as pollution, lack of transparency and the widening gap between the rich and poor. The authors propose that instead of the negativity associated with concentrating on these conflicts and trying to resolve weaknesses, the time has come for a positive approach, namely to focus on China's strengths – its unlimited and still largely untapped human resources.

Specifically, the importance of this study is to provide the background for and to add additional empirical evidence to the value that positive psychological capital (PsyCap), as the authors call it, can have for Chinese HRM. A few years ago, this research programme had introduced the concept of psychological capital in an exploratory study of Chinese factory workers. The preliminary results indicated that the workers' positive states of hope, optimism, and resiliency, separately and when combined, significantly correlated with their performance. Now the theory, research and application of psychological capital have been greatly enlarged. The researchers continue that this reflects the progress made vis à vis psychological capital and its relevancy to Chinese HRM. The follow-up study, (N=456 workers in both the largest private and SOE in the copper-refining industry) reported by the authors provides further evidence concerning the significant relationship between Chinese workers' PsyCap and their performance. Of special note is the study's finding that there were no differences between the PsyCap–performance relationship of the workers in the SOE and the private firm in the same industry, using the same technological process.

Since PsyCap has been demonstrated to be open to development and related to performance, the implications for Chinese HRM appear to be evident. Taking a positive approach and focusing on China's major strength, Chinese HRM in both private and especially SOEs, needs to recognize, select, develop and manage the psychological capital of what the authors dub these potentially unlimited, untapped human resources. By taking this positive approach, the researchers conclude that Chinese HRM may greatly contribute to solving the challenges of sustaining and gaining competitive advantage in the global economy not only now and but also in the future.

In the next contribution, Li and colleagues from Hong Kong and the UK define firms that adopt a world-wide strategy as 'global firms' and set out to test whether they have high commitments to human resources in their host countries. They argue that the commitment of multi-nationals (MNCs) to implementing HRM in their host countries is positively related to their level of what the authors call 'globalness'. The reasons are as follows: First, as the level of a firm's globalness increases, the demand for timely business information in its host countries also increases. To satisfy this demand, MNCs have to have qualified staff to collect and analyse this information. Without qualified human resources, MNCs may have difficulty in collecting and processing local information effectively. Accordingly, if MNCs engage in effective HRM in their host countries, then they will be able to recruit competent employees to collect and process local information, which in turn will help them to perform competitively in terms of their global rationale.

Second, as their level of globalness increases, MNCs need to try harder to obtain the support and goodwill of the governments of their host countries. Previous research has shown a negative relationship between the proportion of local human resources among MNCs and the perception of local governments that these MNCs are 'hostile' in their local operations. In other words, if the MNC engages in good HRM practices in a host country, then the local employees may feel more satisfied and the firm may find it easier to maintain a good relationship with the government locally. This link will, it can be argued, in its turn be beneficial to the firm's performance in the country, and will in turn help increase its globalness ranking.

Third, research has shown that the higher the level of globalness of an MNC, the stronger the need for direct networking and local expertise. Accordingly, to improve their global character, MNCs need to recruit competent local employees who, with appropriate local knowledge, can help them to develop local networks and local expertise. If an MNC has a strong commitment to HRM activities in its host countries as demonstrated through effective recruitment and employee training activities, then it will be more likely to obtain competent local employees. The presence of competent local employees should then make it easier for the MNC to develop local networks and obtain local expertise, which in turn will help it to perform well in international markets and increase its global scope.

Finally, as the level of globalness grows the demand for fast local responsiveness increases. MNCs with a high level of global reach must be able to react efficiently to changes in local markets and other local environmental developments. Such local responsiveness should again have a positive relationship with commitment to HRM.

The MNCs with a strong commitment to local HRM should have qualified human resources that can help them to enhance their local responsiveness and achieve a global competitive advantage.

With data and observations from multi-national enterprises (MNCs) operating in China, the researchers tested the above arguments and found evidence that challenges the view that global firms should have less commitment to human resources in their host countries. Specifically, the data suggest a positive relationship between MNCs' adoption of global strategy and their commitment to human resources in their host countries. Moreover, they found that the firms' commitment also has a positive relationship with their overall performance in global competition.

Following on, Zhu and colleagues from Australia and the PRC investigate the extent to which devolvement, as part of strategic HRM, is practised in firms operating in China and look at the consequent effect of this process on firms' performance. The devolvement of HR practices is defined by the authors as the involvement of front-line managers in the execution and administration of HR practices. The line manager's primary function, they continue, is the achievement of predetermined organizational objectives. Researchers, they claim, have long argued that devolution of HR responsibilities to line managers is seen as something of a 'defining' issue in HRM. Furthermore, there is an increasing recognition of the need to explore beyond the relationship between HRM practices and firm performance, also to explore the context within which HRM operates, the ways HRM practices are conducted, and the role of the devolvement of HRM to line managers.

Zhu and colleagues' findings are based on a survey of managers in state-owned enterprises, domestic/private and foreign-invested firms operating in the Jiangsu Province of China. Drawn from a list of the HR Managers Directory of Jiangsu Province HRM Institute, 2400 questionnaires were distributed. After excluding non-managerial respondents, a sample of 618 or a response rate of 25.8% was achieved. Respondents included 26.4% from HRM/Personnel department, while the remaining respondents were from other departments.

The results of this study indicate that there was little evidence of devolvement of HR practices to front-line managers in the sample. However, middle managers were engaged in performing some HR practices, notably employee training and performance assessments. The regression analyses showed that variation in the degree of devolvement to front-line managers was not found to be predictive of perceived firm–market performance or organizational effectiveness. Interestingly, devolvement to middle level managers was positively related to organizational effectiveness. The results also show that the proportion of front-line/middle managers formally trained to perform HR practices was positively related to market performance and organizational effectiveness.

The authors propose that future research might examine the extent to which HRM was integrated into the organizations' core business operations, i.e. the level of strategic integration in both vertical and horizontal directions. Also research should examine the relationship between upward and downward integration and the impact of this relationship on firm performance. Further analysis needs to be conducted to provide full explication of the roles and relationships of HRM with regard to organizational business strategy and firm performance.

Based on this research study and the emerging circumstances in China, the authors propose that there are four major areas that demand the attention of HR practitioners in China. First, there is a need to identify appropriate sources and attract strong candidates to fill HR roles. The next challenge then becomes the development of talent in the HR function. A third area for attention is that HR professionals will also benefit by forming networks in the HRM community outside their own organization. Finally, and perhaps most relevant to this research, the researchers propose that HR practitioners will need to work with line managers to build their competencies, in order for devolvement to be successful.

In the next study, Rotondo and Xie from Canada, discuss organizational citizenship behaviour (OCB) and counterproductive work behaviour (CWB) in Chinese enterprises. They argue that, historically, the measurement of employee-level job performance in Western cultures has only focused on task-related behaviour specific to a workers' job. Against this, they observe that in the modern workplace, a wider range of employee behaviour is considered as being positively linked to overall job performance, including organizational citizenship behaviour and counterproductive work behaviour. Some examples of OCBs would include volunteering and helping co-workers, while CWBs may involve tardiness or harassment, for instance. Only a limited amount of research to date has investigated how generalizable these categories of performance behaviour or their content are to other cultures. This study attempts to rectify this lacuna.

Convergence theorists have argued that regardless of the cultural context in which a firm operates, certain specific management functions and practices are necessary for administration and coordination in an industrialized economy. Hence, such theorists argue that management practices derived in Western cultures should be capable of generalization to other industrialized settings. On the other hand, divergence theorists posit that the values and attitudes of different societies and cultures may influence the design and content of management practices, suggesting that management practices are adapted to the specific culture in which the business operates. The conflict between the convergence and divergence theorists is clearly an important one that needs to be dealt with by researchers in the field.

The growing role of China in the world economy makes its culture an important one to consider, argue the authors, as its importance in the global arena continues to increase by the day. This culture also represents an interesting one for study, mainly as it is known to be very different from that of the West. More specifically, cross-cultural research has characterized China as being a 'collectivist' society, in which the greater good of the group is given precedence over 'individual' goals. In contrast, Western cultures, such as Canada and the US, score higher on individualism, as they appear to emphasize individual-goals over group-goals.

This study contributes to job performance research in two important ways. First, Study 1 investigates whether CWB in China is described by similar or different behaviour, as in Western-based literature. A sample of 160 Chinese managers and executives were asked to describe five kinds of behaviour considered to be counterproductive. A different sample of 30 Chinese managers was asked to sort the Chinese CWBs into different categories of their choosing. Multidimensional scaling was used to determine the structure underlying the Chinese CWB. Findings from Study 1 reveal that Chinese managers are similar to North American managers, both in content and structure of CWB. More specifically, the Chinese CWBs were defined by the two dimensions of interpersonal-organizational CWB and the degree of task-relevance. Second, Study 2 examines the importance that Chinese managers place on task-performance, OCB and CWB in ratings of overall job performance. A different sample of 198 Chinese managers and a sample of 114 Canadian managers read hypothetical profiles of employees (in which was embedded information about the employee's OCB, CWB and task performance) and rated their overall job performance. The findings from Study 2 indicated that Chinese managers value all three groups of behaviour when rating overall performance and place greater emphasis on task performance and less emphasis on CWB compared to North American managers. The results suggest that cross-cultural research on job performance needs to take both convergence and divergence perspectives into account, which is a very important conclusion and one which will no doubt increase our understanding.

After this, a contribution by Choi from Hong Kong discusses how both academic research and practice in HRM and other related activities have long focused their efforts on understanding the factors that tend to cause life stress among employees. According to the work–family interface perspective, he argues that work and family as two primary domains of adult life are known to influence employees' life stress. Although a number of studies have been conducted that adopt this interface view, he continues, several limitations in the literature prevent us from fully understanding the relationship between employee stress and stressors, both in the work and family domains.

First, because most of the existing research in this area has been conducted in a Western setting, he points out that very little is known as to whether demands in the work and family domains are also two key sources of life stress among employees in developing countries, such as the PRC. Second, little is known about the relative importance of work and family demands vis à vis life stress among employees. Finally, it is unclear what the role of work–family conflict, defined as a form of inter-role conflict in which work and family role demands are mutually incompatible so that meeting demands in one domain makes it difficult to meet demands in the other, is in determining life stress among employees. This study based in the Chinese enterprise was designed to fill these gaps in the existing HRM literature. More specifically, he investigated the life stress of 239 Chinese employees, based on the work–family interface perspective. In this context, he hypothesized that role demands in both domains are positively related to life stress. Since extra work may be legitimized or even encouraged in the PRC, he proposed that among Chinese employees, the roles in the work domain will be more salient than those in the family domain, and thus expected that work demands should be more likely to promote life stress than would family demands. Moreover, it was hypothesized that work and family demands would amplify the life stress of Chinese employees through the mediation of work–family conflict. From the survey undertaken, he found that work and family demands were positively related to life stress among Chinese employees. Contrary to expectations, however, the relationship of family demands with life stress appears to be a little stronger than that of work demands. Some additional analyses demonstrate that the relative importance of work and family demands varies as a function of gender: for women employees, family demands had a greater influence on life stress than work demands; for men employees, work demands had a stronger impact on life stress than family demands.

Furthermore, while the effect of family demands on life stress is fully mediated by work–family conflict, work demands affect life stress both directly and indirectly through work–family conflict. Altogether, although it appears that the findings presented here are in line with those of previous studies conducted in Western settings to some extent, there is also further evidence that points to the unique nature of Chinese society. Thus, the research study concludes that the detailed picture on how work and family demands specifically affect employee stress – and how these influences are mediated by work-family conflict – may vary across different societies. The results are particularly relevant to the theme of this symposium.

Next, Gamble and Huang, both working in the United Kingdom, investigate how organizational commitment is believed to be critical to organizational effectiveness and how it has been studied extensively by Western management scholars. Some claim that the organizational commitment construct as developed in Western contexts is valid across both nations and cultures and is a global predictor of intention to quit. The application of this research to the Chinese context would appear to be highly relevant. In this study, the authors seek to understand whether organizational commitment differs between various cultures, by exploring that of local employees in the Chinese subsidiary stores of a UK multinational retailer and this variable's relationship to employees' willingness to stay. They argue that China constitutes an important location to test such theories given its rapid integration into the global economy, along with increased levels of labour turnover that have become a serious problem for many foreign-invested enterprises. It is thus timely to investigate the factors that underlie both labour turnover and retention in China and to explore whether organizational commitment contributes to retention. The multinational enterprise they selected for the research study operates over 50 stores, which are based in 23 cities in the PRC, and has become the country's third largest foreign retailer and its largest home-improvement chain store.

The empirical data presented is drawn from a survey of 394 employees at four major stores owned by this firm (two in Shanghai and one each in Beijing and Shenzhen respectively) and three months' in-depth ethnographic study at one of the sites. Several hypotheses are tested, based on the literature and taking into consideration elements that are perceived as particularly important in the Chinese context: relationships between management and employees, 'face', and job security.

The contributions of this research are fourfold. First, it examines employees' organizational commitment in the retail sector, an industry that is under-researched. Second, it not only examines the construct of organizational commitment as a combined scale of several items, as used in previous research, but also takes one step further and looks at the impact of individual components of organizational commitment on willingness to stay with the organization. Third, it investigates relationships and 'face', organizational commitment and willingness to stay. Fourth, added insights are provided by combining survey-findings with ethnographic data that sheds light on the often subtle and nuanced processes that underpin organizational commitment.

Among the main findings the authors discuss are that loyalty to organization and belief in company values, dimensions found to be important in Western contexts, are not associated with employees' willingness to stay. By contrast, factors seen as more important and relevant to the Chinese HRM context, feeling proud of working for the company, good relationships between management and employees, and job security, are good predictors of employees' willingness to stay. The findings have implications for other transitional economies, which have similar situations to China, and particularly those in transition from state-planned labour systems to uncertain labour-markets, in which social capital plays an important role.

In a further insightful and related study, Yingyan Wang, who is based in Japan, looks at emotional bonds between supervisors and co-workers, with their relationship to organizational commitment in China's foreign-invested companies. In a society where personal relationships are emphasized in the social life of individuals, good relations with other kinds of close members might play a significant role in improving relationships in the workplace. However, the linkage with significant others in the Chinese context has not been thoroughly examined, especially the influence of the linkage between an employee and co-workers has not yet received sufficient attention in the HRM context. More research is needed in the aspects of clarifying and presenting the role of emotional attachment with particular constituencies within an organization. Also, the theory should be able to account for how the emotion-focused aspects between organization members and the organization as a whole are related.

Consequently, the author aims to address three research questions. First, what are emotional bonds with supervisor and co-workers in the Chinese context? Second, given that organizational commitment has been regarded widely as a multi-dimensional concept, what are the relationships between emotional bonds with supervisor and co-workers and different dimensions of organizational commitment? Third, considering the concerns of high turnover rates in foreign-invested enterprises in China, what are the practical implications for HRM in light of the role played by emotional bonds with supervisor and co-workers?

Recent research concerning relationships with supervisors tends to be conducted in terms of cognitive and behaviourial approaches. In contrast to the cognitive and behaviourial perspectives, the present research examines the relationship with supervisors in an emotional perspective. The meaning of emotional bonds with co-workers shares some common ground with the emotional bond with a supervisor, in that an individual is encouraged to form pleasant interpersonal relationships, valued as a traditional social norm, with co-workers.

Wang's earlier 'construct of organizational commitment' in the Chinese context is composed of a five-dimensional model, i.e. affective commitment, active continuance commitment, passive continuance commitment, normative commitment and value commitment. The five-dimensional organizational commitment model has been extended from a transposition of Western methodology to a Chinese context and reflects more Chinese characteristics. Applying the five-factor component model of organizational commitment in a sample of 1160 industrial employees, the author indicates that emotional bonds with both supervisor and co-workers were related to normative commitment and active continuance commitment. Furthermore, emotional bonding with co-workers accounts for passive continuance commitment, while an emotional bond with a supervisor is associated with affective and value commitment.

The findings help confirm that emotional bonds among various organizational members have different impacts on the way in which individuals create and visualize their relationships with the organization. Implications for HRM in foreign-invested companies are relevant here. It can be inferred from the analysis that, in designing appropriate measures aimed at fostering commitment levels of employees in foreign-invested companies, top managers should recognize the importance of appropriate policies to increase emotional bonds of employees with their co-workers and supervisor. It is also suggested that varying HRM practices to promote a range of emotional bonds might be considered, if management recognizes the exact sub-dimension of the organizational commitment which needs to be improved.

In the next research study, Si and colleagues from the United States, Hong Kong and the PRC, discuss how to attract and retain valuable human resources and how to create a mutually beneficial relationship between organizations and managers, always important issues for multinational enterprises as well as domestic companies. One highly topical issue related with the above questions in the field of international/strategic HRM is the psychological contract. A psychological contract is a set of perceptions of what managers and workers owe their organizations and what their organizations owe them. This contract has important implications for managers' and workers' job satisfaction and motivation, as well as for the effectiveness of the organization.

The study investigates a sizeable sample, 524 managers in total, with a high response rate of 87%, and examines the effect of organizational psychological contract violation on managers' behaviour in the Chinese mixed-economy context, a blend of market-driven, government-controlled and guanxi-based culture. It identifies four categories for exploring the effect of organizational psychological contract violations: managers' exit, voice, loyalty and neglect (EVLN). This study indicates that a psychological contract between organizations and their managers has three dimensions: (1) the dimension of the transactional psychological contract; (2) the dimension of the relational psychological contract; and (3) the dimension of the managerial psychological contract. It then uses structural equation modelling (SEM) to examine the relationships between the above three dimensions of a psychological contract and the four categories of the managers' exit, voice, loyalty and neglect in the Chinese context. This investigation follows a two-step procedure to test the relationships. First, it examines the factor structure of the organization-manager psychological contract and psychological contract violation to examine the discriminate validity of the two constructs. Second, it examines the factor structure of all the variables in the study, seeking a basis for the structural relationship among the variables. After confirming the factor structures, the study forms composite variables for each construct from their respective items and uses those composites as single indicators of their respective factors.

The results provide valuable information to clarify the relationships among organization-manager, organization-manager psychological contract, and organization-manager psychological contract violation. They also provide valuable information on the ways of measuring and interpreting managers' EVLN behaviour. The research finds that Chinese managers tend to place their heaviest emphasis on the managerial psychological contract and the transactional psychological contract. It also suggests that organizational psychological contract violations, of either or both the managerial psychological contract and the transactional psychological contract, may tend to increase managers' tendencies towards destructive behaviour and decrease managers' tendencies towards constructive behaviour.

Next, the senior Chinese management academic, Zhongming Wang and his collaborator, Sheng Wang, based respectively in the PRC and US, look at modelling regional HRM strategies. With the rapid development of organizational change and globalization in China, most Chinese firms are preparing themselves for doing business across regions and going global through effective strategies and HRM. This study examines the relationship between two general HRM practices (i.e. performance management and career development), strategic entrepreneurship, and organizational performance in order to build up cross-regional strategies and HRM models. Based on prior research, in-depth interviews, and pilot testing, the authors identified four dimensions of strategic entrepreneurship, including adaptive capability, resourceful innovation, proactive change, and risk anticipation. Performance management and career development were of particular interest because of the unique context in China. In the past, especially before the economic reform in 1978, state-ownership dominated the economy and HRM practices were limited to more technical activities; because of the Chinese tradition of harmony, great differentiation among employees was discouraged, affecting changes in traditional HRM practices especially performance management and career development. Despite the economic reforms, it is difficult for many organizations to completely change their old practices in a very short time (due to 'institutional continuity') and to allow HRM practices to contribute to organizational performance. Participants in this field study included 103 firms from 11 different cities and provinces. In each city, the study sampled about 10 companies. In each company, three types of surveys were distributed: an HRM practice survey (career development and performance management), a strategic entrepreneurship survey and a business performance survey among two HR managers, two to three executives and two to three top management members. Altogether 606 managers and executives participated in this study across regions of China. The results showed that performance management had a positive effect on all three organizational performance indicators including competitiveness, profitability, and market share. Among the four dimensions of strategic entrepreneurship, proactive change was found to have a positive effect on organizational performance whereas risk anticipation showed a negative effect. Although the results did not show a direct influence of adaptive capability and resourceful innovation on performance, the authors found moderating effects of adaptive capability on the relationships between the two HRM practices and competitiveness. Moreover, the performance management–competitiveness and performance management–profitability relationships varied across regions. The implications of the findings and suggestions for future research are then discussed. In particular, proactive change and risk anticipation should receive special attention as they showed direct relationships with organizational performance and building adaptive capability may help firms better utilize and coordinate human resources to enhance their competitiveness. More research is needed on resourceful innovation and adaptive capabilities and how they might interact with other resources and contextual factors to affect firm performance. Also, some specific practices related to human resources, such as performance management for example, may provide needed support to achieving organizational goals. An understanding of how HRM practices influence firm performance across regions will be valuable for entrepreneurs who are interested in starting up or doing business in different areas.

The last contribution, from Björkman and colleagues from Finland and the UK, looks at, first, to what extent do subsidiary practices resemble those found in the foreign parent organizations ('MNC standardization') and in local firms ('localization'); and second, what role is played by the HR function in the MNC subsidiaries? Although a fair amount of research has been attempted on HRM in foreign MNCs in China and India, the two up-and-coming economic superpowers, to the best of the authors' knowledge this study is the first comparative one of HRM in MNC units located in these two major emerging markets and one of the first studies to examine the role played by foreign subsidiary HR departments.

Perhaps the most striking result of this investigation, once we get to the detail, has been the importance of 'location' as a major factor. The authors note that HR departments in Western-owned units located in India tended to be seen to be playing a considerably stronger strategic role than were the China-based subsidiaries. Furthermore, the HRM practices were more locally adapted (that is, more similar to those of local corporations) and marginally less similar to those of the MNC parent. These differences appear to be consistent with the 'institutional theory' arguments presented. India, having an institutional legacy as a part of the British Empire, had not been as secluded from Western influences as China was for much of the period after World War II and English remains an important language in education and business. These factors may at least partly help to facilitate the transfer of organizational practices from the parent corporation and tend to boost processes of convergence of HRM practices.

Two other factors helped explain a significant part of the variance in both HRM practices and the HR department roles. First, the background of HR managers appears to matter for both the degree of MNC standardization and the role played by the HR department. Seen from an institutional theory perspective, HR managers tend to enact what they have been exposed to in their past and refrain from supporting unfamiliar roles – thus, persons recruited from local organizations are less likely to adopt HR department roles from the MNC parent. However, it is also conceivable that the roles played by the HR function are contingent on the expectations held by top and line managers, which may at least partly be an outcome of the perceived competency of the HR managers, with managers being recruited from other units of the focal MNC or other (leading) MNCs being perceived as more competent and thus in a better position to enact a strategic role.

Second, the higher the number of expatriates, the more similar the HRM practices were to those of the MNC parent companies. This finding is consistent with those obtained in previous research on foreign subsidiaries in the US, and corroborates general observations in the literature concerning the key roles played by expatriates in the transfer of practices and (embedded) knowledge in MNCs. The number of expatriates was also (marginally) positively related with the perceived roles of the HR department in corporations.

Discussion

Most of the studies we have outlined above have a number of common characteristics. Of the twelve discussed here, a few take a broad-brush approach and deal with macro-issues for the most part. Others look mainly at the micro-level; some take a psychological approach, others a sociological one, many mixed with an interpretive business/economics dimension. A number are commendably interdisciplinary. The majority are all based on field-studies in enterprises. They all offer specific findings linked to wider conclusions, relating to the future role of China in international business specifically and the global scene generally. The researchers involved all have sound background experience of carrying out research in China, not always a straightforward matter, and reveal an understanding of Chinese institutions and values. Many of the studies have relatively large samples, of either enterprises or individuals studied. Most link a range of independent variables to an outcome, namely performance.

They cover in their contributions six important themes, as set out below:

Empirical
Enterprise-based
Generalizability/specificity
Convergence/divergence
Personnel management/HRM
Performance

The main focus within these broader categories is on the following specific topics:

Human capital
Psychological capital
'Globalness'
Counterproductive work behaviour
Devolvement of HRM functions
Organizational commitment
Life stress
Emotional bonds
Psychological contract
HRM/entrepreneurial
HRM strategies

The above foci encompass an important set of topics, which are of theoretical as well as practitioner interest. What is particularly interesting about the empirical studies summarized above is the range of topics covered and their timeliness. The authors also come from a wide variety of academic backgrounds and disciplines (some senior hands, others aspirant), with an encouraging mixture of Chinese and Western authors, sometimes collaborating on the same research, in the case of the latter either as researchers based on Chinese mainland campuses or in the case of others, those abroad. The contributors teach and/or research in universities in Australia, Canada, Finland, Hong Kong, PRC, the UK and US.

The conclusions arising from the specific research projects vary from finding confirmation of initial hypotheses, to falsification of them. Most studies only deal with a Chinese sample but at least a few feature comparative data from both the PRC and other countries. A number even concern themselves with wider generalizations about the past, present and future state of HRM. We hope that they will enhance the reader's insight into and knowledge of the subject.

Concluding remarks

The summary and discussion above of the HRM research covered in this symposium shows how far Chinese theory and practice of people-management has progressed since the economic reforms were initiated close to three decades ago, perhaps supporting the conjecture that people-management in China has moved further along the road than what we might have conceded a decade ago, to what we might now call 'bounded convergence'.[23]

It is hard to predict where HRM 'with Chinese characteristics' will advance to in the coming years, particularly since so much of it is dependent on a continuation of present economic trends. The world financial crisis of late 2007 has rung alarm bells throughout Asia. A global recession in 2008 might reverse much of the optimism now prevalent in China. Civil unrest, environmental disasters, military conflicts or natural catastrophes might also unhinge any projections one might make. In the light of the overview discussion we made earlier, we conclude by surmising possible directions. Given that the three pillars of our argument in the introduction (based on the 'core' variables set out earlier in Figure 1), namely, the economic set as determinants of possible human resources outcomes (with 'values' as the contextual/intervening variables) may all be seen as phenomena in flux, we can conclude that the relationship between them should perhaps ultimately be seen as dynamic rather than static. The marketization of the Chinese economy clearly encompasses a fast-changing set of forces, as it moves into 'the knowledge society', as does in turn the HRM configuration in enterprises in its recognizable embodiment where 'knowledge workers' may become more predominant (see Warner 1999b; Sun et al 2007). The intervening variables, such as 'values' (part of 'with Chinese characteristics') may also be less constant than some would think. Therefore, the three sets of force-fields are often simultaneously interacting with each other.

The way the resolution of these dynamics vis à vis the future evolution of HRM in China takes shape will surely depend on their rates of change, many of which are less than wholly predictable, with its direction probably determined by the 'path dependency' resulting from past trends.[24]

Acknowledgement

I am grateful to the many anonymous referees who reviewed the contributions set out above and also to the many others who have generously helped with their present advice and/or past collaboration, including John Child, Daniel Z. Ding, Wei Huang, Keith Goodall, Grace O.M. Lee, Jane Nolan, Peter Nolan, Riccardo Peccei, Michael Poole, Zhongming Wang, Shuming Zhao and many others.

I also draw on recent work on Asia with John Benson, Chris Rowley and Ying Zhu and a symposium generously organized by the University of Melbourne. At the University of Cambridge, the Judge Business School, as well as Wolfson College, have been, as ever, highly supportive, as has been the Cass Business School, City University, London. The following universities must be thanked for hosting me in recent years, City University of Hong Kong and the University of Hong Kong, as well as Nanjing University, Tsinghua University and Zhejiang University. As usual, Penny Smith provided the expected admirably efficient administrative back-up at the journal. I must also acknowledge, on the publisher's side, the backing of Alan Jarvis and Peter Sowden, at Routledge as well as Gail Carter for her invaluable help.

Notes

1. This phrase is attributed to Deng Xiaoping, but long before that Mao Zedong had observed that socialism had to be adapted to Chinese circumstances. He formally called for the 'sinification' of Marxism in October 1938 at the Sixth Plenum of the Sixth Central Committee (Schram 1989, p. 84).
2. Gerd Hofstede has measured values in over 40 countries – see his 'Confucian dynamic' vis à vis Chinese culture (Hofstede 2001).
3. Deng Xiaoping, who launched his reform programme in the late 1970s, observed that, 'Some people are afraid that China will take the capitalist road if it tries to achieve the Four Modernizations with the help of foreign investment. No, we will not take the capitalist road. The bourgeoisie no longer exist in China. There are still former capitalists, but their class status has changed. Although foreign investment, which belongs to the capitalist economy, occupies a place in our economy, it accounts for only a small portion of it and thus will not change China's social system. Achievement of common prosperity characterizes socialism, which cannot produce an exploiting class' (Deng 1979, p. 1).
4. Wang (2007, p. 118) describes how China needed 'to adopt the prevailing international norms of rational management, meritocracy, rule of law and adaptation to replace the old system of irrational management, virtuocracy and seniority, rule of man and rigidity' (2007, p. 18). With regard to globalization, she continues, most Chinese policymakers recognize it as 'inevitable and potentially beneficial to China' (2007, p. 18). This strategy led to joining international bodies such as the World Trade Organization (WTO), as well as the International Labour Organization (ILO). Citing the contemporary Chinese philosopher Li Zehou, whose message was mixing 'Western essence with Chinese function' (*xiti zhongyong*), she argues that modernization has even been identified with Westernization as an intrinsic element. However, conservatives may want to limit its influence to the economic sphere; they do not want to see Chinese 'values' compromised (2007, p. 19).
5. See Luthans et al. in this collection on looking beyond such negative aspects to the positive ones, such as what they call 'psychological capital'.
6. The lower figure was due mainly to the underestimate built into the official figures, as they formerly did not count the first three years of those laid-off (*xiagang*) (see Lee and Warner 2007).
7. Some observers think cosmetic reforms are not enough, 'Social injustice in China has structural roots. Without substantial changes to China's economic structure, any policy aimed at improving income disparities and increasing social justice can hardly be effective. Despite the establishment of the policy discourse of building a "harmonious society," it is still unclear what effective measures the Chinese leadership will take to realise this ambitious goal' (Zheng and Chen 2007, p. 1).There are many critics of the Chinese labour laws who see them as inadequately protecting the workers' interests and anticipating a 'melt-down' of worker-management relations (see for example, Chan 2001; Cai 2006; Lee 2007). Regular accounts of labour rights abuses appear on the *China Labour Bulletin* website: http://www.clb.org.hk/public/main
8. According to the ACFTU, a total of 862,000 collective contracts were signed nationally in 2006, involving 112.5 million workers. The figures were putatively up 14.3% and 8.3%, respectively, on the previous year (*China Daily* 2007a, 25 May).
9. But there are many critics of the system who see it as not adequately protecting the workers' interests (see for example, Chan 2001; Cai 2006; Lee 2007).

10. A recent report 'A Resolution on the Major Issues Concerning the Building of a Socialist Harmonious Society' adopted at the Sixth Plenum of the Sixteenth CCP Central Committee 11 October 2006, sets this out as follows, 'Social harmony is the intrinsic nature of socialism with Chinese characteristics and an important guarantee of the country's prosperity, the nation's rejuvenation, and the people's happiness. The building of a socialist harmonious society is an important strategic task, which was put forward partly under the guidance of Marxism-Leninism, Mao Zedong Thought, Deng Xiaoping Theory, and the important thinking on the "Three Represents"', ... It continues further, 'No society can have no contradictions. Human society has been developing and progressing amid movements of all kinds of contradiction. The building of a socialist harmonious society is a sustained process during which social contradictions are resolved'. After dealing with ideological and institutional considerations, the text goes on to propose the ways of ensuring social equality and improving the income distribution system, for example, 'We should strengthen regulation and control over enterprise wages, increase guidance in this regard and bring the guiding role of information about the wage guiding line, labour-market price, and industrial labour cost into play in the wage level'. It goes on to specify how the Party can act out a greater role in the building of a socialist harmonious society. It continues, 'They should step up the improvement of the party's leadership over trade unions, the Communist Youth League (CYL), women's federations, and other mass organizations and support them in playing their role in maintaining close ties with the masses, serving and educating, and protecting their legitimate rights and interests.' (See Quarterly Chronicle and Documentation 2007, pp. 261ff).

11. See Shuming Zhao on 'Human Capital' in the PRC in this collection.

12. Replication 'occurs via people observing one another, through training and education, learning appropriate rules of behaviour and interacting with machines and documents' (Aldrich and Ruef 2006, p. 24). There may, on the other hand, be limitations to 'inter-organizational learning', where there are 'impermeable organizational boundaries' (2006, p. 25).

13. On the relationship between the 'globalness' of MNCs and HRM, see the paper by Li et al. in this volume.

14. For example, see contributions in this collection by respectively: Choi; Rotondo and Xie; Gamble and Huang; Wang; Si et al.

15. See Cherrie Zhu et al.'s study on the devolution of HRM practices, in this volume, for example.

16. We can also see in the research by Wang and Wang, in this collection, that the regional factor is an important one to consider.

17. Xu et al. (2006) found that both domestic non-state-owned firms and foreign-invested enterprises performed better than SOEs. However, three categories of Chinese firms – privately owned, collectively owned, and shareholding – enjoyed higher performance levels than the foreign-invested enterprises.

18. Like many academic and other visitors to China in the early days of the economic reforms, the present writer was taken to see the vast steel-works like Shougang and to interview managers, workers and trade union officials there. It was a 'show-case SOE', together with joint ventures like Beijing Jeep and various Ministries and Institutes (see Warner 1995). Interviews conducted over many years witnessed the transformation from personnel management to HRM in its people-management.

19. See Ji Li et al. on 'globalness' in this volume.

20. The present writer interviewed the General Motors HR Director in the early days of the JV's existence in Pudong. It was far ahead of its time in its selection and recruitment procedures, being the only encountered at that date in the late 1990s that used psychometric tests.

21. Again, See Ji Li et al. on 'globalness' in this collection.

22. Also see Björkman et al. comparing HRM in China and India in this volume.

23. The present writer has also previously referred to this as a 'soft convergence' (see Warner 2004).

24. On China's 'path-dependence', see Guthrie (1999) and Liew (2005) for further details.

References

Aldrich, H.E., and Ruef, M. (2006), *Organizations Evolving*, London and New York: Sage.

Asian Development Bank (2006), "Privatization and Reform," *ADB Review*, April-May, retrieved 22 June 2007 from: http://www.adb.org/Documents/Periodicals/ADB_Review/2006/vol38-1/privatization-reform.asp

Asian Development Bank (2007), "Asian Development Bank and the People's Republic of China," *Asia Development Bank*, retrieved 13th May 2007 from: http://www.adb.org/Documents/Fact_Sheets/PRC.pdf

Benson, J., and Zhu, Y. (1999), "Market, Firms and Workers: The Transformation of Human Resource Management in Chinese Manufacturing EPLEA Enterprises," *Human Resource Management Journal*, 9, 4, 58–74.

Benson, J., and Zhu, Y. (eds) (2005), *Unemployment in Asia*, London and New York: RoutledgeCurzon.

Bhalla, A.S., and Qui, S. (2004), *The Employment Impact of China's WTO Accession*, London and New York: RoutledgeCurzon.

Björkman, I., and Lu, Y. (2001), "Institutionalization and Bargaining Power Explanations of HRM Practices in International Joint Ventures: The Case of Chinese-Western Joint Ventures," *Organization Studies*, 22, 3, 491–512.

Budhwar, P.S. (ed.) (2004), *Managing Human Resources in Asia-Pacific: Past, Current and Future HR Practices in the Industrial Sector*, London and New York: Routledge.

Bian, M.L. (2005), *The Making of the State Enterprise System in Modern China: The Dynamics of Institutional Change*, Cambridge, MA: Harvard University Press.

Braun, W., and Warner, M. (2002), "Strategic Human Resource Management in Western Multinationals in China: The Differentiation of Practices across Different Ownership Forms," *Personnel Review*, 31, 5, 553–579.

Bray, D. (2005), *Social Space and Governance in Urban China: The Danwei System from Origins to Reform*, Stanford, CA: Stanford University Press.

Cai, Y. (2006), *State and Laid-off Workers in Reform China*, London and New York: Routledge.

Chan, A. (2001), *China's Workers under Assault: The Exploitation of Labour in a Globalizing Economy*, Armonk, NY: M.E. Sharpe.

Cheng, Y. (2004), "The Development of Labour Disputes and the Regulation of Industrial Relations in China," *International Journal of Comparative Labour Law and Industrial Relations*, 20, 2, 277–295.

Child, J. (1994), *Management in China during the Era of Reform*, Cambridge: Cambridge University Press.

China Daily (2004), "People hold Deng in High Esteem," 2nd August, retrieved 12th May 2006 from: http://www.chinadaily.net/english/doc/2004-08/02/content_356766.htm

China Daily (2007a), "Workers to get power to negotiate, union says," 25th May, retrieved 28th June 2007, http://en.chinagate.com.cn/news/2007-05/25/content_2451495.htm.

China Daily (2007b), "China Adopts Law to Streamline Labor Arbitration," 29th December retrieved on 29th December 2007 from: http://www.chinadaily.co.cn/china/2007-12/29/content_6359423.htm

Cooke, F.L. (2005), *HRM, Work and Employment in China*, London and New York: Routledge.

Croll, E. (2006), *China's New Consumers: Social Development and Domestic Demand*, London and New York: Routledge.

Davies, D.J. (2007), "Wal-Mao: The Discipline of Corporate Culture and Studying Success at Wal-Mart China," *The China Journal*, July, 58, 1–30.

Deng, X. (1979), "We Can Develop a Market Economy under Socialism," *Interview*, 26th November, retrieved 7th July 2007 from: http://www.china.org.cn/english/features/dengxiaoping/103388.html

DiMaggio, P.J., and Powell, W. (1983), "The Iron Cage Revisited: Institutional Isomorphism and Collective Rationality in Organizational Fields," *American Sociological Review*, 48, 147–160.

Ding, D.Z., Ge, L., and Warner, M. (2001), "A New Form of Chinese Human Resource Management? Personnel and Labour–Management Relations in Chinese TVEs," *Industrial Relations Journal*, 32, 328–343.

Ding, D.Z., Goodall, K., and Warner, M. (2002), "The Impact of Economic Reform on the Role of Trade Unions in Chinese Enterprises," *International Journal of Human Resource Management*, 13, 3, 431–449.

Ding, D.Z., Ge, L., and Warner, M. (2004), "Evolution of Organizational Governance and Human Resource Management in China's Township and Village Enterprises," *International Journal of Human Resource Management*, 15, 4/5, 836–852.

Economist Intelligence Unit, The. (2007), *China: Country Report*, London: The Economist Intelligence Unit, 28th June, retrieved 22nd July 2007 from: http://www.economist.com/countries/China/profile.cfm?folder = Profile-Forecast

Farhoomand, A., and Sethi, K. (2005), "Motorola in China; Failure of Success," *Harvard Business Online*, retrieved 23rd June 2007 from: http://harvardbusinessonline.hbsp.harvard.edu/b01/en/search/searchResults.jhtml;jsessionid = S4BKZCWXHIKAYAKRGWDR5VQBKE0YIISW?Ntx = mode + matchallpartial& Ntk = Author%20Name&N = 0&Ntt = Ali + Farhoomand

Financial Times (2007), "China's Labour Law Raises US Concerns," 2nd May, retrieved 27th June 2007 from: http://www.ft.com/cms/s/09d35e16-f8c4-11db-a940-000b5df10621,dwp_uuid = 9c33700c-4c86-11da-89df-0000779e2340.html

Frazier, M.W. (2002), *The Making of the Chinese Industrial Workplace: State, Revolution and Labour Management*, Cambridge: Cambridge University Press.

Gadiesh, O., Di Paola, P., Caruso, L., and Oi, C.L. (2007), "Preparing for China's Next Great Leap," *Strategy & Leadership*, 35, 1, 43–46.

Gamble, J. (2001), "Shanghainese Consumerism," *Asia Pacific Business Review*, 7, 3, 88–110.

Garnaut, R., Song, L., Tenev, S., and Yao, Y. (2005), *China's Ownership Transformation*, Washington, DC: IFC.

Goodall, K., and Warner, M. (1997), "Human Resources in Sino-foreign Joint Ventures: Selected Case Studies in Shanghai, Compared with Beijing," *International Journal of Human Resource Management*, 8, 5, 569–594.

Granick, D. (1990), *Chinese State Enterprises: A Regional Property Rights Analysis*, Chicago, IL: University of Chicago Press.

Guthrie, D. (1999), *Dragon in a Three-piece Suit: The Emergence of Capitalism in China*, Princeton, NJ and Oxford: Princeton University Press.

HRM Guide (2006), "Employee Retention Problems in China," *HRM Guide: Global Labour-market*, retrieved 13th December 2006 from: http://www.hrmguide.net/international/china–retention.html

Hofstede, G. (2001), *Culture's Consequences: Comparing Values, Behaviors, Institutions and Organizations across Nations*, Thousand Oaks, CA and London: Sage.

Hodgson, G.M. (1997), *Economics and Evolution: Bring the Life Back into Economics*, Cheltenham: Edward Elgar.

Iyengar, J. (2004), "Uphill Task for Lenovo," *Asian Times*, 24th December, retrieved 25th May 2006 from: http://www.atimes.com/atimes/China/FL24Ad05.html

Kaple, D. (1994), *Dream of a Red Factory: The Legacy of High Stalinism*, Oxford and New York: Oxford University Press.

Khan, A.R., and Riskin, C. (2005), "China's Household Income and its Distribution, 1995 and 2002," *The China Quarterly*, 182, June, 356–384.

Korzec, M. (1992), *Labour and the Failure of Reform in China*, London and New York: Routledge.

Krug B. (ed.) (2007), *The Chinese Economy in the 21st Century: Enterprise and Business Behaviour*, Cheltenham: Edward Elgar.

Lardy, N.R. (2002), *Integrating China into the Global Economy*, Washington, DC: Brookings Institution.

Lee, C.K. (2007), *Against the Law: Labour Protests in China's Rustbelt and Sunbelt*, Berkeley, CA: University of California Press.

Lee, G.O.M., and Warner, M. (eds.) (2007), *Unemployment in China: Economy, Human Resources and Labour-markets*, London and New York: Routledge.

Lee, G.O.M., and Warner, M. (2008), *The Political Economy of SARS: The Impact on Human Resources in East Asia*, London and New York: Routledge.

Li, B., and Walder, A. (2001), "Career Advancement as Party Patronage: Sponsored Mobility into the Chinese Administrative Elite, 1949–1996," *American Journal of Sociology*, 106, 1371–1408.

Li, J. (2003), "Strategic Human Resource Management and MNEs' Performance in China," *International Journal of Human Resource Management*, 14, 2, 157–173.

Liew, L. (2005), "China's Engagement with Neo-liberalism: Path Dependency, Geography and Party Self-reinvention," *Journal of Development Studies*, 41, 2, 331–352.

Ling, Z.J., and Avery, M. (2006), *The Lenovo Affair: The Growth of China's Computer Giant and Its Takeover of IBM–PC*, Singapore: Wiley Asia.

Liu, J. (2007), *Gender and Work in Urban China: Women Workers of the Unlucky Generation*, London and New York: Routledge.

Lu, X., and Perry, E. (1997), *Danwei: The Changing Chinese Workplace in Historical and Comparative Perspective*, Boulder, CO: M.E. Sharpe.

Luo, Y. (2006), "Lenovo Wrestles Dell on the Mainland," *China Today*, retrieved 23rd May 2007 from: http://www.chinatoday.com.cn/English/e2006/e200607/p22.htm

Motorola (2007), *MotorolaCareers* >retrieved 22nd May 2007 from: http://www.motorolacareers.com/moto.cfm?cntry = China

Naughton, B. (1996), *Growing out of the Plan: Chinese Economic Reforms, 1978–1993*, Cambridge: Cambridge University Press.

Naughton, B. (2006), *The Chinese Economy: Transitions and Growth*, Cambridge, MA: MIT Press.

Ng, S.-H., and Warner, M. (1998), *China's Trade Unions and Management*, Basingsoke: Macmillan/ New York: St Martins Press.

Ngo, H.-Y., Foley, S., and Lau, C.-M. (2008), "Strategic Human Resource Management. Firm Performance, and Employee Relations Climate in China," *Human Resource Management Journal*, 47, 1, 73–91.

Nolan, P. (1994), "The China Puzzle: 'Touching Stones to Cross the River.'" *Challenge*, 37, 1, Jan/Feb, 25–31.

Nolan, P. (1998), *Indigenous Large Firms in China's Economic Reform: The Case of Shougang Iron and Steel Corporation*, London: Contemporary China Institute.

Nolan, P. (2003), *China at the Crossroads*, Oxford: Blackwell Publishers.

People's Daily Online (2004a), 20th May, retrieved 22nd September 2006 from: http://english.peopledaily.com.cn/200405/20/eng20040520_143812.html

People's Daily Online (2004b), 8th November, retrieved 24th October 2006 from: http://english.people.com.cn/200411/08/eng20041108_163154.html

People's Daily Online (2005), 12th September, retrieved 20th May 2006 from: http://english.people.com.cn/200509/12/eng20050912_208112.html,15

People's Daily Online (2006), 9th August, retrieved 12th June 2007 from: http://english.peopledaily.com.cn/200608/19/eng20060819_294782.htm

People's Daily Online (2007), 9th August, retrieved 12th August 2007 from: http://english.people.com.cn/90001/90778/6235539.html

Perkins, D.H. (2006), *The Challenges of China's Growth*, Washington, DC: AEI Press.

Perry, E., and Selden, M. (eds) (2000), *Chinese Society: Change, Conflict and Resistance*, London and New York: Routledge.

Qian, Y. (2000), "The Institutional Foundations of Market Transition in the People's Republic of China", working paper, 9, Manila: Asian Development Bank, retrieved 12th June 2007 from: http://venus.icre.go.kr/metadata/10921_wp09.pdf

Quarterly Chronicle and Documentation (2007), *The China Quarterly*, 189, March, 232–285.

Rawski, T.G. (2006), "SARS and China's Economy," in *SARS in China: Prelude to Pandemic?*, eds. A. Kleinman and J.L. Watson, Stanford, CA: Stanford University Press, Watson, pp. 105–121.

Recruitment Advertising (2007), "Chinese Companies are Better Employers". *Recruitment Advertising*, retrieved 10 May 2007 from: http://www.recruitmentadvertising.cn/index.htm

Reuters (2007), "China's Shougang Steel to Slash Jobs as Plant Moves," *Reuters*, 9th March, retrieved 12th May from; http://www.alertnet.org/thenews/newsdesk/PEK2842.htm

Rovai, S. (2005), "HRM Practices in Foreign MNCs Operating in the PRC: A New Hybrid Form?," *International Journal of Human Resources Development and Management*, 5, 3, 284–301.

Rowley, C., Benson, J., and Warner, M. (2004), "Towards an Asian Model of Asian HRM: A Comparative Analysis of China, Japan and Korea," *International Journal of Human Resource Management*, 15, 4/5, 917–933.

Rowley, C., and Warner, M. (2004a), "Asian Financial Crisis: Impact on HRM," *International Studies in Management and Organization*, 34, 1, 3–9.

Rowley, C., and Warner, M. (2004b), "HR Development in the Asia Pacific," *Journal of World Business*, 39, 4, 308–310.

Schram, S. (1989), *The Thought of Mao Tse-Tung*, Cambridge: Cambridge University Press.

Schurman, F. (1968), *Ideology and Organization in Communist China*, Berkeley, CA: University of California Press.

Shue, V., and Wong, C. (eds.) (2007), *Paying for Progress in China: Public Finance, Human Welfare and Changing Patterns of Inequality*, London and New York: Routledge.

Si, L., and Sato, H. (eds.) (2006) *Unemployment, Inequality and Poverty in Urban China*, London and New York: Routledge.

Steinfeld, E.S. (1998), *Forging Reform in China: The Fate of State-owned Industry*, Cambridge: Cambridge University Press.

Solinger, D. (1999), *Contesting Citizenship in Urban China*, Berkeley, CA: University of California Press.

Sun, Y., von Zedwitz, M., and Simon, D.F. (eds.) (2007), "Global R&D in China," *Asia Pacific Business Review*, 13, 3, Special Issue, 311–480.

Taylor, B., Chang, K., and Li, Q. (2003), *Industrial Relations in China*, Cheltenham: Edward Elgar.

The Economist (2007a), "Chinese Bankruptcy: Euthanasia for Companies," *The Economist*, 31st May, retrieved 25th July 2007 from: http://www.economist.com/finance/displaystory.cfm?story_id = 9267817

The Economist (2007b), "Economic and financial indicators," *The Economist*, 21st July 97.

The Economist (2007c), "Red Flag". *The Economist*, 28th July, p. 74.

Thireau, I., and Hua, L. (2003), "The Moral Universe of Aggrieved Chinese Workers: Workers' Appeals to Arbitration Committees and Letters and Visits Offices," *The China Journal*, 50, July, 83–106.

Walder, A.G. (1986), *Communist Neo-traditionalism: Work and Authority in Chinese Industry*, Berkeley, CA: University of California Press.

Wal-Mart (2007), "Career Information," *Wal-Mart China*, retrieved 12th October 2007 from: http://www.wal-marchina.com/english/career/othercity.htm

Wang, H. (2007), "Linking Up with the International Track: What's in a Slogan," *The China Quarterly*, 189, March, 1–24.

Wang, M.-L., Zhang, S., and Wang, X. (2007), *WTO, Globalization and China's Health Care System*, Basingstoke and New York: Palgrave Macmillan.

Wang, Y. (2006), "China in the WTO: A Chinese View," *China Business Review Online*, retrieved 12th July 2007 from http://www.chinabusinessreview.com/public/0609/yong.html

Warner, M. (1995), *The Management of Human Resources in Chinese Industry*, Basingstoke: Macmillan/New York: St Martin's Press.

Warner, M. (1996), "Economic Reforms, Industrial Relations and Human Resources in the People's Republic of China: An Overview," *Industrial Relations Journal*, 27, 3, 195–210.

Warner, M. (1997), "China's HRM in Transition: Towards Relative Convergence?," *Asia Pacific Business Review*, 3, 4, 19–33.

Warner, M. (1999a), "Human Resources and Management in China's 'Hi-tech' Revolution: A Study of Selected Computer Hardware, Software and Related Firms in the PRC," *International Journal of Human Resource Management*, 10, 1, 1–20.

Warner, M. (ed.) (1999b), *China's Managerial Revolution*, London/ Portland, OR: Frank Cass.

Warner, M. (ed.) (2000), *Changing Workplace Relations in the Chinese Economy*, Basingstoke: Macmillan/New York: St Martin's Press.

Warner, M. (2004), "China's HRM Revisited: A Step-wise Path to Convergence?," In *The Management of Human Resources in the Asia Pacific Region: Convergence Reconsidered*, eds. C. Rowley and J. Benson, London/Portland, OR: Frank Cass, pp. 15–31.

Warner, M. (ed.) (2005), *Human Resource Management in China Revisited*, London and New York: Routledge.

Warner, M. (2008), "Trade Unions in China: Towards the Harmonious Society," in *Trade Unions in Asia*, eds. J. Benson and Y. Zhu, London and New York: Routledge, pp. 140–156.

Warner M., and Ng, S.-H. (1999), "Collective Contracts in Chinese Enterprises: A New Brand of Collective Bargaining under 'Market Socialism'," *British Journal of Industrial Relations*, 37, 2, 295–314.

Warner M., Edwards, V., Polansky, G., Pucko, D., and Zhu, Y. (2005), *Management in Transitional Economies: From the Berlin Wall to the Great Wall of China*, London and New York: RoutledgeCurzon.

Wellins, R.S., Brandt, J.R., Taninecz, R., and Tong, R.T.L. (2005), "Super Human Resource Management in China: Practices, Performances, and Opportunities among China's Manufacturers," *Development Dimensions International*, working paper, retrieved 12th June 2007 from: http://64.233.183.104/search?q = cache:9K49HR7iwEJ:www.ddiworld.com/pdf/superhrchina

World Bank (2004), *An Evaluation of World Bank Assistance*, Washington, DC: World Bank, available from: http://www.worldbank.org.cn/English/Content/china_cae.pdf

Wu, Y. (2003), *China's Economic Growth: A Miracle with Chinese Characteristics*, London/ New York: Routledge.

Xu, D., Pan, Y., Wu, C., and Yim, B. (2006), "Performance of Domestic and Foreign-invested Enterprises in China," *Journal of World Business*, 41, 3, 261–274.

Yan, Y., Child, J., and Chong, C.Y. (2007), "Vertical Integration of Corporate Management in International Firms: Implementation of HRM and the Asset Specificities of Firms in China," *International Journal of Human Resource Management*, 18, 5, 788–807.

Zhang, W. (1996), *Ideology and Economic Reform under Deng, 1978–1993*, New York: Columbia University Press.

Zheng, Y., and Chen, M. (2007), "China's Recent SOE Reform and its Social Consequences," briefing paper, Nottingham: University of Nottingham, China Policy Institute, p. 13.

Zhu, C.J. (2005), *Human Resource Management in China: Past, Current and Future HR Practices in the Industrial Sector*, London and New York: RoutledgeCurzon.

Zhu, Y., and Warner, M. (2001), "Taiwanese Business Strategies vis-à-vis the Asian Financial Crisis," *Asia Pacific Business Review*, 7, 3, 139–156.

Zhu, Y., and Warner, M. (2004a), "HRM in East Asia," in *International Human Resource Management* (2nd ed.), eds. A.W. Harzing and J.V. Ruysseveldt, London: Sage, pp. 195–220.

Zhu, Y., and Warner, M. (2004b), "Changing Patterns of Human Resource Management in Contemporary China," *Industrial Relations Journal*, 35, 4, 311–328.

Zhu, Y., Warner, M., and Rowley, C. (2007), "Human Resource Management with 'Asian' Characteristics: A Hybrid People-Management System in East Asia," *International Journal of Human Resource Management*, 18, 5, 745–768.

Application of human capital theory in China in the context of the knowledge economy

Shuming Zhao

Introduction

Ideas about human capital have developed over a number of centuries, but these ideas were to form as a theory in the West in the 1960s. The contributions of the theory of human capital to economy and culture are widely recognized. This theory evolved on the basis of Western economic growth theory and studies of human behaviour. The determinant of economic development in Western countries has been changed from physical materials to human capital, and the focus on human behaviour has attracted more and more attention from both theoretical and industrial perspectives since the creation of the school of human relations. The conceptualization and theorization of human capital has been promoted and prevailed in Western nations and the research outcomes of human capital and related theories have made great contributions to social, economic, and corporate development. In this study, we shall now apply these theories to the People's Republic of China (PRC) drawing on both Western and Chinese research sources.

Since the implementation of the policy of economic reform and opening to the outside world from 1979 onwards, Chinese economists and entrepreneurs have obtained a great deal of successful experience in applying the theory of human capital in the reform process (Zhao 2001) but there still exist issues worthy of study. In spite of recent growth, China is still a developing country with a vast land-area, a large population and a relatively weak industrial structure. Currently, multiple and complex changes are taking place in its economic and social structure. Traditional agriculture is turning into modern, traditional industry into modern, industrial society to knowledge economy society, extensive economic growth pattern to intensive, and the dominant industry of the whole society is being transformed from resources- and energy-consumption-based to knowledge- and intellectual-based. For these changes, the theory of human capital provides strong theoretical support to help the social economic structures and emergent corporations under reform conditions to establish a series of effective mechanisms for human capital investment and development to promote corporate development, social evolution and economic growth.

At the same time, the development of a knowledge-based economy is a challenge that aspires to elevate China to a new stage of social evolution. Hui Yongzheng (2006), Vice Minister of the Ministry of Science and Technology of China, in a policy statement noted that: 'Implementing a strategy of "revitalizing the nation through science and technology" will help China reinforce its economic power, and we should focus more on promoting industries related to the knowledge-based economy, such as computer software, telecommunications, environmental protection, finance, computer-aided services, technological consulting, education and professional training industries'. A knowledge economy provides us with many opportunities and challenges to change our enterprises, education, policies, society, even our mind, and also create conditions to further apply classical human capital theories in every aspect, from country-level to individuals, and from government-level to enterprises. Based on a literature review, the current situation of Chinese human capital formation and development and the application of human capital theories in the context of a knowledge economy is now discussed.

Literature review

Knowledge economy and knowledge management

The knowledge economy has entered our economic life, driven by commercialization of knowledge, skills and information, and has come to dominate the world economy taking the place of the material economy. The authoritative explanation of the knowledge economy is proposed in the report on *The Knowledge Based Economy* issued by OECD in 1996 (Kim and Maugborgne 1997), which says it is an economy based on the production, distribution and application of knowledge and information. Its major economic features are as follows: first is commercialization of knowledge, skills and information; second, intellectual property rights system; third, price mechanism of knowledge; fourth, wide application of information technology; and last, the industrial structure with human capital as the centre. The typical phenomenon of the knowledge economy is the wide application of information technology, the foundation for development of knowledge economy development is talent, and the core of the knowledge economy is innovation.

In the knowledge economy, the success of corporations relies more on knowledge possessed by corporations. That is to say, how to apply existing knowledge to create sustainable competitive advantages is the new challenge faced by corporations. With the intensity of competition in the market, the increasingly uncertain aspects in the environment and the growing turnover of employees, corporations will need to provide value-added service for more diversified customers, which requires them to have stronger capabilities in communication, knowledge acquisition, knowledge creation and knowledge transmission. Successful knowledge management demands corporations shape a knowledge-sharing corporate culture, and set up trust-based message transmission mechanisms and operational procedures. In addition, corporations are required to master the values, scarcity, and non-imitability of knowledge, and to utilize knowledge and resources acquired and created to establish proper organizational structures to ensure the full use of knowledge and resources. From the aspect of knowledge, the main task of corporations is to integrate the special knowledge acquired by individuals and convert that knowledge into products and services; while from the aspect of corporations, the capability of finding opportunities in markets and locating resources is decided by existing storage of knowledge and the ability of creating and converting new knowledge. As the carrier of knowledge, human talent is the new source of competitive advantage for corporations. Hence, knowledge creation and knowledge management should be included in corporate strategy to gain sustainable competitive advantage when integrating human capital management into corporate management.

The trend of knowledge economy and knowledge management has brought many changes in Chinese society in recent years. During the past decade, China has placed more importance on reforming and modernizing its information and communication technology (ICT) sector than any other developing country. At the first session of the 10th National People's Congress in 2003, the Chinese leadership was strongly committed to making ICT as one of the most important national goals – from transforming Chinese society at home to pursuing its ambitions as a world economic and political power (National People's Congress 2003). The current leadership under President Hu Jintao and Premier Wen Jiabao continues to devote massive material and political resources to what it called "informatization" as a key strategic element for advancing the final goals. Within the next couple of years, several important policy decisions should be made under the Chinese leadership that will shape domestic and possibly global ICT performance and will affect a variety of other key matters such as economic efficiency, growth rates, international competitiveness, and patterns of political participation for many years. Some examples of data can demonstrate the size and direction of changes in Chinese ICT sectors. For instance, China's Ministry of Information Industries (MII) predicts that the ICT industry will continue to grow about 20% annually, or around three times the growth rate of GDP. The China Centre for Information Industry Development (CCIID) estimates that China's PC industry will grow 11.5% in market sales annually from 2004 to 2010. CCIID estimates that China's PC industry will reach a value of US$1450 billion by 2010 (China Electronics News 2007).

Theory of human capital

Traditional classical economics regards human labour as pure physical strength input, with little need for knowledge and skills, in other words – a homogeneous capability inherent in all labour. This idea had not been changed substantially until the 1960s. T.W. Schultz (1961), the American economist, put forward the concept of human capital for the first time in the early 1960s, and afterwards the theory of human capital developed rapidly. Although this was a new theoretical framework, the ideology of economics using humans as a kind of capital can be traced back to earlier times. At this point, William Petty (1690), a classical economist, used the concept of human capital to compare losses in soldiers, weapons and other instruments of war. A century later, Adam Smith (1776) argued in his works about how human capital investment and labouring skills affect individual earnings and pay structure, and regarded labourers' skills as an important resource for economic growth and increasing welfare. Schultz first proposed the explicit concept of human capital with the idea that human capital includes abilities, knowledge, skills and qualifications possessed by individuals. Later, Gary S. Becker (1962) connected human capital with the factor of time in a further way, indicating that human capital includes time, health and life expectancy in addition to the factors named above. When the idea first emerged, there were criticisms of the idea of human capital and the expansion of the theory of capital to human beings. Some criticized this referring to skills and producing knowledge storage in individuals as 'human' capital. Mincer (1993) indicates that some traditional economists, such as Stigler, Reder and Bjerke, argued that it was a mistake in morality and justice, depreciation in the status of 'free men/women' and that it violated everyday convention to treat humans as a kind of capital. However, this criticism should be viewed in the context of its times. We believe that any concept proposed is a real demonstration of that historical period, neither belonging to that period and neither transcending nor lagging behind this is of any great significance. Therefore, the concept of human capital involved in regarding humans as a 'commodity', was for them contrary to common customs then and to some extent it is still so even in modern times.

With the conceptualization of human capital, the theory of human capital was developed accordingly, which impelled the development of new management theories and practices. The first is the theory of human capital wealth, which studies the issue of human capital input and revenue in terms of the relations between human capital and personal wealth. This theory brought brand new attention to human capital revenue distribution and career choices. The second is the theory of human capital growth, which studies the effects of human capital, especially the impact of the various components of human capital on economic growth, using quantitative models. In the 1980s, David Romer (1986) and R.E. Lucas (1988), representatives of this theory, held that economic growth has its roots in the expanding of human capital storage, and that most income disparities are caused by the different quantity of human capital investment. Romer and Lucas see increases in human capital investment as the basic factor needed in reducing personal income disparities. The third is the theory of human capital properties, which was elaborated by several Chinese scholars in exploring the theory of modern corporations. In the People's Republic of China (PRC), Weiyin Zhang (1996), Qiren Zhou (1996) and others discussed the issues of the ascription of human capital properties and relative income distribution on the basis of property as part of corporation theory in their new system economics. The main points of this theory are as follows: (1) as an inherent personal property, human capital can naturally be held under the personal ownership of the labourer; (2) as a dynamic property, human capital can be utilized not by extortion but only by motivation; (3) with values of uncertainty, human capital has a great potential for exploitation, and has the possibility of becoming valueless at the same time; and (4) the theory of human capital allocation, which involves the issue of reasonably transferring and reallocating human capital among different regions and departments. Transference is a special way of deploying human capital, the real driving force behind which is net income increase both financially and non-financially. It is the fundamental principle of pursuing environment improvement that motivates individuals and families to improve incomes; and it is the fundamental principle of maintaining an open and highly efficient economic system that enhances greatly the welfare of human beings (Zhu 2005).

Education, as the most direct means of improving the value of human capital, has been paid more attention from the last century on. Preparing for the knowledge economy era, China has carried out ambitious plans to modernize its education system on the basis of a full understanding of human capital theory, which can be regarded as an important measure of human capital investment. For example, in 1998, the Ministry of Education announced its '211 Project' which selected some 60 universities in a national programme to upgrade college facilities and improve teaching systems. The plan was drawn up in the mid-1990s by the Chinese government to build 100 mega-universities which can achieve the same level as universities in developed countries. Ministry officials say that 350 key specialities in the 60 universities will receive funds for renovation, and an educational computer network and document system will be established to link universities nationwide and internationally The country has also invested more than 13 billion RMB /yuan (about US\$1.71 billion) in the project, which is the largest investment in the educational sector since new China was founded in 1949 (Ministry of Education 1998).

Intellectual capital and psychological capital

In the era of a new economy driven by information and knowledge, changes in information networks and human relations models are currently receiving more attention in the academic field. Hence, the concept of intellectual capital was put forward on the basis of the theory of organization, the theory of human capital and accounting of human capital. As the synonym for human capital, the term 'intellectual capital' was brought forward by N.W. Senior (1836), who thought it referred to knowledge and skills acquired by humans. John Kenneth Galbraith, the American economist (cited in Hudson 1993), mentioned the concept of intellectual capital and noted that the nature of intellectual capital is not only a static intangible asset, but a kind of process of 'ideological morphing-formation' and a method of 'goal-reaching'. He clearly moved the idea forward from that proposed earlier by Senior, but it is a pity that he did not form a more complete definition of intellectual capital. Later, Thomas A. Stewart (1997) defined intellectual capital as 'the sum of what all members in a corporation know that can help obtain competitive advantages in the market.' Also, he divided intellectual capital into three aspects – external (relations with customers) capital, internal (some scholars call this structure capital or organizational capital) capital, and human capital. However, P.N. Rastogi (2000) doubted this way of division and held that the three aspects of intellectual capital cannot be separated. As a dynamic system, a corporation keeps changing with the changes of internal and external factors, environments, relations and markets. Intellectual capital should be considered as a corporation's capability to create wealth after effective integration of a variety of knowledge components. This idea of integration and unification is also a new challenge in the study of intellectual capital in the field of management, urging more emphasis on the flow of intellectual capital management and measurement of intellectual capital during the course of value-creation, value-extraction and value-transformation.

When studies focus on human capital, intellectual capital and the relations between socio-economics and organizational performance on the macro level, the psychology of employees on the micro level is ignored. Luthans, Luthans and Luthans (2004) first presented the concept of psychological capital, further expanding the study on relations between human and intellectual capital and organizational performance to the micro level of psychology. Luthans et al. held that psychological states that help with personal positive development should include: (1) confidence in work challenges; (2) optimism maintained for now and the future; (3) hope and goal setting; and (4) fortitude when facing difficulties. At the same time, they thought that personal psychological capital could be developed through microcosmic adjustment in three psychological states indices, which are hope, optimism and mental toughness. In 2004, working with several Chinese scholars, Luthans et al. (2004) examined the relations between psychological capital conditions and performance with these three indices using 422 workers in three factories in China as the sample. The results showed that there is a significant relationship between these three indices separately or together as a core psychological capital variable and work performance. Their study pioneered a new direction in the category of human capital, and can serve as supplement for traditional work re-designing and newly developed human capital competence, promoting the relations between human capital and performance to a subtle micro level.

Human-based management thought

Peter Drucker (1967) elevated management to a lofty level through comprehending the effects of management in human society once again. Humanism is an essential pursuit running though Drucker's management thought. At first, he established the principle of the human as the core of management, advocating setting up management humanism with the human as the core of organizations. Then, he presented the idea of harmonious relations between individuals and organizations, seeking the organic harmony of positive collaboration of individuals and organizations. Finally, he attributed ultimate responsibility of management to individuals' self-management, trying to realize personal ultimate values through self-management. The humanism pursued by Drucker formed an organic and consistent ideological system, and elevated substantially the theory of humanistic management through proposing the idea of self-management (Drucker 1967, Chinese version, 2005, p. 20).

There are four humanistic features in the idea of self-management as set out by Drucker: a *goal*, that is, to realize an individual's life meaning and integrated development through self-management; a *subject*, to raise the awareness of subject in individuals through self-reflection and self-evaluation and leveraging individual self-determination, enthusiasm and original creation; *responsibility*, to make individual choices on the basis of personal obligations and attitude towards social values. A sense of responsibility is the premise for that of achievement; *effectiveness*, to inspire and use personal potential and advantages to the highest extent possible, and to pursue values through accomplishments. Drucker believed that the key issue of management and organization is the human, with the relations between the organization and the individual to be the foundation and premise for reaching humanistic goals, and self-management as the key to self-realization. His classical theory of self-management has great significance to human resource management in all kinds of enterprises, and we believe that the purpose of the organization is to permit ordinary persons to do uncommon things (Drucker 1967, Chinese version, 2005, pp. 182–185). Drucker's (2005) book is very popular among Chinese managers and provides many valuable suggestions for them on employee training.

Discussion: The current situation of Chinese human capital formation and development

Based on the above theories, the present author argues that intellectual capital has special meaning in relation to research on Chinese human capital in the context of the knowledge economy. The knowledge economy endows this era with special resources and advantages, as it promotes the progress of society bringing with it all kinds of challenges. China, a country well known for creating 'Chinese miracles', has a special background of economy, culture and society. It is important to research human capital in the current context of Chinese society, enterprises and citizens taking into account the background – one that combines tradition and modernity, East and West, theory and practice. Therefore, we present a detailed discussion identifying hypotheses based on the special background.

Hypothesis 1:   The hypothesis of complex men/women.

The hypothesis of complex men/women proposes that human beings have complex characteristics of being both lazy as well as industrious, which are decided by different conditions. It also emphasizes human beings' individual differences and advocates flexible management measures according different situations.

Hypothesis 2:   China is moving towards a new society with characteristics of a knowledge
economy.

The knowledge economy brings special resources and advantages and has its special characteristics of knowledge, science and information. First, as the core of knowledge economy, knowledge magnifies the human being's labour by permeating workers' labour, labour-materials and labour-objects; second, scientific labour provides rational theories and methods for the development of the social economy; third, information technology is now increasingly apparent in all kinds of fields of society.

Hypothesis 3:   Chinese transitional economy has special characteristics.

During the transitional stage, the hypothesis proposes that the Chinese economy has special characteristics, such as large regional differences, unbalanced economic development, fewer reserves, a lower quality of current human capital, an incomplete market system, and labour-denseness economy among others.

Hypothesis 4:   Chinese enterprises in the process of transformation have their special
characteristics.

Chinese enterprises have specific, special characteristics during the transitional stage, such as lack of a labour-market for managers and associated innovations relating to human resource management for example.

Hypothesis 5:   Knowledge economy brings many opportunities for society, economy,
enterprises and individuals.

Knowledge economy improves the progress of society by accelerating the speed, increasing efficiency and the appearance of scientific labour. All kinds of sectors benefit from the knowledge economy, for example, through the formation of human capital that is accelerated in the context of the knowledge economy.

Rate of return on human capital investment

The costs of human capital investment can be specified as educational investment, which means the sum of direct and indirect costs payable by an individual during the course of education. The costs can be divided into *social costs* and *personal costs*. Social costs are the expenses assumed by public authorities on behalf of the persons receiving the education, such as government and corporations, in which education expenses assumed by society and nation are direct costs, and the loss of opportunities for the individual being educated to create value for society during the period of education are indirect costs. For individuals, education costs are the expenses borne by those educated themselves, including expenses directly assumed by the educated and possible income and effect lost due to spending time and energy obtaining education instead of working and leisure, that is, opportunity costs. In addition, time values, risk costs and other factors during the course of education should be taken into consideration. Obversely, investment in human capital can be returned in the following five ways: (1) higher salary; (2) more career opportunities; (3) sound health capital; (4) reasonable consumption; and (5) benefits in culture and education for future generations. It is not hard to calculate the rate of return on human capital investment in a certain period with the help of Becker's simplified (1962) model.

Compared with other countries in the world, the rate of return on human capital investment is lower in China, the main reason for which is that due to the restriction of traditional notions – the current income distribution system of China cannot yet fully embody the principle of distribution according to work, and a salary cannot depend entirely on labour skills, namely human capital. Also, wide income disparities exist in different areas of China, which not only include the disparity of salary categories between cities, but also includes the rather large salary disparities between rural and urban areas. All these non-economic factors have had great effects on the rate of return on human capital investment in China.

The formation of human capital

The most important thing is to clearly understand the conditions of demand and supply of human capital in order to fully comprehend the basic concepts of human capital formation in China. The current conditions are as follows: first, the capacity of the market restricts the demands of corporations and society for human capital; second, physical capital assists the formation of human capital from the two aspects of employment opportunity and salary level; third, the desire and reasonable expectation for a high salary will influence the formation of human capital; fourth, time and preference have some effects on the demand for human capital formation. In accordance with demands, the power of supply in human capital formation is decided by investment ability and investment aspiration, and is also influenced by income, rate of birth, inflation and expectation for human capital potential.

The general picture of Chinese human capital is disequilibrium between supply and demand and co-existence of labour shortages and labour lying idle. Shortages lie in the fact that the whole sum of human capital is insufficient, and structured human capital is critically lacking, while in contrast a large quantity of human capital is left unused, which represents deficiency in effective demand under the traditional system. At the same time, monopoly is formed in human capital, with little or no freedom in job choice. In addition, various factors in distribution and education systems cause the inevitable phenomenon of human capital lying idle, leading to a huge waste in social production capabilities.

Optimal allocation of human capital

The key issue of human capital allocation research relates to signal-transmission, that is, how to put the right person in the right position, which corresponds to the idea of allocating personnel, described a long time ago by Confucius in the Analects: 'A man of honour recruits people according to their abilities' (Confucius 1973 edition, p. 117).

According to the basic categories of human capital, the author thinks that it can be illustrated as follows: at first, the common signal of human capital allocation is determined by the situation of compulsory education completely implemented in one country. In China, compulsory education exists on a wide scale. With further development of a market economic system, knowledge and skills improving, and reforms in education system in recent years, the scale is continually expanding. The second, the signal of skilled human capital is decided by professional education and training. Combined with the situation in China, it is clear that there are restrictions over education choices, and skilled human capital is not only determined by education, but also by experience. Therefore, this will cause shortages of appropriate people to fill higher-level positions. The present system will not deploy skilled human capital according to the education-signal, resulting in a distortion of the pure education-signal. The third, the signal of organizational management of human capital depends on accumulation of experience. Experience not only means experience of work, but also all abilities accumulated through work performance, that is, competence. Competence tests are becoming an important measure for modern corporations to select, assess, and motivate employees, which is of significance to human resource management systems (formerly known as personnel administration systems) and corporate recruitment mechanisms. Finally, the most important resource to maintain the sustainable development of national economy is entrepreneurial human capital, the model of which was proposed by Weiyin Zhang (1996). He states that the signal of entrepreneurial human capital allocation is the combination of personal fortune, capabilities, personal performance and experience. If only education and performance work as the transmission signal, fake entrepreneurs would exclude real ones.

Implications: Application of the theory of human capital in China

MBA education

The Harvard Business School started its Master of Business Administration (MBA) education programme in 1908 and the MBA has since been recognized as the most representative education plan in business administration education. MBA education is also the most critical form to exploit human capital and cultivate professional managers in China, and at present more than 120 business schools (approved by China's Ministry of Education) offer MBA degree programmes in China (Zhao 2005). Today, there are nearly 100,000 MBA students graduating each year in the United States, while the number is only around 20,000 in China, and this number is still deficient according to current domestic demand for MBA graduates. Based on observation of the global situation, China probably needs thousands of additional individuals with these talents; the annual growth rate of 6 to 7% is not enough in terms of total demand. The market demand for MBA-educated human capital is still rather large. At the same time, Chinese MBA education is far from mature with many problems, such as too high entry requirements, poor effects of on-site study, out of date teaching methods, low qualification of teachers, lack of appropriate teaching materials and case study teaching not corresponding to real Chinese practice. What is more, it is reported that most MBA graduates are not satisfied with their salary, and problems with the MBA education and the low salary situation make many students feel disappointed at the future of the MBA, creating a negative effect on the market for Chinese MBA education. For example, the average annual salary of MBA students graduating from one of the top business school in China only was 80,000 RMB/yuan in 2000 (about US\$ 10,000), and rose to 100,000 RMB/yuan in 2002 (about US\$ 12,000). However, we believe that with the reform of MBA education and the large market demand for MBA students, Chinese MBA education will improve in time.

Chinese official MBA education has a history of only 15 years, with many aspects in need of improvement and the issue of practicability is rather prominent since Chinese economy is in a transitional stage. Rather than developing entrepreneurs, MBA education brings up a kind of an 'MBA spirit' for the knowledge economy era, making managers learn and master the theory, knowledge and methods of successful business management and corporation management, and equipping managers with a kind of capability to comprehend and analyse problems at a higher level.

Government support

Education investment

Education is the foundation for the public to stand on its own feet. Chinese education is changing from a welfare education system to a multi-dimensional education system.

The primary source of education investment is the government. In addition, there are many diverse forms of investment in education, such as corporate investment, family and individual investment, social investment, private enterprises, and foreign investment. Educational institutions can be public, private, formal education (regular training) and non-regular training. The current education format covers degree and non-degree education, knowledge and skill education, and national and international education. Inevitably, problems will arise during the development of an educational system, for example, unreasonable education structure, unfairness in the field of education, and education producing graduates that the market does not accept. In addition to increasing education investment, the Chinese government is actively advocating vocational education, putting emphasis on fairness, improving the welfare of compulsory education, and exploring reasonable mechanisms of education costs sharing, aiming to improve the current situation of Chinese education business, marketizing, systematizing and normalizing it.

At present, the primary problem of Chinese education investment is insufficient funds. Compared with other developed countries in the world, the percentage of education investment within GDP is still low. According to the data in Table 1 the percentage of education funds in GDP was lower than in other developed countries and the average world level, while the level in developed countries is 5.1% and average level worldwide is 4.9% (National Bureau of Statistics of China 2006). Besides, more and more scholars pay attention to the education investment on children. Many present research studies test the extent of parental investment in children's human capital by use of intra-household resource allocation models. For example, one research study found that there is more spending on boys aged 13 to 15 but more on girls aged 16 to 18, by using an unusual, comprehensive data set for urban China; this result also suggests that standard human capital theories and traditional perceptions of gender bias do not completely explain educational expenditure decisions (Yueh 2006). What is more, numerous empirical studies from developing countries have noted that parental education has a robust and positive effect on child learning, a result that is often attributed to more educated parents making greater investments in their children's human capital (Brown 2006). It has also been found that more educated parents make greater educational investments in both goods and time and that these relationships are generally robust to a rich set of controls. Evidence suggests that making greater investment in both goods and time stems both from higher expected returns to education for children and from different preferences for education among more educated parents.

Table 1.   Percentage of Chinese education investment in GDP.

	1985	1990	1995	2000	2001	2002	2003	2004	2005
Total of education investment (a hundred million RMB/yuan)	226.9	659.4	1877.9	3849	4637.7	5480	6208	7243	8586
The percentage of education investment in GDP	2.5	3.6	3.21	4.31	4.8	5.4	3.32	4.53	4.12

Data source: National Bureau of Statistics of China (2006).

Health service and public support

Complete health service includes prevention and treatment. Most health service investment is undertaken by government departments. In addition, there are still some issues requiring further improvement, such as criteria for admission to medical training and practice, sanitation supervision and systems to ensure that laws are properly executed. The purpose of all these policy measures is to protect the public from possible health risks. In the middle of the 1960s, a triple-level (county, town and village) health service network was formed integrating prevention and treatment. In the past 20 years, the economic system, including the health service system, went through drastic marketization reform, increasing the health risks of farmers, especially poor groups, due to the fact that public support for health care was inadequate. The government does not regard public health expenses as human capital investment, but as a kind of welfare consumption, and plans to solve the problem of cost control with the help of the market. However, market forces cannot solve the basic problems in the nation's health and the gap between rural and urban areas will widen. In contrast, although urban populations, especially jobless families, suffer the impact of health service marketization, they can enjoy the priority of health care service availability, since the health care investment by central and local governments focuses on the cities, and social medical insurance and rescue system development have emphasized the cities. Recently, the Chinese government has recognized the situation and is trying to establish regional or district health care network systems in the rural areas (Gao and Yao 2004).

To gain public support and lay the foundations for a harmonious society, social public service in China needs to address its problems, for example, the structure of resource allocation still needs adjustment, the unbalanced situation between urban and rural areas – even within different regions – should be changed soon and so on. The main function of the social public service is to improve social conditions and environment constantly, to enhance people's living standard and material benefits, and to meet the demands of the public's requirement through education, science and technology and economic development. At present, however, the problems existing in the Chinese public service need urgent resolution. For example, the Chinese social security system mainly covers the employees in government organizations, non-profit organizations and part state-owned enterprises, while employees in collective enterprises, private enterprises, and especially people in the rural areas, still cannot enjoy the guarantee (Sun 2006).

Labour flow and allocation

Labour flow and allocation is characterized by cross-region migration of human capital. Take the policies of Shenzhen as an example. Shenzhen, one of the early Chinese Special Economic Zones (SEZ) set up in the 1980s, is an overseas-oriented and economically developed city, adjacent to Hong Kong. Once a small village with a few thousand people, it has now been transformed into a city of 8.5 million residents, in an urban region of 17 million citizens with the highest population density in China. According to a recent government report, the number of Shenzhen's long-term residents totalled 8.46 million at the end of 2006 with its population density growing to 4240 people per square km, more than three times that of Guangdong's capital city, Guangzhou (*China Daily* 2007). It has a rather high rate of external reliance, and it needs to depend on strong talent support to obtain international competitive advantages. On the coast of Southern China, Shenzhen ranks third in the list of 50 cities in human talents competence in China. The size of the employed labour force in Shenzhen is the sixth in terms of human capital quantity, and the rate of employed people in the urban area is growing rapidly. In terms of human capital quality, the coverage rate of varieties of professional employees in all employed people in Shenzhen is rather high, the growth rate of professional employees is increasing fast, the city does well on indices of entrepreneurial opportunity, and the education level of employed people is high. Regarding human capital allocation, Shenzhen, as a SEZ, attracts many highly talented individuals, making the availability of advanced talents in Shenzhen the top in the 50 cities. In the aspect of human capital education, the Shenzhen government invests a lot in education, and public education spending per capita in Shenzhen is also ranked first in the list of 50 cities in human talent competency in China. However, the rate of students at medium level and above and the size of adult higher education enrolment still need improvement. Shenzhen is a migrant city, and talent cultivated locally cannot satisfy all the local needs for talent. Therefore, attracting talent from other places is the key to Shenzhen development. The policy, mechanism, and environment for talent in Shenzhen make it a gathering place of excellent talented people from all over China, and have helped build Shenzhen as a centre of qualified people (Guangdong Government nd).

Open labour-markets

Government input is not the sole way to make human capital investment. We should promote the accumulation of human resources and provide more training programmes. Mechanisms in the labour-market can increase the human capital investment. In this regard, the labour-markets that have emerged in Beijing, Shanghai and Shenzhen have been performing effectively. Therefore, we need to open up labour-markets, to raise salaries and promote fairness for employees. However, immature labour-markets in developing countries and special characteristics in the social economy bring some market distortions. For example, the Chinese labour-market has at times caused the salary of skilled workers to increase in the short-term, reducing competitiveness.

Furthermore, labour-markets provide us with detailed and accurate information about domestic supply and demand of professions. It is very important for government to have this information in order to adjust policies, for units to select employees and so that individuals can choose suitable jobs. For example, from the detailed information of the domestic labour-market, we found that 101 cities in China have many special characteristics in the fourth quarter of 2006. First, the supply of labour was still greater than the demand for labour in the market; second, the structure of industry requirements was relatively stable, with the characteristics of service industry leading; third, 66.3% of labour demand was centralized in the manufacturing industry, wholesale and retailing industry, hotel and food industry, and resident service industry (Jin and Miao 2006).

Corporate behaviour

On-site training

Training, arguably, is the most important method for corporations to develop human capital. Currently, one bold step in developing vocational education and training in China is to depend on corporations and industries to conduct vocational education and training. In addition, many corporations have begun to introduce and establish corporate internal training systems, helping employees build up the idea of training, form the habit of training and build learning organizations through setting up training management departments within corporations, supervisors' training, and improving techniques for motivation. Data show that corporate employee training is playing a more and more important role

Table 2. Training investments of Chinese enterprises in 2004.

Percentage of training budget out of salary	Seldom	<1%	1–2%	2–3%	3–4%	>4%
Percentage of samples	35	28.2	19.7	10	3.8	3.3

Data source: Zhao and Wang 2006.

in corporate management, human resources development and the overall corporate benefits scenario. For example, the investment in on-site training of Chinese enterprises had increased in 2004 compared with 1996, and from data in Table 2, we can find that Chinese enterprises have paid more attention to on-site training investment, although this still needs further improvement (Zhao and Wang 2006).

Incentive mechanism

Another contribution of human capital theory to the corporation is that it boosts the establishment and implementation of incentive mechanisms to promote entrepreneurship. Take state-owned enterprises as an example: as the owner of capital, the state possesses the entire or most of the surplus claiming and controlling rights to capital. The benefits and status of human capital ownership in enterprises cannot materialize. Therefore, benefits conflict leads to low efficiency in business operations. The core of an entrepreneurial incentive mechanism is property rights, to be specific, possessing surplus claiming and controlling rights and gaining the whole or part of excess profits. Incentives for entrepreneurs include: compensation, short-term incentives and long-term incentives. Short-term incentives are usually in the form of bonuses, and long-term incentives are in the form of stock options. This diversified incentive model enhances enthusiasm for work and heightens the total efficiency of organizational human resource management (Xie 2001, pp. 61–96).

Property rights system reform

In accordance with Chinese traditional ideas, a corporate system should be 'who invests, who owns and who gains', without regard to the role of human capital in corporations, which leads to many inappropriate short-term behaviours. In order to solve this problem, many newly developed hi-tech corporations apply the theory of human capital to replace the old ideas. As a key component, human capital property rights can be converted into stock options to quantify the contribution of each human capital owner to the corporation, which clarify the human capital property rights. For example, Wang Xuan and Zhang Yufeng, the founders of Beijing Founder Electronics Co., Ltd, developed printing technology for Chinese characters with their own intellectual efforts and successfully set up a well-known modern hi-tech enterprise (Zhao 2002). Lenovo Group Limited (formerly Legend Group Limited), is the biggest computer company in China, which for a long period has been prominent in the computer industry, due to the excellent management provided by Liu Chuanzhi and the development of the Legend Chinese card and other innovative products by Ni Guangnan. The company recently acquired the PC Division of IBM.

Human resources accounting

In the process of social development and corporation changes, the scarcity of human capital requires accounting to bring human capital into its scope, which is in accordance with the common rules of accounting development. Although the importance of human resource accounting in corporate business management is beyond doubt, no common agreement has been reached on the application of human resource accounting. There are two problems facing the development of human resource accounting: one is an ethical viewpoint that it depreciates the idea of humanity to treat humans as a kind of capital. The other problem is an accounting idea that human resource accounting cannot meet the stipulation in the popular definition of properties to regard humans as resources, and that as of now there is no effective accounting and auditing system to quantify human resources. Hence, the field is still full of arguments about whether human capital can be definitely included in the scope of accounting (Zhao 2001). The present Corporate Accounting Standards do not give a clear prescription to answer these questions. However, the Chinese Ministry of Finance is organizing a group of scholars and experts to further explore the issue and make changes to the standards (Chinese Ministry of Finance nd).

Human capital pricing

Three kinds of foreign-invested enterprises, namely, wholly-foreign owned, joint ventures, and cooperative firm, in post-WTO China bring limitless challenges for Chinese enterprises. What Chinese state-owned enterprises and/or private firms fear the most is the attraction of high salaries offered by these foreign-invested enterprises. In foreign countries, the corporate revenue distribution model of human capital pricing has been continuously modified and improved, and the systems of human capital categories and formats participating in distribution of rewards (bonuses, performance-based salary plans, profit sharing, and stock option plans) have been greatly expanded. In China, after the entry into WTO in December 2001, an important method appeared to enhance Chinese corporate international competitiveness, which is to bring the corporate management and distribution system in line with international practice (Xiao and Li 2005). Therefore, we must establish a model of Chinese corporate human capital, taking into account corporate revenue distribution, vis à vis Chinese enterprises and future human capital development.

Individual investment

Individual investment in human capital may take the forms of education investment and health investment. Chinese education system reform has promoted college education integration. In recent years, the costs of personal education investment have been increased greatly, since there has been a movement towards self-supported post-graduate education within China in addition to the phenomenon of very large numbers of Chinese spending significant amounts of money to study outside China. Thus, it is necessary to have a sound employment system and career counselling mechanism to match with personal education investment policy implementation. Health investment includes food and clothing, exercising time, and health services for the purpose of sound health, in line with which, individuals are consumers and investors at the same time. Health is also the result of investment. Under the same other conditions, health depends on individual behaviour choice, such as smoking, drinking, psychological adjustment, and work and rest-schedules. Although health is composed of various products, services and time, the standard measure of health investment is medication and health care only, since medical treatment cost is the most direct way to quantify and measure health investment (Health Management 2005).

Conclusion and future studies

In the context of the knowledge economy, first, we should take effective measures to support the rural population to become a more important source of human capital, so that it can fully contribute to the development of the economy; second, we should make more efforts to construct an information-infrastructure and improve traditional industries to move to higher levels of technology, step up our efforts to restructure enterprises using information technology and make technological breakthroughs relating to agriculture; and third, a knowledge-based economy also requires the constant qualitative improvement of the population through continuous education and training. The transformation of education, such as MBA, higher education and on-job training in enterprises, should be given more attention. Last but not least, changing our 'mind-set' and improving our social system will surely be the foundation of further human capital development.

The theory of human capital not only enriches the treasury of human ideology but may also boost the growth of the economy, corporations and individuals. Compared with more mature studies in foreign countries, Chinese theoretical research in this field to date is insufficient, with much more to explore. From the aspect of a practical examination of human capital theory in China, some policies and measures instituted on the basis of human capital theory still need perfecting further. For example, we need changes and improvements in national education investment policy, health policy and human capital measurement. In addition, there should be improvements in pricing, allocation and motivation in corporations devising optimized plans that are more suitable for China's current economic situation and corporate development. All of this reminds us of the heavy responsibilities on the shoulders of its HRM scholars and researchers to push forward the development of the theory and practice of human capital.

Acknowledgements

The study is part of the research for the National Natural Science Foundation of China (Project No: 70572048). The author would like to thank the Foundation for the financial support. Many thanks also for very helpful comments and ideas from Michael Poole and Malcolm Warner, as well as the reviewers of this paper.

References

Becker, G.S. (1962), "Investment in Human Capital: A Theoretical Analysis," *Journal of Political Economy*, 70, 5, 9–49.
Brown, P.H. (2006), "Parental Education and Investment in Children's Human Capital in rural China," *Economic Development and Culture Change*, Chicago, 54, 4, 759.
China Daily (2007), "Keep Adjusting China's Homegrown Policies," July 5, www.chinadaily.com.cn
China Electronic News (2007), "Enhancing the Independent Innovation Competence and Building an Innovational Country," March 22, www.einnews.com/china/newsfeed-china-electronics
Chinese Ministry of Finance (nd), available online at: www.mof.gov.cn
Confucius (1973), *The Confucian Analects*, Beijing: Qinghua University Press (The original work was published in 500 BC; translated by James Legge, 1893, an English version is available online at: at http://www.sacred–texts.com/cfu/conf1.htm).
Drucker, P. (1967), *The Effective Executive*, New York: Harper & Row. Chinese translation of 2005, China: China Machine Press.
Gao, M., and Yao, Y. (2004), "Gender, Life-cycle and Intrahousehold Health Investment," *Economic Research Journal*, 7, 12, 115–125.
Guangdong Government (nd), available online at: www.gd.gov.cn
Health Management (2005), "Investment for Health," 8, available online at: www.HUWEIMIN.com
Hudson, W. (1993), *Intellectual Capital: How to Build It, Enhance It, Use It*, New York: John Wiley.
Hui, Y. (2006), available online at: www.most.gov.cn

Jin, X., and Miao, D. (2006), "Research Extensions of Human Capital Theory and Practice," *Journal of Beijing Normal University*, 4, 5–11.

Kim, W.C., and Maugborgne, R.A. (1997), "Fair Process: Managing in the Knowledge Economy," *Harvard Business Review*, 75, 65–75.

Lucas, R. (1988), "On the Mechanics of Economic Development," *Journal of Monetary Economics*, 22, 3–42.

Luthans, F., Luthans, K.W., and Luthans, B.C. (2004), "Positive Psychological Capital: Beyond Human and Social Capital," *Business Horizons*, 1/2, 47, 1, 45–50.

Mincer, J. (1993), *Studies in Human Capital, Collected Essays of Jacob Mincer* (Vol. 2.), Chichester: Edward Elgar Publishing Ltd.

Ministry of Education (1998) available online at: www.moe.edu.cn

National Bureau of Statistics of China (2006), *Chinese Statistics Annual*, Beijing: China Statistics Press.

National People's Congress (2003), available online at: www.educenter.com.cn

Petty, W. (1690), *Political Arithmetic* (Chinese translation, 1960), Shanghai: The Commercial Press.

Rastogi, P.N. (2000), "Knowledge Management and Intellectual Capital – The New Virtuous Reality of Competitiveness," *Human Systems Management*, 19, 1, 39–48.

Schultz, T.W. (1961), "Investment in Human Capital," *The American Economic Review*, 51, 5, 1035–1039.

Senior, N.W. (1836), *An Outline of the Science of Political Economy*, London: Clowes & Sons.

Smith, A. (1776), *An Inquiry into the Nature and Causes of the Wealth of Nations* (Chinese translation, 1981), Shanghai: The Commercial Press.

Stewart, T.A. (1997), *Intellectual Capital: The New Wealth of Organizations*, New York: Doubleday/Currency.

Sun, X. (2006), "Reform in Public Service: An Ethnic Perspective," *Teaching and Research*, 4, 26–29.

Wan, X. (2005), "Review on the Theory of Intellectual Capital," *Economics Trend*, 5, 82–86.

Xiao, W., and Li, S. (2005), "A Human Capital Pricing Model Based on Hierarchical Structure," *Chinese Journal of Management*, 5, 17, 582–590.

Xie, K. (2001), *Enterprise Incentive Mechanism and the Design of Performance Evaluation*, Zhongshan University Press, 9, 61–96.

Yueh, L. (2006), "Parental Investment in Children's Human Capital in Urban China," *Applied Economics*, 38, 18, 2089–2111.

Zhang, W. (1996), "Ownership, Corporate Governance, and Principal–Agent Relationship," *Economic Research Journal*, 9, 3–15.

Zhao, S. (2001), *Research on Human Resource Management*, Beijing: China RenMin University Press.

Zhao, S. (2002), *Human Resource Strategy and Planning*, Beijing: China RenMin University Press.

Zhao, S. (2005), "Life Force of MBA Lies in Practice," *Business Management*, 10, 48.

Zhao, S., and Wang, Y. (2006), "Company Training Under the Context of Independent Innovation: International Comparison and Implications," *Reform*, 3, 85–93.

Zhou, Q. (1996), "Corporations in the Market: A Special Contract between Human Capital and Non-human Capital," *Economic Research Journal*, 6, 7–79.

Zhu, B. (2005), "On the Rise of the Theory, Technology and Practice of the Modern Human Capital Theory," *Journal of Nanjing University of Science and Technology*, 18, 2, 45–49.

More evidence on the value of Chinese workers' psychological capital: A potentially unlimited competitive resource?

Fred Luthans, James B. Avey, Rachel Clapp-Smith and Weixing Li

China's fast-paced economic growth never ceases to amaze and simultaneously worry both the Chinese, and rest of the world's economists, politicians and business people. Hovering around 10% growth over the past 5 years, there seems little doubt that the Chinese economy is poised to surpass the United States in terms of purchasing power (*Economist* 2007) and has already become the world's second largest exporter behind Germany, but ahead of both Japan and the US. While these statistics have gained the attention of global corporations for several years (e.g., over 400 of the Fortune Global 500 are doing business in China), there is increasing concern among Chinese leaders, and with outside investors, whether such a booming economy can be sustained, let alone continue to grow. Most of the concern and focus has been on keeping up with advancing technology and the need for financial capital and some passing interest in environmental protection and transparency. Very little attention has been devoted to the virtually unlimited human resources of China. Instead of concentrating only on the obvious technological and economic challenges and trying to fix the weaknesses such as pollution, transparency and piracy, the time has come to take a positive approach by recognizing and leveraging Chinese human resources for contribution to sustained growth and competitive advantage.

Despite having very different employee obligations than most countries in the world, both private and state-owned Chinese enterprises need to update their understanding and effective practice of human resource management (HRM). Chinese employees are becoming increasingly mobile and the market economy embedded in a socialist political system (i.e. 'one country–two systems') poses challenges for the employer/employee contract. Most notable, state-owned enterprises (SOEs) are frequently criticized for inefficiencies largely due to the obligation they have to maintain what amounts to a surplus of human resources. In order to gain a competitive advantage under such unique and trying circumstances, SOEs must better leverage this excess human capital for a higher return and competitive advantage. The same is true for private enterprises operating in China. Simply competing on the basis of low-cost labour is no longer sufficient in a China that is now in the mainstream of the global economy with increasing wages and competition for talent (i.e. the so-called 'War for Talent' is reaching a China-front).

Using results of an exploratory study conducted a few years ago, that found a significant relationship between Chinese factory workers' 'psychological capital' (or simply PsyCap) and their performance outcomes (see Luthans, Avolio, Walumbwa and Li 2005) as a point of departure, the purpose of this study is to determine if the now more refined core construct of PsyCap's impact on performance can be updated and better understood. If similar results are obtained, then there is additional evidence and even more confidence in the value of such a positive approach to managing and leveraging Chinese human resources for sustaining and gaining competitive advantage into the future. After first providing a brief overview of the current Chinese context for managing human resources and what is meant by psychological capital in relation to this context, the study methods, results, and implications of the role that PsyCap may have in Chinese HRM and, in turn, the country's future path in the global economy conclude the study.

The Chinese context for HRM

Today's environment facing Chinese organizations' human resource management is a unique dilemma: How can a market-oriented economy function within the current boundaries and recent history of a socialist political system? In other words, Chinese HRM must operate within the constraints and challenges of a country with two seemingly conflicting systems. Gross domestic product growth rates do not provide evidence for hindered economic growth under the dual systems. However, the ghosts of the not too distant past (e.g., the early Communist and Cultural Revolution Eras) are often used to explain the inefficiencies of especially the state-owned enterprises (e.g., see Chen 2004). In addition, China's rapid rise in the world economy has left the society as a whole, and the human resources of organizations in particular, experiencing considerable uncertainty and stress (Gifford 2007).

In the last 25 years, the Chinese economy has shifted such that SOEs accounted for 80% of the country's GDP in 1978, but as of 2003, they accounted for only 17%. However, SOEs still employ half of the nation's industrial workforce (much greater than the entire US workforce) and still over half of China's industrial assets (Desvaux, Wang and Xu 2004). To address some of the inefficiencies associated with SOEs, the Chinese government adopted a reform approach during the 1980s that has increased managers' autonomy, implemented forms of financial incentives, and made reductions in some unneeded workers (Chen 2004). Although such measures have improved productivity, the profitability of SOEs remains a problem. While privatization of smaller SOEs has occurred over the last few years, complete privatization is unrealistic given the social responsibilities (i.e. employment opportunities) that SOEs carry on behalf of the state. Thus, the major challenge facing Chinese HRM as well as the entire country is how to leverage and effectively manage its unlimited human resources to meet the goals of both the economic and political systems.

We propose that this daunting challenge facing China and its organizations today may be helped by not just lamenting on the negative conflict between the two systems or trying to fix the weaknesses inherent in the rapid change and growth, but instead taking a positive approach. A positive HRM approach aimed at better understanding, development, and effective management of China's strength of unlimited, and still largely untapped, human resources may be a key solution. As evidenced in this volume, increased attention is finally being given to Chinese HRM. Our contribution is to provide increasing evidence of the value of the positive psychological capital of Chinese human resources. We next provide the meaning and role that this recently emerging core construct of positive psychological capital can play and then present the results of a follow-up study that provides additional evidence that the PsyCap of Chinese workers relates to their performance.

The meaning of positive psychological capital

Over the past few years, increasing recognition has been given to the value of positivity in human resource management. Particular attention has been given to how to strengthen the psychological resources of employees and improve their performance. Positive psychology (e.g., see Seligman and Csikszentmihalyi 2000; Synder and Lopez 2002), positive organizational behaviour (Luthans 2002; Luthans 2003; Wright 2003; Luthans and Youssef 2007; Nelson and Cooper 2007); positive organizational scholarship (Cameron, Dutton and Quinn 2003), and positive emotions (Fredrickson 1998, 2000) have all provided evidence that individuals flourish when the focus shifts from fixing what is wrong with people to strengthening what is right. The application of this positive movement to the workplace in general, and human resource management in particular, can be found in psychological capital or, simply, PsyCap (see Luthans and Youssef 2004; Luthans, Youssef and Avolio 2007b).

Since we first introduced the notion of psychological capital in relation to the Chinese workforce a few years ago (see Luthans et al. 2005), theory, research and application have greatly expanded. For example, PsyCap is now recognized to go beyond just human capital (i.e. what employees know, their education and experience). PsyCap represents who employees are (i.e. their psychological self) and what they can become. PsyCap is defined as: 'An individual's positive psychological state of development that is characterized by: (1) having confidence (self-efficacy) to take on and put in the necessary effort to succeed at challenging tasks; (2) making a positive attribution (optimism) about succeeding now and in the future; (3) persevering toward goals and, when necessary, redirecting paths to goals (hope) in order to succeed; and (4) when beset by problems and adversity, sustaining and bouncing back and even beyond (resiliency) to attain success' (Luthans et al. 2007b, p. 3).

An expanding body of research demonstrates that PsyCap is both open to development (e.g., see Luthans, Avey, Avolio, Norman and Combs 2006; Luthans, Avey and Patera 2008) and has performance impact (Luthans, Avolio, Avey and Norman 2007a). As indicated, a few years ago our exploratory study utilizing some of the components of PsyCap (hope, optimism and resiliency, but our model now also includes efficacy) found a relationship with the performance of a sample of Chinese factory workers (Luthans et al. 2005). We feel the time has now come to extend this initial finding with the now more fully developed and tested PsyCap core construct (e.g., see Luthans et al. 2007a, 2007b) and solidify the contribution it can make to the future of Chinese HRM.

As defined above, PsyCap is a core construct that consists of hope, efficacy, optimism, and resiliency. To gain clearer insight into how the PsyCap of Chinese workers can be better understood and then developed, leveraged and managed for competitive advantage, it is first necessary to clarify the contribution of each component state in relation to the Chinese context.

The role of hope

In positive psychology, hope is comprised of two dimensions: willpower and pathways (Snyder 2000; Snyder, Feldman and Taylor 2000; Snyder and Lopez 2002). Willpower is the expectancy and motivation individuals have for attaining a desired goal. Pathways complement this willpower by providing psychological resources that help find multiple alternative pathways to the goal. This alternative pathways thinking helps individuals achieve goals despite the presence of obstacles.

Applying the hope of human resources in organizations in China, the willpower dimension facilitates them to recognize and set goals that lead either an SOE or a private firm to attain desired performance outcomes. As China has been found to be relatively high in power distance and social collectivism (House, Hanges, Javidan, Dorfman and Gupta 2004), such goals may be identified by either an individual organizational leader and/or by the group of workers. However, each of the individual employees must internalize such goals to drive their own behaviour and make them personally relevant. In order to achieve the desired goals, particularly in a rapidly changing environment such as China is currently experiencing, individuals will make a greater contribution and be more effective when they utilize the alternate pathways dimension of hope. This is because they will have the resources to recognize and immediately implement alternative options to achieving goals. This hope factor of PsyCap is further strengthened when complemented by the confidence or efficacy to succeed at workplace activities, especially in the fast changing Chinese organizations.

The role of efficacy

Self-efficacy is the positive belief or confidence in one's ability to perform specific tasks (Bandura 1997). It has been found to be a universal state, although it manifests itself differently in various contexts (Bandura 2002). For instance, even in cultures with a high degree of group collectivism, such as in China, individuals utilize their efficacy to assess their ability to contribute to and execute workplace activities. However, the area in which efficacy varies across cultures is the manner in which it is developed. For example, it has been found that individuals from countries with a level of collectivism tend to develop efficacy more readily in a group context (Earley 1994).

This confidence component of PsyCap has been clearly shown to relate work-related performance in the US (Stajkovic and Luthans 1998) and in other cultures (Earley 1994; Luthans, Zhu and Avolio 2006; Luthans and Ibrayeva 2006). Human resource management practices that develop efficacy will be more successful in the Chinese context by utilizing a group training technique. In Bandura's (1997) conceptualization of self-efficacy, optimism is a critical component to more successfully apply to specific tasks. Optimism, therefore, is still another psychological state that strengthens the effectiveness of hope and efficacy and contributes to the overall core construct of PsyCap.

The role of optimism

Optimism is characterized by a positive explanatory style. When individuals experience instances of optimism, they tend to internalize positive events and externalize negative events (Seligman and Schulman 1986; Seligman 1998). As a result, optimists will have more positive expectancies of outcomes from specific events. Therefore, a higher level of optimism should aid Chinese employees in having more positive expectations of outcomes in the fast-paced, changing work environments.

In his description of today's China, Gifford (2007) explains that a tremendous optimism is apparent in the booming business centres such as Shanghai. However, other portions of the country, once one leaves the development and futuristic technology of Shanghai, are more depressed and worried about the future of China. Such a lack of optimism in the polluted industrial centres in provinces west of Shanghai may deeply affect the performance of employees. Thus, to improve performance, human resource managers may need to focus on developing positive expectancies (i.e. optimism). Such optimism for future outcomes and the role they may have for individuals, families and the greater Chinese society will be further reinforced when combined with the fourth recognized component of PsyCap – resiliency.

The role of resiliency

Resiliency is the capacity to bounce back from adverse or stressful situations (Masten, Best and Garmezy 1990; Masten 2001; Luthans 2002). Within the Chinese context, although rapidly developing business centres such as Shanghai may have a more positive outlook for the future, both developed and less developed regions of the country have undergone and will continue to undergo tremendous change at an unprecedented rate. This change, regardless of how positively or negatively it is perceived, as we have indicated is creating considerable stress and uncertainty that can be debilitating in the absence of resiliency.

At one time thought to be very rare and even 'magical', resiliency is now recognized to be a psychological capacity that all individuals possess (Masten 2001), but it needs to be developed and unleashed. In other words, everyone seems to have the potential for resiliency and what varies is their ability to call on this resource in times of stress (positive or negative) or adversity. The power of resilience is that once activated, it not only allows individuals to bounce back, but it also allows them to flourish even beyond their previous equilibrium state. Thus, by developing resilience, in conjunction with hope, efficacy and optimism, Chinese human resources may overcome the stress and uncertainty they are facing now and especially in the future.

Overall PsyCap

The four components – hope, efficacy, optimism and resiliency – that meet the PsyCap inclusion criteria of being based on theory, research and valid measurement and open to development (i.e. state-like) with performance impact (Luthans 2002; Luthans and Youssef 2007; Luthans et al. 2007b), on the surface appear very similar. However, there is now considerable evidence, both conceptually (e.g., Bandura 1997; Snyder 2000, 2002; Luthans et al. 2007b) and empirically (Magaletta and Oliver 1999; Carifio and Rhodes 2002; Bryant and Cvengros 2004), that they are independent constructs. However, as seen in the definition of PsyCap given earlier, there is also a common underlying linkage of positivity and striving to succeed among the components and empirical evidence supporting PsyCap as a core construct (Luthans et al. 2007a). Specifically, overall PsyCap has been found to predict performance better than the individual components (Luthans et al. 2005, 2007a).

Applying PsyCap to the Chinese context, we propose that the mindset of Chinese human resources needs to be changed to cope with the unique one-country, two-systems context. As China deals with a market-oriented economy and a socialist system, as well as the global competitive requirements and pressures as a member of the WTO, both SOEs and private firms must find new, we propose positive, approaches to HRM. These new approaches are needed not only to help employees maintain their present level of performance, but to help bounce them beyond current levels to overcome the inefficiencies at SOEs and the uncertainties and stress of employment in private firms. Based on the above foundation and our preliminary findings from the earlier study (Luthans et al. 2005), we hypothesize that the positive psychological capital of Chinese workers will have a positive relationship on their performance in both the SOE and private firm in our sample. We turn next to the methods used to test this hypothesis and the results and implications.

Methods

In this study, 456 workers from both the largest copper refining SOE and largest private copper refining factory in China using the same technological processes completed survey instruments in Mandarin Chinese. The survey instrument included demographic questions and the 12-item Psychological Capital Questionnaire (PCQ-12, see Luthans et al. 2007b for the full 24-item measure). Additionally, the worker's supervisor rated their performance on a multi-item measure on a scale of 1–10. A Chinese member of the research team familiar with the two organizations supervised the data collection. He gave a brief orientation on site to the study participants and supervisors in terms of the procedure for filling out the questionnaires and assured them of confidentiality and that the results would be used for basic research only. Of the 456 participants in the two firms, there were 367 males and 86 females (three individuals did not indicate gender). The average age was 39.8 years with an average work experience of 9.42 years. Of the participants, 46% had not completed high school, 41% had completed high school and no more, and 11% had completed the equivalent of a Bachelor's degree. Since the technological process and demographics of the two firms were not significantly different, they were combined into one sample for the analyses.

All scales were translated into Mandarin Chinese using back translation methodology (Brislin 1970, 1980). That is, the questionnaire was first translated from the original language (English) into the Mandarin Chinese by a bilingual native Chinese linguist. Next, the translated Chinese language version was "back translated" into English by a second bilingualist. Finally, the translated English version was compared to the original and any discrepancies were resolved by mutual agreement between the two linguists.

As indicated, positive psychological capital was measured with a reduced version (12 items) of the original 24-item PCQ (Luthans et al. 2007b). This 12-item PCQ included 3 items for efficacy, 4 items for hope (2 agentic capacity, 2 pathways thinking), 2 items for optimism and 3 items for resilience. Although the reliability of this translated 12-item PCQ ($\alpha = .68$) was not as high as has been found in multiple American samples using the original 24-item version (e.g., see Luthans et al. 2007a), it was still very close to the standard acceptable levels. In fact, a meta-analysis of Cronbach's alpha indicates that .60 is reasonable (Peterson 1994) and other researchers' published findings using back translations similarly fell just short of the .70 alpha level (e.g., see Sagie 1998; Van Vegchel, De Jonge and Landsbergis 2005) and specifically with a Chinese translation (Hui and Law 1999).

Performance was measured with a 5-item scale that supervisors rated each of their employees. This approach has been used in a number of studies that have tested the relationship of PsyCap and its components with performance (Luthans et al. 2005; Youssef and Luthans 2007). Example items of this instrument were 'Please rate his/her contribution to the organization's mission and goals' and 'Please rate his/her overall job-related ability'. This performance scale had an internal reliability of $\alpha = .92$. The demographic variables were measured by self-report. Specifically, employees were asked to list their work experience, education, age and gender.

Study results

All means, standard deviations and correlations of the study variables are shown in Table 1. The workers' PsyCap, tenure and education were all significantly related to manager rated performance. To determine the meaningfulness of the relationship between PsyCap and performance, a regression analysis was conducted. Specifically, tenure, education, gender and age were entered into Step 1 of a linear regression model. Next, PsyCap was entered into Step 2 to determine the extent to which PsyCap predicted performance above and beyond the demographic variables.

As seen in Table 2, tenure positively predicted performance while age negatively predicted manager rated performance. In Step 2 of this regression model, PsyCap predicted variance in the performance dependent variable above and beyond the covariates ($\beta = .26$, $p < .001$). In addition, PsyCap explained an additional 7% variance in the performance outcome.

Discussion

The purpose of this work was to conduct a follow-up investigation of the potentially powerful role that positive psychological capital may play in Chinese HRM. As evidenced in this sample, which included workers from both state-owned and private enterprises, as was found in an earlier exploratory study (Luthans et al. 2005), positive PsyCap does indeed seem to be a significant and unique predictor of employee performance. For example, while the widely recognized human capital component of work experience was found to be an important predictor of performance, adding psychological capital to the model significantly increased the amount of variance explained in the performance outcome, although work experience continued to be a significant independent variable.

Table 1. Means, standard deviations and bivariate correlations of study variables.

	Mean (S.D.)	PsyCap	Performance	Education	Tenure	Age	Gender
PsyCap	4.33 (.46)	1.00					
Performance	7.01 (1.13)	.25**	1.00				
Education	1.69 (.82)	.11**	.15**	1.00			
Tenure	9.42 (7.44)	.01	.39**	.06	1.00		
Age	39.79 (8.95)	.05	−.04	−.40**	.26**	1.00	
Gender	.18 (.39)	.04	−.06	−.03	.09	.03	1.00

**$p < .01$.

Table 2. Performance predictors.

	Performance	
	Step 1 β	Step 2 β
Education	.093	.048
Tenure	.392**	.407**
Age	−.079	−.119*
Gender	−.034	−.044
PsyCap		.260**
ΔR^2		.07**

*$p < .05$; **$p < .01$.

This finding suggests that PsyCap complements and adds value to the traditional human capital view of HRM rather than replaces it. Both human capital (e.g., work experience) and psychological capital accounted for separate and meaningful components of performance. In effect, by considering both human capital and psychological capital, there may be a more comprehensive and effective approach to Chinese HRM.

Before exploring the specific implications, as in any research there are certain methodological limitations to the study that must be noted. However, there are strengths that are also important to note. Specifically, this study does not suffer from common method variance or the impact when the independent and dependent variables are collected with the same method, at the same time, and from the same person. In this study the participant workers completed the independent variable(s) and their immediate supervisor completed the performance evaluation. However, in terms of limitations, first, the 12-item PsyCap scale was slightly below the threshold of generally accepted reliability at .68, indicating that further refinement of the Chinese translated measure may be required. Specifically, back translation methodology, while helpful, does not guarantee the meaning of items across cultures, only that they were, as far as possible, accurately translated grammatically and linguistically. Therefore, future research should include a more rigorous approach than back translation when studying PsyCap in Chinese organizations. In addition, future studies may consider item response theory on the individual items of the PCQ when applying them in contexts such as Chinese organizations.

Implications and conclusion

There are multiple implications and conclusions from this study for Chinese HRM. First, the unlimited human resource potential of China would seem to be an overwhelming opportunity for any investor or manager who understands the Chinese environment. As found in the first study and reinforced in this study, the performance of Chinese workers, and likely subsequent profitability of their organizations, may at least in part depend on the ability to select and especially develop and manage workers who are generally higher in PsyCap. Recent research (Luthans et al. 2007a) provides evidence that PsyCap is less stable (i.e. more 'state-like') than personality traits, suggesting that PsyCap is more open to be developed and managed. On the other hand, PsyCap was also found to be more stable than emotions, suggesting it does not fluctuate in the short term, e.g., from hour to hour. Therefore, by hiring employees who are predisposed to being higher in PsyCap and coupling this human resource selection practice with HRD programmes targeted toward developing employees' hope, optimism, efficacy and resilience (i.e. their PsyCap), Chinese organizations could enhance performance and over time their competitive advantage. This developmental attribute of PsyCap is critical. Not only may private firms hire and train based on PsyCap, but importantly SOEs that have an obligation to current employees to keep them on the payroll, may also develop their PsyCap in order to leverage them as a value-added resource, rather than just a costly liability.

In addition to the practical implications for performance improvement, another major implication for the current transition going on in China today was the lack of significant difference in the relationship between PsyCap and performance in the SOE and the private firm in the same industry using the same technological processes. Thus, regardless of a state-owned or private organizational context, PsyCap appears to be a meaningful predictor of individual performance. In particular, this result provides empirical evidence that SOEs may utilize the human resource management practice of developing PsyCap in their workers in order to overcome the challenges of surplus labour.

Still another important implication of the study results is the uniquely important role that positivity in general and PsyCap in particular may play in using HRM to meet China's unique and difficult challenges. In a country that has, in recent decades, fostered the collective mindset, discouraged individualism, and generally avoided enabling individual hope, confidence, optimism and resilience, this positive approach in general, and using PsyCap in HRM in particular, can have intuitive, and importantly from two empirical studies, evidence-based appeal to the Chinese at all levels – political, economic, and social. As more Chinese take on individualistic mindsets and the society as a whole continues to recover from the Maoist reforms of the Cultural Revolution, such positivity provides a means to integrate market-oriented individualistic thinking and behaviours with a collectivistic, socialist tradition. In sum, as China continues to emerge as a world economic leader, developing and managing this untapped positivity and PsyCap in their unlimited human resources may become the 'tipping point' for Chinese organizations and the country as a whole. This approach to HRM may allow the Chinese to continue to, and even better to, compete with Western corporations and adhere to the requirements and pressures of the WTO and full entrance into the global economy.

In conclusion, results from previous research and this study suggest that Chinese HRM may make a significant contribution to the great challenges facing China today. Chinese HRM needs to recognize, develop and manage the psychological capital of their unlimited human resources. Although economic, technological, political and social challenges certainly lie ahead, and the negative conflict of the two systems – one country and the fallout of rapid growth are certainly realities that must be addressed, the time seems right also to take a positive approach and emphasize China's strength of unlimited, untapped human resources. We propose, and our research supports, that the psychological capital of Chinese workers may indeed be a potentially unlimited competitive resource for China now and in the future.

References

Bandura, A. (1997), *Self-efficacy, The Exercise of Control*, New York: Freeman.
Bandura, A. (2002), "Social Cognitive Theory in Cultural Context," *Applied Psychology: An International Review*, 51, 269–290.
Brislin, R. (1970), "Back-translation for Cross-Cultural Research," *Journal of Cross-Cultural Psychology*, 1, 185–216.
Brislin, R. (1980), "Translation and Content Analysis of Oral and Written Material," in *Handbook of Cross-Cultural Psychology*, (Vol. 2), eds. H.C. Triandis and J.W. Berry, Boston: Allyn and Bacon, pp. 389–444.
Bryant, F.B., and Cvengros, J.A. (2004), "Distinguishing Hope and Optimism," *Journal of Social and Clinical Psychology*, 23, 273–302.
Cameron, K.S., Dutton, J.E., and Quinn, R.E. (eds.) (2003), *Positive Organizational Scholarship*, San Francisco, CA: Berrett-Kohler.
Carifio, J., and Rhodes, L. (2002), "Construct Validities and Empirical Relationships between Optimism, Hope, Self-Efficacy, and Locus of Control," *Work*, 19, 125–136.
Chen, J.J. (2004), "Corporatization of China's State-owned Enterprises and Corporate Governance," *Corporate Ownership and Control*, 1, 82–93.
Desvaux, G., Wang, M., and Xu, D. (2004), "Spurring Performance in China's State-owned Enterprises," *The McKinsey Quarterly*, special edition, 96–105.
Economist (2007), "Still no. 1," July, 11.
Earley, C.P. (1994), "Self or Group? Cultural Effects of Training on Self-efficacy and Performance," *Administrative Science Quarterly*, 39, 89–117.
Fredrickson, B.L. (1998), "What Good Are Positive Emotions?," *Review of General Psychology*, 2, 300–319.
Fredrickson, B.L. (2000), "Why Positive Emotions Matter in Organizations, Lessons From the Broaden-and-Build Model," *Psychologist-Manager Journal*, 4, 131–142.
Gifford, R. (2007), *China Road: A Journey into the Future of a Rising Power*, New York: Random House.
House, R.J., Hanges, P.J., Javidan, M., Dorfman, P.W., and Gupta, V. (2004), *Culture, Leadership, and Organizations, The GLOBE Study of 62 Societies*, Thousand Oaks, CA: Sage.

Hui, C., and Law, K.S. (1999), "A Structural Equation Model of the Effects of Negative Affectivity, Leader-member Exchange, and Perceived Job Mobility on In-role and Extra-role Performance," *Organizational Behaviour and Human Decision Processes*, 77, 3–21.

Luthans, F. (2002), "The Need for and Meaning of Positive Organizational Behaviour," *Journal of Organizational Behaviour*, 23, 695–706.

Luthans, F. (2003), "Positive Organization Behaviour (POB), Implications for Leadership and HR Development and Motivation," in *Motivation and Leadership at Work*, eds. R.M. Steers, L.W. Porter and G.A. Begley, New York: McGraw-Hill/Irwin, pp. 187–195.

Luthans, F., Avey, J.B., and Patera, J.L. (2008), "Experimental Analysis of a Web-based Intervention to Develop Positive Psychological Capital," *Academy of Management Learning and Education*, 8, in press.

Luthans, F., Avey, J.B., Avolio, B.J., Norman, S.M., and Combs, G.M. (2006), "Psychological Capital Development, Toward a Micro-intervention," *Journal of Organizational Behaviour*, 27, 387–393.

Luthans, F., Avolio, B.J., Avey, J.B., and Norman, S.M. (2007a), "Psychological Capital, Measurement and Relationship with Performance and Satisfaction," *Personnel Psychology*, 60, 541–572.

Luthans, F., Avolio, B.J., Walumbwa, F.O., and Li, W. (2005), "The Psychological Capital of Chinese Workers, Exploring the Relationship with Performance," *Management and Organization Review*, 1, 247–269.

Luthans, F., and Ibrayeva, E.S. (2006), "Entrepreneurial Self-efficacy in Central Asian Transition Economies, Quantitative and Qualitative Analyses," *Journal of International Business Studies*, 37, 92–110.

Luthans, F., and Youssef, C.M. (2004), "Human, Social, and Now Positive Psychological Capital Management, Investing in People for Competitive Advantage," *Organizational Dynamics*, 33, 143–160.

Luthans, F., and Youssef, C.M. (2007), "Emerging Positive Organizational Behaviour," *Journal of Management*, 33, 321–349.

Luthans, F., Youssef, C.M., and Avolio, B.J. (2007b), *Psychological Capital, Developing the Human Competitive Edge*, Oxford: Oxford University Press.

Luthans, F., Zhu, W., and Avolio, B.J. (2006), "The Impact of Efficacy on Work Attitudes across Cultures," *Journal of World Business*, 41, 121–132.

Magaletta, P.R., and Oliver, J.M. (1999), "The Hope Construct, Will and Ways, Their Relations with Self–Efficacy, Optimism and Well-being," *Journal of Clinical Psychology*, 55, 539–551.

Masten, A.S. (2001), "Ordinary Magic, Resilience Processes in Development," *American Psychologist*, 56, 227–239.

Masten, A.S., Best, K.M., and Garmezy, N. (1990), "Resilience and Development, Contributions from the Study of Children Who Overcome Adversity," *Development and Psychopathology*, 2, 425–444.

Nelson, D., and Cooper, C.L. (eds.) (2007), *Positive Organizational Behaviour, Accentuating the Positive at Work*, Thousand Oaks, CA: Sage.

Peterson, R. (1994), "A Meta-analysis of Cronbach's Coefficient Alpha," *Journal of Consumer Research*, 21, 381–391.

Sagie, A. (1998), "Employee Absenteeism, Organizational Commitment and Job Satisfaction, Another Look," *Journal of Vocational Behaviour*, 52, 156–171.

Seligman, M.E.P. (1998), *Learned Optimism*, New York: Pocket Books.

Seligman, M.E.P., and Csikszentmihalyi, M. (2000), "Positive Psychology," *American Psychologist*, 55, 5–14.

Seligman, M.E.P., and Schulman, P. (1986), "Explanatory Style as a Predictor of Productivity and Quitting Among Life Insurance Agents," *Journal of Personality and Social Psychology*, 50, 832–838.

Snyder, C.R. (2000), *Handbook of Hope*, San Diego, CA: Academic Press.

Snyder, C.R. (2002), "Hope Theory, Rainbows in the Mind," *Psychological Inquiry*, 13, 249–276.

Snyder, C.R., Feldman, D.B., and Taylor, J.D. (2000), "The Roles of Hopeful Thinking in Preventing Problems and Enhancing Strengths," *Applied & Preventive Psychology*, 9, 249–269.

Snyder, C.R., and Lopez, S.J. (eds.) (2002), *Handbook of Positive Psychology*, Oxford, UK: Oxford University Press.

Stajkovic, A., and Luthans, F. (1998), "Self-efficacy and Work-related Performance, A Meta-analysis," *Psychological Bulletin*, 44, 580–590.

Van Vegchel, S., De Jonge, J., and Landsbergis, P.A. (2005), "Occupational Stress in (Inter)action, The Interplay Between Job Demands and Job Resources," *Journal of Organizational Behaviour*, 26, 535–560.

Wright, T.A. (2003), "Positive Organizational Behaviour: An Idea Whose Time Has Truly Come," *Journal of Organizational Behaviour*, 24, 437–442.

Youssef, C.M., and Luthans, F. (2007), "Positive Organizational Behaviour in the Workplace: The Impact of Hope, Optimism, and Resiliency," *Journal of Management*, 33, 774–800.

Human resource management and the globalness of firms: An empirical study in China

Ji Li, Gongming Qian, Stacy Liao and Chris W. L. Chu

Introduction

This study examines the relationship between the commitment of firms to human resource management (HRM) in their host countries and their level of globalness. Despite numerous studies on the relationship between HRM and firm performance, it remains unclear how HRM commitment on the part of multinational corporations (MNCs) in their host countries influences their globalness. It is of interest to study this issue for several reasons:

- First, for academic researchers, our review of the literature on the relationship between HRM and firm performance gives rise to the conclusion that insufficient research has been conducted on the issue of the HRM of MNCs in their host countries. It would therefore be of use to academic researchers to obtain more empirical evidence on this issue from the MNCs with different levels of globalness.

- Second, for practitioners, this study will also be helpful in several ways. For instance, as it focuses mainly on HRM in a country that plays host to many major MNCs – China – the findings may also help the management of MNCs to formulate better HRM strategies and achieve a competitive advantage in this fast-growing market. The findings may also be useful for MNCs in developing competitive strategies for other emerging markets.

- Finally, this work will be of significance for both academic researchers and practitioners because it will help us to understand the relationship between globalness and the localization of human resources among MNCs. The results of this study should also improve our understanding of the competitiveness of MNCs that is derived from the human resources that they possess in their host countries.

This study is structured as follows. We first provide a brief review of the research on the relationship between firm globalness and HRM commitment. Based on this review, we then discuss the actual HRM activities and performance of MNCs in China and present the hypotheses for the empirical testing. Finally, we report the results of this testing, which are based on a set of data that was collected from large MNCs operating in China.

Literature review

The relationship between the commitment of MNCs to local HRM and firm performance has been studied by a number of authors (e.g., Farley, Hoenig and Yang 2004; Jaw and Liu 2004). Generally, the research suggests that the commitment of MNCs to HRM in their host countries is positively related to their level of globalness. First, as the level of a firm's globalness increases, the demand for timely and actual business information in its host countries also increases (Luo 2005). To satisfy this demand, MNCs must have qualified staff to collect and analyze this information. Without qualified human resources, MNCs may have great difficulty in collecting and processing local information. Accordingly, if MNCs engage in effective HRM in their host countries, then they will be able to recruit competent employees to collect and process local information, which in turn will help them to perform well in terms of globalness.

Second, as their level of globalness increases, MNCs need to make greater efforts to obtain the support and goodwill of the governments of their host countries. Previous research has shown a negative relationship between the proportion of local human resources among MNCs and the perception of local governments that these MNCs are hostile in their local operations (Kriger 1988). In other words, if an MNC engages in good HRM in a host country, then the local employees will feel satisfied and the firm may find it easier to maintain a good relationship with the local government. This good relationship will be beneficial to the firm's performance in the country, and will in turn help increase its globalness ranking.

Third, research has shown that the higher the level of globalness of an MNC, the stronger the need for direct networking and local expertise (Mizruchi 1997). Accordingly, to improve their globalness, MNCs need to recruit competent local employees who can help them to develop local networks and local expertise. If an MNC has a strong commitment to HRM activities in its host countries as demonstrated through effective recruitment and employee training activities, then it will be more likely to obtain competent local employees. The presence of competent local employees should then make it easier for the MNC to develop local networks and obtain local expertise, which in turn will help it to perform well in international markets and increase its globalness.

Finally, as the level of globalness increases, the demand for fast local responsiveness also increases (Roth and O'Donnell 1996). MNCs with a high level of globalness must be able to react efficiently to changes in local markets and other local environmental developments. Such local responsiveness should again have a positive relationship with commitment to HRM. MNCs with a strong commitment to local HRM should have qualified human resources that can help them to improve their local responsiveness and achieve a global competitive advantage.

In summary, previous research has found that the commitment of MNCs to HRM in their host countries has a positive relationship with their globalness. In the following, we further discuss this issue by focusing on the HRM of MNCs in China.

Globalness and the HRM activities of MNCs in China

In this section, we focus on the specific dimensions or activities of HRM based on the performance of MNCs in China, and propose some testable hypotheses to study the relationship between the globalness of MNCs and their commitment to each specific dimension of HRM.

Recruitment

Recruitment can be defined as the process of seeking and attracting a pool of qualified candidates for a job vacancy, and is said to be a major cause of strategic changes in firms today (Li, Liao and Chu 2006). A firm with a high level of globalness must be able to attract qualified employees in its host countries otherwise it may have a competitive disadvantage.

According to research and empirical observations, many competitive MNCs that are operating in the Chinese market today commit a large amount of their resources to employee recruitment (e.g., Hulme 2006; *Wall Street Journal* 2006). For example, a study in September 2006, conducted by Shanghai's Fudan University, showed that over 70% of the MNCs operating in China wanted to hire managers from the local area (see http://202.120. 224.5/fudannews 2006). A common practice of these firms is to recruit new graduates from major Chinese universities. For example, Procter and Gamble (P&G) does not usually recruit its managers directly from the labour market, nor does it try to attract managers from other firms, but prefers to recruit new graduates from over 20 major universities in China and systematically train them according to its demand. In recruiting new graduates, P&G has detailed and specific requirements about the attributes that they are looking for, which include creativeness, perseverance, leadership, good decision-making, good communication and cooperativeness. Only those who have no 'poor' scores in any of these dimensions can enter the second round of interviews, which may eventually lead to a job in the firm (Wang 1999, p. 85). Intel recruits university graduates from 12 key universities in eight Chinese cities, but also accepts applications from students from other universities (Li et al. 2006).

In contrast, it is evident that overseas firms with a low level of globalness usually commit fewer resources to employee recruitment. For example, many overseas Chinese firms, such as those from Hong Kong, have a lower level of globalness than the large MNCs from the West, and these Hong Kong firms normally commit fewer resources to employee recruitment (Li et al. 2006). This leads us to predict the following:

Hypothesis 1:   Firms with a high level of globalness usually commit significantly more resources to employee recruitment than firms with a low level of globalness.

Employee training

Employee training is a very important element of HRM. Training basically refers to activities that teach employees how to perform better in their current job. According to research and empirical observations in China, MNCs with a high level of globalness commit substantial resources to employee training (Hymowitz 2005; Hulme 2006). For instance, General Electric (GE), an MNC with one of the highest levels of globalness according to the *Fortune* ranking, is well known for its commitment to employee training in China. So far, GE has established over 24 joint ventures and wholly owned firms in China, and the majority of its local Chinese managers and engineers receive overseas training on joining the firm. GE also spends millions of dollars annually in China to train its local employees (Wang 1999).

Many firms with a high level of globalness set up their own training centres in China. For example, in 1996 Motorola established a training centre in the northern Chinese city of Tianjin. According to reports, this centre has nine classrooms, two computer laboratories, six seminar rooms, a library, and various other facilities, such as language-training and software-writing facilities (Wang 1999, p. 86).

In contrast, it has been observed that international firms with a low level of globalness usually commit few resources to the training and development of their employees. For example, many overseas Chinese firms, such as those from Hong Kong, have a lower level of globalness than the large MNCs from the West. And they normally commit little resource to employee training and development (Li et al. 2006). We therefore predict the following:

Hypothesis 2:   Firms with a high level of globalness usually conduct significantly more employee training than those with a low level of globalness.

Job description

According to the literature, international firms with a high level of globalness usually write accurate and effective job descriptions. A job description refers to a written statement that explains why a job exists, what the holder of the job actually does, how they should do it, and under what conditions the job is performed. Although there is no standard format for writing a job description, most job descriptions contain information on job identification, objectives, duties and responsibilities, relationships, knowledge, problem solving, accountability, authority, special circumstances, performance standards, and licences. To help employees and potential job applicants to understand their job requirements and other related issues, it is vital that international firms provide clear and detailed job descriptions. For reasons that have been discussed, the better the job descriptions that an international firm writes, the better they will perform in terms of globalness.

Job descriptions are arguably related to employee career development, which can be defined as activities that prepare employees for their future career or greater responsibility. If employees understand the specific jobs that are available in their firm and how to perform these jobs well, then they will be able to better prepare themselves to take on these roles, which will benefit their career in the firm.

According to research and empirical observation in China, firms with a high level of globalness usually provide clear job descriptions and career development programmes for their employees. For example, Fedex stresses that the most important characteristic of its HRM is to provide the best opportunities for career development for its employees. Every employee can receive US\$ 2500 from the firm annually to study for an MBA or other qualifications. The firm also has a leadership discovery and assessment programme that allows employees to recommend themselves to attend training programmes and be promoted to management positions (Hou 2006, pp. 35–36). All these may improve the firms' human resource and give them a greater competitive advantage, which in turn can improve their performance in terms of globalness.

Accordingly, we predict the following:

Hypothesis 3:   Firms with a high level of globalness usually provide significantly better job descriptions than firms with a low level of globalness.

Job appraisal or assessment

It is necessary for international firms with a high level of globalness to carry out effective performance appraisals or assessments. Performance assessment refers to activities that are related to the determination of how well employees are performing in their jobs, the communication of that information to employees, the agreement on new objectives with the employees, and the establishment of a plan for performance improvement. If an MNC carries out these activities well, then it will be likely to gain competitive advantages to become more successful in its global expansion. In other words, it will become more globally competitive.

According to research and empirical observation in China, firms with a high level of globalness often have an open and transparent performance appraisal system. Citibank, for example, requires all parties that are involved in an appraisal report to sign it after the report has been completed to ensure that appraisals are conducted fairly and objectively. This means that an appraisal or assessment record is invalid without the signature of the employee who has been assessed. Moreover, employees can check their appraisal records and the supporting documentation if they require. The results of the appraisals are directly linked to promotions and pay increases. Furthermore, Citibank continues to improve its appraisal system in accordance with changes in the business environment and the firm's global growth (Hou 2006, p. 89).

All these lead us to predict the following:

Hypothesis 4:   Firms with a high level of globalness usually conduct significantly better job appraisals or assessments than firms with a low level of globalness.

Internship

Internship is a method that is widely adopted by MNCs to discover and attract competent employees. It can be difficult for HRM managers to assess the quality of job applicants in a few hours or even a few days. Internships, however, allow a firm to have more time to observe the performance of applicants in a comprehensive way. This advantage has led many international firms competing in the Chinese market to provide sound programmes of internship for Chinese university students, who are the major source of new employees for these MNCs. For example, in 2006 Siemens offered over 100 internship positions through its Chinese Web site. On average, the firm has over 200 internship trainees working in its dozens of sub-units. GE accepts applications from Chinese university students through the Internet, and then selects candidates through three rounds of interviews. If candidates perform well in all of the interviews, then they are given a three-month internship. Those who show excellent performance in the internship eventually become formal employees (Li et al. 2006; http://y.sina.com.cn).

To attract the best candidates to their internship programs, many firms, such as IBM, P&G and Siemens, also offer scholarships to major Chinese universities (Luo 2001, p. 119). MNCs also organize activities at university campuses to attract the attention of students. These activities include making donations to schools and taking part in sports or other extracurricular activities (Li et al. 2006).

In contrast, it has been observed that international firms with a low level of globalness usually provide few or no internship programmes in China. For example, overseas Chinese firms with a low level of globalness, such as those from Hong Kong, usually do not provide any internship programmes for Chinese students (Li et al. 2006).

We therefore predict the following:

Hypothesis 5:   Firms with a high level of globalness usually offer significantly more internships than those with a low level of globalness.

Method

As indicated above, we selected China as the platform for this study. The reasons are: (1) The country has long been one of the largest recipients of foreign direct investment. Almost all of the firms on the *Fortune* lists have business operations in the country. As a result, there has been a growing interest in the HRM issues in China (see Warner 2004); and (2) Using a single country can help to control for the country effect, which might significantly affect the commitment to HRM. Hence, China provides a good setting for this research.

Sample

The sample for this study was selected from firms that were ranked by *Fortune* magazine as the World's Most Admired Companies in the four years from 2003 to 2006. Every year *Fortune* conducts an annual survey of some 10,000 directors, executives and analysts in industries from all over the world and rates companies on their globalness and performance in other areas. We selected the top 10 firms each year according to their globalness scores and compared their HRM with that of the bottom 10 firms. This comparison will help us to understand the relationship between the globalness of MNCs and their HRM in their host countries. Chinese firms were excluded from the sample as the focus of this study is non-Chinese MNCs.

Measures

The key variable in this study is *globalness*. As has been mentioned, the score for this variable was obtained from *Fortune* magazine based on their annual survey. However, *Fortune* did not actually publish the scores of all 500 international firms. The only complete data on globalness that were available were the scores for the top 10 and bottom 10 firms. Given this limitation, we decided to measure this variable as a dummy. Specifically, if a firm was among the top 10 firms in terms of globalness, then the dummy was assigned a value of 1. Otherwise it was zero.

To measure the HRM activities of the firms in China, we obtained information from two other sources. One was the websites of the MNCs in our sample that contained relevant information about HRM, and the other was telephone and e-mail communications. When visiting these websites, we paid particular attention to the information that was provided by these firms to potential job applicants. Two final-year university students were invited to visit the websites and code the relevant information about the HRM activities of the firms.

We also conducted e-mail and telephone interviews with staff members of the firms. When the information about the HRM of an MNC that was available on its website was insufficient or incomplete, we e-mailed or telephoned the firms to ask for more information. This allowed us to develop better and more comprehensive measures of the HRM practice of MNCs in China, which are discussed in detail in the following:

1. *Firm internship* was measured by the number of internship programmes that are provided to the Chinese university students. The majority of the MNCs in our sample provide this information on their websites.
2. *Employee recruitment* was measured by three items. Two were dummies that were based on whether an MNC set up both an English and a Chinese recruitment website. If the firm set up an English website for recruitment purposes, then this dummy was assigned a value of 1, otherwise it took a value of 0. Using the same

approach, we also measured the number of Chinese websites. Finally, we also coded the number of university recruitment centres that had been set up by each firm in China. We added the values of these three items together to obtain a measure of commitment to employee recruitment.

3. *Employee training* was measured by the number of training programmes that are provided by the MNCs for their Chinese employees, which we coded from information from the websites or from the telephone interviews.

4. *Job description* was measured by the perceived specificity of the job information that is provided by each firm on their website. We used the same two third-year student helpers to code this information on a seven-point scale, where seven represents 'very clear' and one represents 'not clear.' The inter-rater correlation for this measurement was higher than 80%.

5. *Performance appraisal or assessment* was measured by the perceived clearness of the description of the performance assessment. This information was taken from the websites of the MNCs. Again, this variable was coded by the two student helpers on the same seven-point scale. The inter-rater correlation was again higher than 80%.

Control variables

The proportion of human resources in China was measured by the ratio of the number of employees of a firm in China to its total number of employees. The effect of this variable was considered because a firm may not commit much resource to HRM activities in China if the proportion of total employees that are located in the country is very small.

Results

Table 1 shows the descriptive statistics of the data. The data suggest significant correlations among the different dimensions of HRM in these MNCs, which seems to indicate that a single construct – the HRM practice of the MNCs – can be computed based on the measurements. In the second half of this study, we present a reliability analysis to test whether this construct really exists.

To test the proposed hypotheses, we conducted one-way ANOVAs. The ANOVA is a type of analysis that allows us to compare the mean scores of the firms with a high level of globalness with those of the firms with a low level of globalness. These scores include the measures of the recruitment commitment, training and internship of the MNCs. Table 2 shows the results of these analyses.

Table 1.   Descriptive statistics.

Variable	Mean	S.D.	1	2	3	4	5	6
Independent variable								
1. Globalness	0.5000	0.50422	1					
Dependent variables								
2. Employee recruitment	4.7161	4.77668	0.306*	1				
3. Internship	2.9167	5.41902	0.499**	0.195	1			
4. Training	4.0833	5.35294	0.449**	0.265*	0.210	1		
5. Job description	5.3667	2.21678	0.713**	0.365**	0.471**	0.437**	1	
6. Performance assessment	7.7667	3.57186	0.828**	0.384**	0.488**	0.612**	0.844**	1

*Correlation is significant at the 0.05 level (2-tailed); **Correlation is significant at the 0.01 level (2-tailed).

Table 2.   One-way ANOVA analysis.

		Sum of Squares	df	Mean Squares	F	sig
Employee recruitment	Between groups	136.15	1	126.15	5.997	0.017
	Within groups	1220.033	58	21.035		
	Total	1346.183	59			
Internship	Between groups	432.017	1	432.017	19.266	0.000
	Within groups	1300.567	58	22.424		
	Total	1732.583	59			
Training	Between groups	340.817	1	340.817	14.645	0.000
	Within groups	1349.767	58			
	Total	1690.583	59			
Job description	Between groups	147.267	1	147.267	59.87	0.000
	Within groups	142.667	58	2.46		
	Total	289.933	59			
Performance assessment	Between groups	516.267	1	516.267	126.629	0.000
	Within groups	236.467	58	4.077		
	Total	752.733	59			

The data in Table 2 support all of the hypotheses that are proposed in this study. First, firms with a high level of globalness are significantly different in their recruitment commitment to those with a low level of globalness ($p < .05$). Second, firms with a high level of globalness offer significantly more internship programmes than those with a low level of globalness ($p < .001$). Third, firms with a high level of globalness provide a significantly greater number of training programmes than those with a low level of globalness ($p < .001$). Fourth, firms with a high level of globalness develop significantly clearer job descriptions than those with a low level of globalness ($p < .001$). Finally, firms with a high level of globalness conduct significantly better performance appraisals or assessments than those with a low level of globalness ($p < .001$).

As the data in Table 1 suggest a strong correlation among the different dimensions of HRM, we conducted a reliability analysis to show that the dimensions can be considered as items that measure the same construct, which we call *HRM Commitment*. The reliability alpha of this construct is .7204 (see Table 3).

Using the construct, we employed the Cox regression (proportional hazards regression) to test the relationship between the HRM commitment of the firms and their globalness scores. The Cox regression was first developed in the biological sciences, but in recent years has been adopted by social scientists to explore a variety of phenomena. A major advantage of this approach over other cross-sectional methods, such as logit or probit regression, is its explicit

Table 3.   Reliability analysis – item-total statistics.

	Scale mean if item deleted	Scale variance if item deleted	Corrected item-total correction	Alpha if item deleted
Employee recruitment	20.1333	165.1684	0.3626	0.7223
Internship	21.9333	150.7073	0.3941	0.7216
Training	20.7667	144.3175	0.4629	0.688
Job description	19.4833	184.8302	0.7094	0.6582
Performance assessment	17.0833	150.9929	0.7832	0.5761

Reliability Coefficients: N of cases = 60; N of items = 5; Alpha = 0.7204.

Table 4.   Cox Regression analysis of the firm with top level of globalness.

Cox Regression	B	SE	Wald	df	Sig.	Exp(B)	− 2logl	Model Chi-square
Model 1							175.767	7.332
HRM	0.030	0.011	7.429	1	0.006	1.030		
Model 2							168.374	0.061
HRM	0.031	0.011	7.186	1	0.007	0.031		
China proportion	0.422	1.628	0.067	1	0.795	1.525		

Table 5.   Cox Regression analysis of the firm with bottom level of globalness.

Cox Regression	B	SE	Wald	df	Sig.	Exp(B)	− 2logl	Model Chi-square
Model 1							157.884	20.259
HRM	− 0.090	0.027	10.961	1	0.001	0.914		
Model 2							137.607	0.19
HRM	− 0.090	0.027	11.022	1	0.001	0.914		
China proportion	− 0.181	1.354	0.018	1	0.894	0.834		

$N = 60$.

incorporation of the timing of changes in a qualitative dependent variable (Carroll 1982; Tolbert and Zucker 1983). We decided to adopt this approach to better control for the effect of the fast-changing business environment in China because our data were from a period when China was undergoing rapid economic and administrative reforms.

In each of the Cox regressions, the HRM commitment of the firms was entered as the independent variable and their globalness ranking was entered as the dependent variable (Model 1). The proportion of their total number of employees that were located in China was entered as a control variable (Model 2).

Table 4 shows the results of the Cox regression analyses, where a high level of globalness is assigned a value of one. According to the data in this table, the HRM commitment of the firms has a significant and positive effect on their ranking as firms with the highest level of globalness ($p < .01$). The effect of the control variable is not significant.

Using the same approach, we also considered the effect of the HRM commitment of firms being ranked in the bottom 10 in terms of globalness. Table 5 presents the results of this analysis. According to the data in the table, the HRM commitment of the firms has a significant and negative effect on their ranking as the firms with the lowest level of globalness ($p = .001$). Again, the effect of the control variable is not significant.

Discussion and implications

In this study, we focus on the issue of the effect on globalness of the HRM commitment of firms in their host countries. Using empirical data from MNCs operating in a major developing market – China, we obtained evidence on the relationship between the HRM commitment of firms and their globalness. The data show, for the first time, that the

HRM commitment of international firms positively influences their globalness. Firms that perform well in the different dimensions of HRM are more likely to receive a high globalness score from researchers and practitioners, which in turn may have a positive effect on their future performance – both financial and otherwise.

We did not directly test the effects of the commitment of MNCs to HRM on their financial performance, and it is acknowledged that a strong commitment to HRM may not always have a positive effect on financial performance, such as profitability or growth, especially in the short term. In other words, while some authors have suggested a positive relationship (e.g., MacDuffie 1995; Ichniowski, Kochan, Levine, Olson and Strauss 1996; Patterson, West, Lawthom and Nickell 1998), others showed the effects of HRM commitment were not significant (e.g., Lane, Feinbery and Broadman 2002; Mok and Yeung 2005).

There may be several reasons for this unclear relationship. For instance, financial performance can be influenced by other factors, such as the level of competition in a specific market and the technology that is controlled by a firm. A firm that performs poorly in HRM may still be profitable, at least in the short term, if it has effective financial or marketing strategies. Similarly, a firm's growth can often be affected by factors other than HRM practice, such as the external environment and the firm's connections (such as *guanxi* in China) (Yeung and Tung 1996; Luo 1997). Due to the presence of these factors, we did not expect to find a direct effect of HRM commitment on the financial performance of MNCs in this study. However, we believe that the globalness of firms can be treated as a proxy for their performance, both in terms of finance and other dimensions. For example, only when MNCs perform well financially can they obtain sufficient resources to globalize or achieve a high level of globalness, especially in the long term. In this sense, a high globalness score may suggest that a firm is performing well in terms of finance, marketing, and other dimensions of firm performance.

We suggest that more empirical studies should be conducted in different business contexts to gain a deeper understanding of the relationship between the HRM commitment of MNCs and their performance in all of the relevant dimensions, including globalness. Such studies would lead to the development of better theories of international HRM and the international strategy of MNCs.

Another direction for future study is about the interactions between firms' globalness and their HRM practice. Some research has suggested that, as the firms' globalness increases, their global HRM practice may also change. For example, according to a study by the Haygroup, the MNCs with a high level of globalness were more likely to place greater emphasis on centralization than on localization in their international operations. In the study by the Haygroup, the sample firms were divided into two groups. Group 1 included the top three firms in each industry in terms of global efficiency or globalness listed by the *Fortune* survey, and Group 2 included the rest of the firms listed by *Fortune* in each industry. To the argument that local priority should be submissive to the global interests of parent companies, 68% of the managers in Group 1 agreed, whereas only 51% of their counterparts in the Group 2 did so. On the issue of whether a firm should have a centralized and consistent compensation system throughout the world, 83% of the managers in Group 1 said yes, whereas only 55% in Group 2 shared that view. Finally, 79% of the firms in Group 1 reported that they frequently sent their home-country employees abroad as expatriates, whereas only 51% in Group 2 reported the same practice (see Demos 2006). All these findings suggest the interactions between firms' globalness and their HRM practice. It would be helpful for both researchers and practitioners to understand these interactions better.

Finally, this work also presents some interesting empirical data and observations that will hopefully help practitioners – especially those in managerial positions in MNCs throughout the world. Specifically, the data from this study suggest that management of MNCs should try to improve the quality of their firm's HRM in their host countries. According to the findings of this study, an MNC needs to perform well in HRM in its host countries to become a truly competitive firm with a high level of globalness.

Conclusion

In conclusion, the results presented here suggest two interesting points. First, when an MNC has a high level of globalness, it is also more likely to have a high commitment to HRM in its host countries. In other words, those with a higher level of globalness have a significantly higher HRM commitment than those with a lower level of globalness. This finding is contrary to the opinion that global strategy means a lower level of local HRM commitment and a high level of expatriate-transfer from home country to host countries. Second, this HRM commitment in host countries has a significant and positive effect on the average performance score of the most admired firms covered by the *Fortune* surveys. In other words, our data showed, for the first time, that the HRM commitment of global firms positively influences the firm performance in international competition.

References

Carroll, G. (1982), "Dynamic Analysis of Discrete Dependent Variables: A Didactic Essay," Mannheim, Germany: Zentrum fur Umfragen, Methoden und Analysen.

Demos, T. (2006), "Going Global, The Most Admired Companies are More Focused on Managing from the Center than on Local Initiatives," *Fortune*, Feb 24, 52–55.

Farley, J.U., Hoenig, S., and Yang, J.Z. (2004), "Key Factors Influencing HRM Practices of Overseas Subsidiaries in China's Transition Economy," *International Journal of Human Resource Management*, 15, 4, 688–704.

Hou, D.S. (2006), *The Motivation System of 36 Multi-national Companies*, Beijing: China Water Conservancy and Hydroelectricity Press, available online at: http://www.waterpub.com.cn

Hulme, V. (2006), "Short Staffed," *The China Business Review*, 33, 2, 18–25.

Hymowitz, C. (2005), "Recruiting Top Talent in China Takes a Boss who Likes to Coach," *The Wall Street Journal*, April 26, p. B1.

Ichniowski, C., Kochan, T.A., Levine, D., Olson, C., and Strauss, G. (1996), "What Works at Work: Overview and Assessment," *Industrial Relations*, 35, 299–333.

Jaw, B.S., and Liu, W.N. (2004), "Towards an Integrative Framework of Strategic International Human Resource Control: The Case of Taiwanese Subsidiaries in the People's Republic of China," *International Journal of Human Resource Management*, 15, 4, 705–729.

Kriger, M.P. (1988), "The Increasing Role of Subsidiary Boards in MNCs: An Empirical Study," *Strategic Management Journal*, 9, 347–360.

Lane, J., Feinbery, R.M., and Broadman, H. (2002), "Do Labour Strategies Matter? An Analysis of Two Enterprise-level Data Sets in China," *International Journal of the Economics of Business*, 9, 2, 25–38.

Li, J., Liao, S., and Chu, C. (2006), "The HRM Practice of Multi-national Enterprises in China," Hong Kong Baptist University, working paper, series no. 200610.

Luo, J. (1997), "Guanxi and Performance of Foreign-invested Enterprises in China: An Empirical Inquiry," *Management International Review*, 37, 1, 51–70.

Luo, J. (2001), *Strategic Management of Transnational Corporations (TNCs) in China*, Shanghai: Fudan University Press.

Luo, J. (2005), "How does Globalization Affect Corporate Governance and Accountability? A Perspective from MNCs," *Journal of International Management*, 11, 19–41.

Mizruchi, M.S. (1997), "What do Interlocks do? An Analysis, Critique, and Assessment of Research on Interlocking Directorates," *Annual Review of Sociology*, 22, 271–298.

Mok, V., and Yeung, G. (2005), "Employee Motivation, External Orientation and the Technical Efficiency of Foreign-financed Firms in China: A Stochastic Frontier Analysis," *Managerial and Decision Economics*, 26, 3, 175–193.

Patterson, M., West, R., Lawthom, D., and Nickell, S. (1998), "Impact of People Management Practices on Business Performance," *Issues in People Management*, 22, London: Institute of Personnel and Development.

Roth, K., and O'Donnell, S. (1996), "Foreign Subsidiary Compensation Strategy: An Agency Theory Perspective," *Academy of Management Journal*, 39, 678–703.

Tolbert, P.S., and Zucker, L.G. (1983), "Institutional Sources of Change in the Formal Structure of Organizations: The Diffusion of Civil Service Reform, 1880–1935," *Administrative Science Quarterly*, 28, 22–39.

Wall Street Journal (2006), "Firms in China Think Globally, Hire Locally," *Wall Street Journal*, Feb 27, p. B1.

Wang, Z.L. (1999), *American Corporations' Investment in China*, Beijing: Chinese Economy Press.

Warner, M. (2004), "Human Resource Management in China Revisited: Introduction," *International Journal of Human Resource Management*, 15, 4, 617–634.

Yeung, I.Y., and Tung, R.L. (1996), "Achieving Business Success in Confucian Societies: the Importance of Guanxi (connections)," *Organization Dynamics*, 25, 2, 54–66.

Devolvement of HR practices in transitional economies: Evidence from China

Cherrie Jiuhua Zhu, Brian Cooper, Helen De Cieri, S. Bruce Thomson
and Shuming Zhao

Introduction

In this research study, we investigate how human resource management (HRM) function and practices have evolved in firms in China. This evolution has been triggered by the challenge of an increasingly competitive environment brought about by economic reforms, and a series of subsequent reforms in corporate governance and ownership structures, especially after China's accession to the World Trade Organization (WTO) in 2001 (Warner 2004; Warner and Zhu 2004). The present study examines the extent to which devolvement, as part of strategic HRM, is practised in firms operating in China, and the consequent effect on firm performance. First, we review the strategic HRM literature, particularly the literature with a focus on the devolvement of HR practices, in the context of changes in the Chinese business environment, and with reference to prior research on strategic HRM research in China. Second, we present the results of our survey conducted in China. Finally, we consider the implications of the research findings for HRM scholars and practitioners. This research has important implications for HRM practitioners, especially those in the increasing number of foreign firms operating or planning to operate in China.

Strategic human resource management and devolvement

Research and practice in the field of strategic HRM has been developed and widely adopted in market economies (e.g., Bowen, Galang and Pillai 2002; Bowen and Ostroff 2004; Brewster and Hegewisch 1994). Research into strategic HRM emerged in the early 1990s with an emphasis on an integrative and value-driven approach to HRM (Butler, Ferris and Napier 1991; Schuler 1992), supported by both theoretical work such as the resource-based view of the firm (e.g., Wright, Dunford and Snell 2001) and empirical evidence (e.g., Huselid 1995; Becker and Gerhart 1996; Wright, Gardner and Moynihan 2003). This view of strategic HRM assumes that human resources are assets for investment, and the management of human resources is strategic rather than reactive, prescriptive and administrative (Budhwar 2000a; Buyens and De Vos 2001). A widely adopted definition of strategic HRM is the pattern of human resource deployments and activities that are planned to enable an organization to achieve its goals (Wright and McMahan 1992).

The dominant view of HRM has focused on a set of mutually reinforcing policies relating to critical features of employee resourcing, performance management and employment relations. However, recent literature encourages a broader view that covers the whole of people management, including leadership behaviour and organizational climate. This broader view is referred to by Bowen and Ostroff (2004) as the 'HRM system'. Bowen and Ostroff (2004, p. 213) define a 'strong' HRM system as one that fosters 'similar viewpoints such that the situation leads everyone to "see" the situation similarly, induces uniform expectancies about responses, provides clear expectations about rewards and incentives for the desired responses and behaviours, and induces compliance and conformity through social influence'. These authors argue that the impact of the HRM system will not be determined by the content of HRM policies and practices alone but rather by the processes that signal to employees desired and appropriate HRM responses in order to form a collective sense of what is expected. In other words, while many researchers have focused only on measuring a set of HRM practices, Bowen and Ostroff (2004) argue that it is important also to measure, and understand, the way in which the HRM practices are managed and communicated (i.e. supported by senior management and by other managers). Their argument has indicated the necessity of involvement of other managers in HRM, especially the front-line managers who are working with employees on the daily basis.

Underpinning strategic HRM are two important dimensions, i.e. vertically it links HR practices with the strategic management process of the firm and horizontally it allows HR practices to be integrated and supportive of each other. Vertical integration has two directions, namely upward and downward. 'Upward' refers to *strategic integration*, or the involvement of HRM in the formulation and implementation of organizational strategies and the alignment of HRM with the strategic needs of an organization (e.g., Budhwar 2000b), whereas 'downward' refers to the delegation or *devolvement* of HR practices to front-line managers (Currie and Procter 2001).

Downward integration, i.e. the devolvement of HR practices is defined as the involvement of front-line managers in the execution and administration of HR practices (Budhwar 2000a, 2000c), such as performance assessment, selection and training. A common classification of managerial positions divides them into staff or line positions. The line manager's main function is to achieve the predetermined objectives of the organization; any manager directly responsible for production and/or sales at any level could be classified as a line manager. A staff manager's primary goal is to provide advice and services to line managers and to non-managerial employees; in many organizations,

HR managers are considered to be staff, rather than line, managers (Gittler 1966; Armstrong 1988; Heraty and Morley 1995). Typically there are three levels of line management: senior managers, middle managers and first or front-line managers. Front-line managers are commonly referred to as supervisors. Brewster and Larsen (2000) argue that devolution of HR responsibilities to line managers is seen as something of a defining issue in HRM. Paauwe (1996) notes two principal ways of delegating an HRM role, i.e. internally devolving to line managers and externally outsourcing to contractors.

Over the last decade researchers have noted several factors that have influenced the trend for the devolvement, or downward integration, of HRM to line managers. These have included: technological advances (Clark 1993; Mayrhofer, Müller-Camen, Ledolter, Strunk and Erten 2004); increased competition (Colling and Ferner 1992; Heraty and Morley 1995); and globalization (Heraty and Morley 1995; Mayrhofer et al. 2004). These factors have forced a re-examination of organizational structures, which in most cases means flatter organization and decentralization in order to achieve greater levels of the effectiveness and efficiency (Colling and Ferner 1992; Heraty and Morley 1995; Paauwe 1996). Rationales provided for the devolvement of HRM to line managers typically present devolvement as: (1) reducing costs; (2) speeding up decision making; (3) an outsourcing alternative; (4) positioning responsibility with managers most accountable for HRM; and (5) utilizing line managers' knowledge of employees and local environment (Budhwar 2000c; Renwick 2003).

It has also been argued that, to make HR managers more available for participation in strategic decision-making processes, the responsibility of day-to-day HR practices should be delegated to lower-level managers as they have direct and frequent contact with employees and a capacity to understand, motivate, control and respond quickly to employees (Ulrich 1997; Budhwar and Khatri 2001). In addition to providing increased opportunities for involvement of the HR function in strategic decision-making, devolvement may have more direct effects on firm performance because this may increase contact between HR managers and line managers to assist HR managers in understanding front-line business problems, enhance the ability of HR managers to promote changes at a corporate level, and better control costs as line managers would work more directly with employees (Budhwar 2000c; Currie and Procter 2001).

Numerous researchers have stated that the practice of devolvement of HRM to line managers has not led to improved performance because of a lack of line managers' skill, knowledge and time (Colling and Ferner 1992; Renwick 2003; Mayrhofer et al. 2004). Thus, for the benefits of devolvement to be realized, line managers need to possess appropriate skills to execute HR practices competently and effectively (Budhwar 2000c). This means that the senior HR manager needs to be a strategic partner with line managers, providing training, resources, incentive and a communication channel to ensure these HR practices are carried out in accordance with HRM policy (Budhwar and Khatri 2001; Teo 2002; Budhwar 2000c).

Over the past decade, a substantial research effort has been built around exploration of the link between strategic HRM and organizational performance (e.g., Huselid 1995; Guest, Michie, Conway and Sheehan 2003; Bowen and Ostroff 2004; Boselie, Dietz and Boon 2005). Recent research, including the work of Datta, Guthrie and Wright (2005) and Wright, Gardner, Moynihan and Allen (2005), has continued to investigate and refine the measurement of the relationship between HRM and organizational performance. There is an increasing recognition of the need to explore beyond the relationship between HRM practices and firm performance, also to explore factors such as the context within which HRM operates and the ways in which HRM practices are conducted (Brewster 1999;

Youndt and Snell 2004; Neal, West and Patterson 2005), and the role of the devolvement of HRM to line managers (Morley, Gunnigle, O'Sullivan and Colling 2006).

Changing business environment and strategic HRM in China

In this research project, we examined the context of the Chinese business environment, developments over the past three decades in China which could influence the way HRM is conducted in China, and the relationship between HRM and firm performance. As McConville (2006, p. 637) has suggested, HRM 'offers a rich array of practices to allow organizations to adapt and respond to environmental changes'. In the transition from a command to a market economy and the increasing globalization of business, China has experienced and is still undergoing changes (Zhao 2005). Over the past three decades China's economy grew at an average annual real growth rate of 9.39% and by 2004, its gross domestic product (GDP) was 10.32 times larger in real terms than at the beginning of the reform period in 1978 (Statistical Abstract of China 2005, p. 22). China is the second largest beneficiary country of foreign direct investment (FDI), with invested amount increasing rapidly from US\$4 billion in 1990 to US\$72 billion in 2005 (UNCTAD 2006). Meanwhile, China has been ranked as one of the largest outward investors among developing economies, with a cumulative stock of outward FDI of over US\$57.2 billion by the end of 2005 (*People's Daily* 2006, p. 1, Bay Area Council 2006). Though China is emerging as a giant in the world economy, it is still in the process of further opening its previously protected markets and submitting to the rule of international law as a member of the WTO. Thus its government is deepening and facilitating reforms to allow greater economic integration with the rest of the world.

The major changes in Chinese business environment have included a closer interaction with global developments, a more market-driven economic system, and a dramatic separation of government from business operations (Zhao 2001, 2005). For example, the state-owned enterprise (SOE) reform and the flourishing non-state sector have witnessed the economy's move toward decentralization and deregulation and cessation of government administration of enterprises. This has levelled the ground for a more market-oriented competition. Furthermore, reforms in other areas (e.g., social security, labour contract and market system) have led to a fast-growing and floating (i.e. mobile) labour force within a free but plural labour market as different standards have been applied (Zhu 2005). These changes and the government's endeavour to establish a modern enterprise system have led to the reasons why enterprises are experiencing much fewer government constraints and have more autonomy to compete against others with different types of ownership. Given the dynamism of the business environment, demands on the HR system are likely to increase in complexity (Zhao 2001, 2005). This means that HRM needs to be conducted at a strategic rather than operational level and devolvement of HR practices could be applied more widely as part of the strategic HRM practices.

This study explores devolvement as an exemplar of a Western HRM practice and examines its effect on firm performance in Chinese firms. There are several reasons why this is an important issue. It has been pointed out by several researchers (e.g., Brewster 1999; Bowen et al. 2002) that strategic HRM research has been mainly carried out in advanced market economies. They suggest further research is needed in transitional economies to explore whether HRM practices translate into improved productivity at firm level. However, the discussion of strategic HRM to date has largely overlooked investigation of the downward integration or devolvement of HR practices to middle or line managers. At the level of middle or line managers, the effectiveness of HR practices can be determined by comparing them to organizational strategic objectives (Richard and Johnson 2001). Few studies have examined devolvement of HRM (Brown and Brainine 1995). Research that has explored line managers and devolvement of HRM in China has found that devolvement was not occurring in many Chinese enterprises due to the legacy of their traditional centralization of labour and personnel administration, the ideology of managing cadres by the Party (dangguan ganbu), and government bureaucracies (e.g., Di 2002; Peng 2003; Tang 2003; Zhao and Wu 2003; also see the report from China Enterprise Association 2006). Peng (2003) and Zhao and Wu (2003) found that there was little or no involvement of line managers in areas such as promotion, pay and work terms and conditions; the HR/personnel management department remained a specialized function, which in many situations was still focused at operational level. Given developments in the Chinese economy over the past decades, there is a need for more research to examine the application of strategic HRM to the Chinese context and its effect on firm performance.

Furthermore, many researchers have claimed that Western HRM has been practised in China either with Chinese characteristics, hybridized features, or a possibly increasing degree of convergence, reflecting the influence of foreign multinational corporations that have invested in China (Björkman and Lu 2001; Ding, Ge and Warner 2004; Warner 2004; Warner and Zhu 2004; Zhao 2005; Zhu 2005). However, few of these authors have examined the transfer of devolvement of HRM in Chinese firms and its impact on their performance.

Given these issues, we seek to explore two research questions as presented below:

1. To what extent is devolvement of HRM practiced by firms in China?
2. What is the relationship between devolvement of HRM practices and the performance of firms in China?

Method

Sample and procedure

Firms in Jiangsu Province of China formed the sample of this study. Jiangsu is one the most industrialized provinces in China with a population of over 74 million people and among the coastal areas first opened to foreign investment in the early 1980s. Our survey was conducted during the period from May to October 2005. Based on a distribution list of HR Managers Directory of Jiangsu HRM Institution 2400 questionnaires were distributed to respondents in firms on the Directory, with a self-sealed envelope and an explanation sheet. A total of 813 questionnaires were returned, yielding an effective response rate of 33.9%, because of the anonymous nature of the survey, respondents could not be directly compared with non-respondents. The focus of this survey was on managerial level respondents. Excluding non-managerial respondents, this left a sample of 618, among them 26.4% were from HRM/Personnel departments while the remaining respondents were from other departments (e.g., production, marketing, accounting and finance, research and development).

The profile of respondents, including their age, gender, education, types of firm they worked for, the duration in the current job and with the current enterprise, are shown in Table 1.

Over half of the respondents (55.7%) described themselves as middle managers, 29.1% as senior managers, and the remainder (15.2%) as line managers. As shown in Table 1, 68.8% of respondents were between the ages of 30 and 49 years and roughly two

Table 1. Profile of survey respondents.

Variables	Total (%)	Line managers	Middle managers	Senior managers
Age				
Less than 30	21.0	33.0	11.3	2.2
30–39	43.1	52.1	50.9	34.4
40–49	25.7	11.7	26.2	45.6
50–59	9.5	2.1	11.0	16.7
60 and over	0.6	1.1	6.0	1.1
Gender				
Male	67.2	68.1	69.5	86.6
Female	32.8	31.9	30.5	13.4
Education				
High school certificate or less	0.9	0.0	1.5	0.0
Technical secondary school	9.0	8.5	8.8	6.7
Bachelor's degree	32.3	29.8	31.9	24.4
Some post-graduate education	46.4	53.2	46.2	47.8
Post graduate degree	11.4	8.5	11.7	21.1
Firm ownership				
State-sector	23.6	26.6	23.3	22.8
Other non-state firms	64.4	67.0	64.2	63.3
Foreign-owned firms	12.0	6.4	12.5	12.0
Mean (SD) yrs. in current job	8.1 (6.6)	6.9 (5.5)	8.2 (6.4)	8.6 (7.3)
Mean (SD) yrs. with current enterprise	11.4 (8.6)	8.1 (6.3)	11.9 (8.5)	12.0 (11.4)

thirds of the respondents were male. The overwhelming majority (90.1%), had a Bachelor's degree or higher. In respect of ownership structure, respondents who worked in state-owned enterprises accounted for 23.6% of the sample. The others (76.4%) were working in the non-state sector, including shareholding firms, private firms, and foreign/overseas-invested ones. The mean duration of respondents' work experience in their current jobs and enterprises was 8.1 years and 11.4 years, respectively. This level of tenure would imply that respondents have a sufficient knowledge of the HR policies and practices, and related responsibilities, in their firms.

As might be expected, senior managers were older, more likely to be male, and to have more years of experience compared with that of line managers. A higher proportion of senior managers had a post-graduate degree compared with line and middle level managers, which reflected the importance of qualifications for senior managers in China as is encouraged by the government.

Measures

Downward vertical integration or devolvement was measured by asking respondents to report on six items referring to the responsibilities for HR practices at different levels in the organization. The practices included recruitment and selection, compensation, commercial insurance packages, training, performance assessment and job design. Respondents were asked to indicate those who assumed responsibilities of the practices, including senior management, middle management, line management, and HR. Respondents were also asked to indicate the proportion of line/middle managers in the organization formally trained to perform HR practices.

Firm performance was measured using perceptual performance indicators; one set measuring market performance, the other set measuring organizational effectiveness (see Appendix 1 for scales). Market performance was measured by three items related to return on equity and assets and profitability (Cronbach's alpha = .85). Organizational effectiveness was measured by five items related to the company's competitiveness by timely adaptation of its products/services and strategy, maintaining its quality, and achieving employee and customer satisfaction (Cronbach's alpha coefficient = .87) (Geringer, Frayne and Milliman 2002).

There are two *control variables*. The first was the *changing business environment in China* and was measured by four items, each rated on a five-point scale ranging from 1 'strongly disagree' to 5 'strongly agree'. The items were: (1) since the accession to the WTO, competition has increased dramatically in both domestic and foreign markets; (2) business environment is improving for more equal competition; (3) government regulations are rapidly changing to accommodate the requirements of the WTO; and (4) the technology in our product/service is complex. Cronbach's alpha coefficient for this scale was .74. The scores on the four items were averaged to form a composite measure (possible range of scores is 1 to 5), with higher scores indicating greater changing business environment in China. This measure was included as a control variable because of its predicted impact on firm performance.

Firm ownership, the second control variable, was categorized as follows: state-sector enterprises (including both state and collectively owned firms), foreign- overseas- (i.e. Hong Kong, Macau and Taiwan) invested firms including joint ventures and wholly foreign-owned firms, and other non-state firms (mainly state-owned turned, with mixture of ownership and domestic privately owned firms). In our regression analyses, firm ownership was measured with two dummy variables (state-owned firms were used as the reference category).

Results and discussion

Table 2 shows results for devolvement, measured by the responsibilities assumed by managerial staff at different levels for major HR practices conducted in the firm, including recruitment and selection, pay administration, commercial social insurance design, training, performance management and job design. All the organizations sampled employed at least one line or middle manager. Addressing our first research question, as Table 2 shows, there was little evidence of devolvement to line managers as most HR practices were carried out by internal senior managers, middle and HR managers. As only 26.4% of respondents were managerial staff from HR/Personnel, senior and middle level managers from other functional departments were also heavily involved in HR practices. It is interesting to see very few HR practices were outsourced (ranging from only 0.3 to 3.1%, see the bottom line in Table 2), or externally devolved as noted by Morley et al. (2006). Line managers were not delegated to conduct HR practices, with less than 10% involved in these practices. Middle managers were more likely than other managers to be involved in employee training and performance assessments. A devolvement index was constructed, ranging from 0 to 6, indicating the number of HR practices assumed by line managers, middle managers and senior managers. As the level of outsourcing was low, this practice was excluded from the index. The resulting index confirmed the low level of devolvement to line managers. Middle managers were slightly more likely than HR or senior managers to conduct HR practices, but the difference was not statistically significant at the .05 level.

Table 2. Devolvement of HR practices.

	Recruit & select applicants (%)	Administer pay and benefits (%)	Design commercial insurance packages (%)	Train employees (%)	Execute performance assessments (%)	Job design (%)	Devolvement Index Mean (SD)
Senior manager	52.8	45.1	41.0	20.1	44.5	51.8	2.53 (1.91)
Middle manager	45.4	39.5	42.9	52.4	56.3	51.7	2.81 (1.96)
Line manager	3.3	4.7	4.8	8.3	8.3	6.1	0.37 (0.97)
HR manager	45.9	43.3	37.5	53.6	37.5	32.2	2.42 (2.35)
Outsourcing	0.5	0.3	0.8	3.1	1.0	0.2	—(a)

Note: The percentages in each column sum to greater than 100 due to the overlapping roles of managers at different levels; (a) excluded from index due to low use of outsourcing.

As shown in Table 3, 41% of respondents reported that less than 30% of line managers in their organization were formally trained to perform HR practices, with 20% of these indicating that less than 10% of line managers were formally trained to perform such roles.

Table 4 presents means, standard deviations, and inter-correlations of the study variables. Table 5 presents the results of multiple regression analyses predicting market performance and organizational effectiveness. Results of evaluation of regression assumptions of normality, linearity, and homoscedasticity were satisfactory. Pairwise deletion was used for missing data (Roth 1994). Collinearity diagnostics using the tolerance test indicated that the regression estimates were not affected by multicollinearity.

Our second research question asked: What is the relationship between devolvement of HRM practices and the performance of firms in China? Controlling for other variables in the model, the results show that the proportion of line/middle managers formally trained to perform HR practices was positively related to both market performance ($\beta = .21$, $p < .01$) and organizational effectiveness ($\beta = .29$, $p < .01$). However, there was no evidence that the degree of devolvement to line managers was related to either market performance or organizational effectiveness. Interestingly, devolvement to middle level managers was positively related to organizational effectiveness ($\beta = .14, p < .01$), which indicates the role played by middle level managers in Chinese enterprises lends support for some researchers' findings that devolvement of HR responsibility to other managers has indicated a transition in HRM (Morley et al. 2006). However, firms need to be aware of the issue of role dissonance when middle level managers were delegated too many HR responsibilities and offered insufficient training to carry out the tasks (McConville 2006).

Of the control variables, the changing business environment had a positive effect on market performance ($\beta = .19$, $p < .01$) and organizational effectiveness ($\beta = .22$, $p < .01$). This has reflected the impact of a more market-driven economy on firm performance and its subsequent pressure on firms to adopt better managerial practices. Compared with state-sector enterprises, foreign-owned firms were more likely to have higher levels of market performance ($\beta = .11$, $p < .05$) and organizational effectiveness ($\beta = .14$, $p < .05$), which is consistent with research findings that foreign-owned firms have normally adopted more HR or "best" practices in their management and become role models for local domestic firms (e.g., Warner 2005; Zhu 2005).

Table 3. Percentage of respondents reporting that line managers are formally trained to perform HR activities.

	Frequency	*% of respondents*
<10%	124	20.1
10–19%	63	10.2
20–29%	66	10.7
30–39%	56	9.1
40–49%	22	3.6
50–59%	48	7.8
60–69%	49	7.9
70–79%	37	6.0
80–89%	35	5.7
>90%	97	15.7
Not known	21	3.4
Total	618	100.0

Table 4. Means, standard deviations, and intercorrelations of study variables.

Variable	M	SD	1	2	3	4	5	6	7	8	9	10
1. Changing business environment	4.08	0.69										
2. State-sector enterprise	0.24	0.43	.06									
3. Foreign-owned firm	0.12	0.32	.11**	-.21**								
4. Other non-state firm	0.64	0.48	-.13***	-.75***	-.50**							
5. Senior management HR	2.53	1.91	.05	-.01	-.07	.06						
6. Middle management HR	2.81	1.96	.13**	.18***	.05	-.19**	.05					
7. Line management HR	0.37	0.97	.04	.06	.13***	-.14***	-.10*	.15**				
8. HR personnel	2.42	2.35	.15***	.16**	-.05	-.11**	.08	-.04	.03			
9. Line management training	5.02	3.29	.20*	.05	-.04	-.02	.09*	.12***	.01	.20**		
10. Market performance	3.68	0.80	.25***	-.02	.09*	-.04	.06	.11*	.00	.08	.27**	
11. Organizational effectiveness	3.80	0.69	.32***	.01	.13***	-.09*	.05	.20***	.05	.13*	.36***	.65**

Note: n ranges from 585 to 618; $*p < .05$. $**p < .01$.

Table 5. Results of regression analyses predicting market performance and organizational effectiveness.

Variable	Market performance β	Organizational effectiveness β
Changing business environment	.19**	.22**
Foreign-owned firms	.11*	.14**
Line management HR	−.03	.01
Middle management	.06	.13**
HR managers	−.01	.04
Senior management HR	.05	.02
Percentage of line-managers formally trained to perform HR activities	.21**	.29**
R^2	.13	.23

Note: β = standardized regression coefficient; *$ap < .05$. **$p < .01$.

The results of this study have indicated that there is little evidence of devolvement of HR practices to front-line managers in the sample of Chinese firms investigated. However, middle managers were engaged in performing some HR practices, notably employee training and performance assessments. The regression analyses showed that variation in the degree of devolvement to front-line managers was not found to be predictive of perceived firm market performance or organizational effectiveness. Interestingly, devolvement to middle level managers was positively related to organizational effectiveness. The results also show that the proportion of front-line/middle managers formally trained to perform HR practices was positively related to market performance and organizational effectiveness. It is, of course, possible that the absence of an effect may be related to the relatively low levels of devolvement, particularly to front-line managers, resulting in restriction of range effects.

Of course, we should acknowledge some limitations of this preliminary investigation. First, the data are cross-sectional and the use of experimental or longitudinal designs would help in future research to strengthen causal inferences about the effects of devolvement on firm performance. Second, the data were gathered using perceptual indicators of firm performance. However, it is important to note that perceptual measures are commonly used in HRM research and have been found to correlate moderately to strongly with more objective measures of organizational performance (Delaney and Huselid 1996). Nevertheless, future studies could obtain measures from different sources, including more objective indicators of firm performance (Wright et al. 2005).

Implications for research and practice

The empirical evidence has indicated a lack of devolvement, which raises questions about the extent to which HRM is vertically integrated in Chinese enterprises (Currie and Procter 2001; Zhu, Cooper, De Cieri and Dowling 2005). We propose that future research might examine the extent to which HRM is integrated into the organizations' core business operations, i.e. the level of strategic integration in both vertical and horizontal directions. Further, such research could examine the relationship between upward and downward integration and the impact of this relationship on firm performance. Further analysis needs to be conducted to provide full explication of the roles and relationships of HRM with regard to organizational business strategy and firm performance.

Over the past three decades the Chinese economy has undergone dramatic growth and change-over. All indications are that this growth will continue and China will be an increasingly important player in the global economy. There are numerous challenges emerging for HR practitioners in China. Several reports have noted the strong competition among firms in China to attract and retain talent; in China, as in many other countries, HR strategies are viewed by many as integral to organizational strategies to gain competitive advantage (e.g., Braun and Warner 2002). Although China is the largest nation in terms of population, there is a critical shortage of talent, particularly among managers and professionals, required to meet China's burgeoning demand (Farrell and Grant 2005; Tung 2007). Based on our research and the emerging circumstances in China, we propose that there are four major areas that demand the attention of HR practitioners in China. First, there is a need to identify appropriate sources and attract strong candidates to fill HR roles in an organization. Many organizations report difficulty in finding and recruiting people in China with HR experience and knowledge, and we suggest that it may be more pragmatic to recruit candidates whose values match those of the organization, rather than seeking specific qualifications or prior experience. The next challenge then becomes the development of talent in the HR function. Requisite competencies of HR professionals operating in dynamic markets such as China include communication and networking skills, to build strong relationships with line managers; and a strong understanding of the HRM system. Building the competencies, and therefore the credibility of HR practitioners with senior and line managers, is an essential step towards development of the strategic role for HRM in any organization (Enns and McFarlin 2005; Farndale 2005; Ulrich and Smallwood 2005). A third area for attention is that HR professionals will also benefit by forming networks in the HRM community outside their own organization. Knowledge sharing among the HRM community can be an important mechanism for designing and managing improvements in HRM policies and practices; in China, the importance of networks or *guanxi* has been widely recognised. Finally, and perhaps most relevant to this research, we propose that HR practitioners will need to work with line managers to build the competencies of line managers, in order for devolvement to be successful. Training programmes and the provision of advice, support and resources are examples of the ways in which line managers' competencies can be built.

Conclusion

This research study provides empirical testing of the transfer of Western concepts and practices to a transitional economy, and contributes to the small but growing body of literature on the emergence of strategic HRM in China. The research is a significant contribution in that the findings will enrich our knowledge about the changing HRM function and practices in China and contribute to theory-building. Further, we have identified several areas for the attention of HR professionals operating in China.

References

Armstrong, M. (1988), *A Handbook of Human Resource Management*, New York: Nichols Publishing Company.
Bay Area Council, Association of Bay Area Governments (2006), "Ties that Bind the San Francisco Bay Area's Economic Links to Greater China," Bay Area Economic Forum, November, pp. 9, retrieved on 2 July 2007 from: http://www.bayeconfor.org/pdf/TiesThatBindFinalWeb.pdf
Becker, B., and Gerhart, B. (1996), "The Impact of Human Resource Management on Organizational Performance: Progress and Prospects," *Academy of Management Journal*, 39, 779–801.
Björkman, I., and Lu, Y. (2001), "Institutionalization and Bargaining Power Explanations of HRM Practices in International Joint Ventures: The Case of Chinese-Western Joint Ventures," *Organization Studies*, 22, 491–512.

Boselie, P., Dietz, G., and Boon, C. (2005), "Commonalities and Contradictions in HRM and Performance Research," *Human Resource Management Journal*, 15, 67–94.

Bowen, D.E., and Ostroff, C. (2004), "Understanding HRM–firm Performance Linkages: The Role of the 'Strength' of the HRM System," *Academy of Management Review*, 29, 203–221.

Bowen, D.E., Galang, C., and Pillai, R. (2002), "The Role of Human Resource Management: An Exploratory Study of Cross-country Variance," *Human Resource Management*, 41, 103–122.

Braun, W.H., and Warner, M. (2002), "Strategic Human Resource Management and Western Multinationals in China: The Differentiation of Practices across the Different Ownership Forms," *Personnel Review*, 31, 553–579.

Brewster, C. (1999), "Strategic Human Resource Management: The Value of Different Paradigms," *Management International Review*, 39, 45–60.

Brewster, C., and Hegewisch, A. (eds.) (1994), *Policy and Practice in European Human Resource Management*, London: Routledge.

Brewster, C., and Larsen, H.H. (2000), "Responsibility in HRM: The Role of the Line," in *Human Resource Management in Northern Europe*, eds. C. Brewster and H.H. Larsen, London: Blackwell, pp. 195–218.

Brown, D.H., and Branine, M. (1995), "Managing People in China's Foreign Trade Corporations: Some Evidence of Change," *International Journal of Human Resource Management*, 6, 159–175.

Budhwar, P. (2000a), "A Reappraisal of HRM Models in Britain," *Journal of General Management*, 26, 72–91.

Budhwar, P. (2000b), "Evaluating Levels of Strategic Integration and Devolvement of Human Resource Management in the UK," *Personnel Review*, 29, 141–161.

Budhwar, P. (2000c), "Strategic Integration and Devolvement of Human Resource Management in the UK Manufacturing Sector," *British Journal of Management*, 11, 285–302.

Budhwar, P., and Khatri, N. (2001), "HRM in Context: Applicability of HRM Models in India," *International Journal of Cross-Cultural Management*, 1, 333–356.

Butler, J.E., Ferris, G.R., and Napier, N.K. (1991), *Strategy and Human Resources Management*, Cincinnati, OH: South-Western.

Buyens, D., and De Vos, A. (2001), "Perception of the Value of the HR Function," *Human Resource Management Journal*, 11, 70–89.

China Enterprise Association. (2006), "Report on Various Aspects of Labour Employment in Chinese Enterprises," (in Chinese), *Enterprise Management*, 5, 90–95.

Clark, J. (1993), "Line Managers, Human Resource Specialists and Technical Change," *Employee Relations*, 15, 22–28.

Colling, T., and Ferner, A. (1992), "The Limits of Autonomy: Devolution, Line Managers and Industrial Relations in Privatized Companies," *Journal of Management Studies*, 29, 209–227.

Currie, G., and Procter, S. (2001), "Exploring the Relationship between HR and Middle Managers," *Human Resource Management Journal*, 11, 53–69.

Datta, D., Guthrie, J., and Wright, P.M. (2005), "Human Resource Management and Labour Productivity: Does Industry Matter?" *Academy of Management Journal*, 48, 135–145.

Delaney, J.T., and Huselid, M.A. (1996), "The Impact of Human Resource Management Practices on Perceptions of Organizational Performance," *Academy of Management Journal*, 39, 949–969.

Di, F. (2002), "How to Deal with Personnel Management in SOEs after the Accession to the WTO," (in Chinese), *Development and Management of Human Resources*, 2, 11–14.

Ding, D.Z., Ge, L., and Warner, M. (2004), "Evolution of Organizational Governance and Human Resource Management in China's Township and Village Enterprises," *International Journal of Human Resource Management*, 15, 836–852.

Enns, H., and McFarlin, D.B. (2005), "When Executives Successfully Influence Peers: The Role of Target Assessment, Preparation and Tactics," *Human Resource Management*, 44, 257–278.

Farndale, E. (2005), "HR Department Professionalism: A Comparison between the UK and other European Countries," *International Journal of Human Resource Management*, 16, 660–675.

Farrell, D., and Grant, A.J. (2005), "China's Looming Talent Shortage," *McKinsey Quarterly*, available online at: http://www.mckinseyquarterly.com

Geringer, J.M., Frayne, C.A., and Milliman, J.F. (2002), "In Search of 'Best Practices' in International Human Resource Management: Research Design and Methodology," *Human Resource Management*, 41, 5–30.

Gittler, H. (1966), "Executive Mobility and the Line/Staff Impasse," *Management Review*, 55, 4–12.

Guest, D., Michie, J., Conway, N., and Sheehan, M. (2003), "Human Resource Management and Corporate Performance in the UK," *British Journal of Industrial Relations*, 41, 291–314.

Heraty, N., and Morley, M. (1995), "Line Managers and Human Resource Development," *Journal of European Industrial Training*, 19, 31–37.

Huselid, M.A. (1995), "The Impact of Human Resource Management Practices on Turnover, Productivity, and Corporate Financial Performance," *Academy of Management Journal*, 38, 635–672.

Mayrhofer, W., Müller-Camen, M., Ledolter, J., Strunk, G., and Erten, C. (2004), "Devolving Responsibilities for Human-resources to the Line Management? An Empirical Study about Convergence in Europe," *Journal for East European Management Studies*, 9, 123–146.

McConville, T. (2006), "Devolved HRM Responsibilities, Middle-managers and Role Dissonance," *Personnel Review*, 35, 637–653.

Morley, M.J., Gunnigle, P., O'Sullivan, M., and Colling, D.G. (2006), "New Directions in the Roles and Responsibilities of the HRM Function," *Personnel Review*, 35, 609–617.

Neal, A., West, M.A., and Patterson, M.G. (2005), "Do Organizational Climate and Competitive Strategy Moderate the Relationship Between Human Resource Management and Productivity?" *Journal of Management*, 31, 492–512.

Paauwe, J. (1996), "Personnel Management without Personnel Managers," in *Managing without Traditional Methods: International Innovations in Human Resource Management*, eds. P.C. Flood, M.J. Gannon and J. Paauwe, Workingham, UK: Addison-Wesley, pp. 185–234.

People's Daily (2005), Overseas Edition (Renming Ribao–Haiwai Ban), 5 September, p. 1 (in Chinese).

Peng, J. (2003), "Focus on the Labour Market in China: Basic Issues and Problems," (in Chinese), *Development and Management of Human Resources,* 3, 4–9.

Renwick, D. (2003), "Line Manager Involvement in HRM: An Inside View," *Employee Relations*, 25, 262–280.

Richard, O.C., and Johnson, N.B. (2001), "Understanding the Impact of Human Resource Diversity Practices on Firm Performance," *Journal of Managerial Issues*, 13, 177–185.

Roth, P.L. (1994), "Missing data: A Conceptual Review for Applied Psychologists," *Personnel Psychology*, 47, 537–560.

Schuler, R.S. (1992), "Linking the People with the Strategic Needs of the Business," *Organizational Dynamics*, 21, 18–32.

Statistical Abstract of China (2005), *2005 Statistics*, Beijing: State Statistical Bureau Publishing House.

Tang, K. (2003), "'A White Page' on the Last 5-year Enterprise Management in China," (in Chinese), *Development and Management of Human Resources*, 1, 4–11.

Teo, S. (2002), "Effectiveness of a Corporate HR Department in an Australian Public Sector Entity during Commercialization and Corporatization," *International Journal of Human Resource Management*, 13, 89–105.

Tung, R.L. (2007), "The Human Resource Challenge to Outward Foreign Direct Investment Aspirations from Emerging Economies: The Case of China," *The International Journal of Human Resource Management*, 18, 5, 868–889.

Ulrich, D. (1997), "Measuring Human Resources: An Overview of Practice and Prescription for Results," *Human Resource Management*, 36, 302–320.

Ulrich, D., and Smallwood, N. (2005), "HR's New ROI: Return on Intangibles," *Human Resource Management*, 44, 2, 137–142.

UNCTAD (2006), *World Investment Report 2006: China.* retrieved on 19th October 2006 from: www.unctad.org/wir

Warner, M. (2004), "Human Resource Management in China Revisited: Introduction," *The International Journal of Human Resource Management*, 15, 617–634.

Warner, M. (2005), *Human Resource Management in China Revisited*, New York and London: RoutledgeCurzon.

Warner, M., and Zhu, Y. (2004), "Changing Patterns of Human Resource Management in Contemporary China: WTO Accession and Enterprise Responses," *Industrial Relations Journal*, 35, 311–328.

Wright, P.M., Dunford, B.B., and Snell, S.A. (2001), "Human Resources and the Resource Based View of the Firm," *Journal of Management*, 27, 701–721.

Wright, P.M., Gardner, T.M., and Moynihan, L.M. (2003), "The Impact of HR Practices on the Performance of Business Units," *Human Resource Management Journal*, 13, 21–36.

Wright, P.M., Gardner, T.M., Moynihan, L.M., and Allen, M.R. (2005), "The Relationship between HR Practices and Firm Performance: Examining Causal Order," *Personnel Psychology*, 58, 409–446.

Wright, P.M., and McMahan, G.C. (1992), "Theoretical Perspectives for Strategic Human Resource Management," *Journal of Management*, 18, 295–320.

Youndt, M.A., and Snell, S.A. (2004), "Human Resource Configurations, Intellectual Capital, and Organizational Performance," *Journal of Managerial Issues*, 16, 337–360.

Zhao, S.M. (2001), *Research on Human Resource Management*, Beijing: Renmin University Press, pp. 17–37.

Zhao, S.M. (2005), *International Business: Human Resource Management* (3rd ed.), Nanjing: Nanjing University Press, pp. 20–22.

Zhao, S.M., and Wu, C. (2003), "Research on the Current Situation of HRM in China''s Enterprises and Corporations," (in Chinese), *Development and Management of Human Resources*, 7, 27–35.

Zhu, C.J. (2005), *Human Resource Management in China: Past, Current and Future HR Practices in the Industrial Sector*. New York and London: RoutledgeCurzon.

Zhu, C.J., and Cooper, B., De Cieri, H., and Dowling, P.J. (2005), "The Problematic Role of a Strategic Approach to Human Resource Management in Industrial Enterprises in China," *The International Journal of Human Resource Management*, 16, 517–535.

Appendix

1. Firm Performance

(a) *Market performance*

How does your company's performance compare with the industry average? Please tick in the box.

	Very poor	Poor	Fair	Good	Very good
Return on equity	☐	☐	☐	☐	☐
Return on assets	☐	☐	☐	☐	☐
Profitability	☐	☐	☐	☐	☐

(b) *Organizational effectiveness*

How does your company's performance compare with the industry average? Please tick in the box.

	Very poor	Poor	Fair	Good	Very good
Timely adaptation of company products and/or services	☐	☐	☐	☐	☐
Timely adaptation of company strategy	☐	☐	☐	☐	☐
Achievement of quality	☐	☐	☐	☐	☐
Achievement of employee satisfaction	☐	☐	☐	☐	☐
Achievement of customer satisfaction	☐	☐	☐	☐	☐

2. Strategic HR Integration

Please circle in each item the number that best describes human resources or personnel activities in your company.
(1=strongly disagree, 2=somewhat disagree, 3=neither, neutral 4=somewhat agree, 5=strongly agree)

1. HR practices help achieve business objectives, e.g., for succession planning, to reduce/expand the workforce   1   2   3   4   5

2. HR strategy is formulated based on business strategy   1   2   3   4   5

3. HR is involved in business decision-making, e.g., to allocate resources, to assist in technology development   1   2   3   4   5

4. The top HR executive is a strategic partner for other senior managers   1   2   3   4   5

5. HR practices, such as recruitment and training, are used to implement business strategies   1   2   3   4   5

6. HR managers or people are involved in the development of work procedures   1   2   3   4   5

7. HR issues are a part of the company mission statement, e.g., commitment to people, people as a key investment   1   2   3   4   5

8. HR is involved in decision-making that co-ordinates your business(es)   1   2   3   4   5

3.   Devolvement

(a) People with responsibility for HR – If your organization engages in the following HR practices, please tick (√) who has responsibility for those HR practices.

	Senior mgt	Middle mgt	Line mgt	HR	Outsourced
1. To recruit and select applicants	☐	☐	☐	☐	☐
2. To administrate pay and benefit	☐	☐	☐	☐	☐
3. To design various commercial insurance packages	☐ ☐	☐ ☐	☐ ☐	☐ ☐	☐ ☐
4. To train employees	☐	☐	☐	☐	☐
5.To execute performance assessments	☐	☐	☐	☐	☐
6. To design job roles	☐	☐	☐	☐	☐

(b) Respondents were also asked to indicate the proportion of line/middle managers in the organization who were formally trained to perform HR practices (see the original question below) Q8. What percentage of line-managers are formally trained to perform HR activities, e.g., performance appraisal, recruitment and selection?

☐ <10%   ☐ 10–19%   ☐ 20–29%   ☐ 30–39%
☐ 40–49%   ☐ 50–59%   ☐ 60–69%   ☐ 70–79%
☐ 80–89%   ☐ more than 90%

Understanding the domain of counterproductive work behaviour in China

Maria Rotundo and Jia Lin Xie

Introduction

Over the past 30 years the globalization of the economy has proceeded at a faster pace than ever. Today, we live in a global community where money, products and talent are flowing across borders with greater ease. Customers, suppliers and employees often come from any part of the globe resulting in an increasingly diverse workforce and business environment. Managers commonly interact with and rate the performance of employees from diverse cultural backgrounds. These circumstances raise questions about whether the Western-based conceptualization of job performance generalizes to other cultures.

One country whose role is increasingly important in the world economy is China. Its sheer size and pace of growth over the last two decades make it a major player. Real GDP grew by 9.7% a year on average from 1990 to 2003; China currently accounts for almost 4% of world output (Kreuger 2005); most other countries' economies are linked to China's. The culture of China contrasts sharply with Western cultures (Hofstede 1991), thus it makes a viable site for cross-cultural research on job performance.

Research on job performance has been centred in North America. This research broadly defines job performance in terms of individuals' actions and behaviours that are under their control and that contribute to the goals of the organization (e.g., Campbell 1990). This research also recognizes that job performance is multidimensional and includes task behaviour, organizational citizenship behaviours (OCB), and counter-productive work behaviours (CWB). Furthermore, a body of research has investigated the extent to which North American managers are influenced by the three categories of behaviours when they form overall impressions about employees (e.g., Rotundo and Sackett 2002). That is, how much weight is given to volunteering to serve on committees or helping co-workers compared to task performance in managers' ratings of employee overall performance. Is it in employees' best interest to devote time and resources to OCBs? Or, to what extent is interpersonal or organizational deviance factored into these global ratings of performance compared to OCB. Research into the importance managers' place on task performance, OCBs, or CWBs answers some of these questions and provides useful information for employees and employers. There has been limited cross-cultural research on performance management. Therefore, questions remain as to what extent the Western conceptualization of job performance applies in other cultures.

There are two important questions in cross-cultural research on performance management. First, do members of non-Western cultures conceptualize job performance differently from how it has been described and measured in the Western cultures? That is, is job performance described by similar behaviours in different cultures? Second, even if the content of job performance generalizes to other cultures, do managers in other cultures value the different performance behaviours to the same degree as managers from Western cultures? The present research was designed to address these two questions. Specifically, Study 1 seeks to examine how counterproductive work behaviour is conceptualized in China using two independent samples of Chinese managers. Study 2 seeks to examine the similarities and differences between Chinese and North American mangers in the relative importance they endorse on task performance, OCB and CWB using another two independent samples of Chinese managers and a sample of Canadian managers.

Theoretical development: convergence and divergence perspectives

Cross-cultural management research has been characterized by debates over the convergence and divergence perspectives – alternative predictions for the relationship between industrialization and the development of managerial values and behaviour (e.g., Brislin 1993; McGaughey and DeCieri 1999; Khilji 2002; Pudelko, Fink, Carr and Wentges 2006; Vance 2006). Convergence theorists argue that industrialization, technology, globalization, and the deregulation of economies are the primary driving forces behind the global merging of workplace attitudes and behaviours. They argue that industrialization necessitates certain managerial practices regardless of the culture in which it occurs. That is, industrial societies share common needs with respect to the economic, technological, coordination and administrative demands that arise from industrialization and that are not dictated by a nation's culture. On the other hand, proponents of the divergence perspective argue that work and personal values are primarily the product of societal-cultural influences. They posit that despite globalization and any economic similarities between nations, individuals hold onto the nation's cultural values and hence management practices are deeply rooted in a nation's culture. They argue that a nation's culture influences the content of the functional areas within an organization, which makes it difficult for global organizations to apply consistent management practices across nations. Hence, they suggest that management practices should be and are adjusted to the local cultural context.

In an effort to address these competing perspectives on the cross-cultural applicability of Western-based management practices, the present study examines the content of counterproductive work behaviour among Chinese managers and analyses this content against the content that has been measured and described in the Western cultures. When analysing the extent to which culture impacts organizational behaviour, cross-cultural organizational psychologists have argued that culture influences those situations where interpersonal or organizational relationships are not constrained by technology or other contingent factors (see review by Markus and Kitayama 1991). Applied to individual level job performance, workplace actions and behaviours that fall under CWB are based firmly on interpersonal relationships and hence they are likely to be impacted by cultural differences. Research has already begun to explore the content of OCB in the Chinese context (e.g., Farh, Earley and Lin 1997; Farh, Zhong and Organ 2004). To our knowledge no research has yet explicitly explored the content of CWB in China. Hence, our research on the Chinese conceptualization of job performance focused on CWB.

Job performance in the Western literature

Traditionally performance appraisal systems were comprised of statements related to the completion of tasks specific to one's job. During the industrial revolution, where manufacturing dominated, jobs were defined primarily by a set of tasks bundled together to form a job (Fleishman and Quaintance 1984). The emphasis at that time was rating employees on the completion of tasks. The 1980s brought about total quality management, the emphasis on cross-functional teams, and the importance of communication. Increased competition and the shift from a manufacturing-based economy to an information-and-service based economy in the new millennium brought greater accountability for production deviance and unethical behaviour and the necessity of sharing knowledge and building relationships. Thus, the modern workplace drew our attention to a category of behaviours that detract from the goals of the organization by harming the well-being of co-workers or the organization. Examples of these forms of behaviour include absenteeism, production deviance, workplace aggression, theft, sabotage or fraud. Various labels have been given to these behaviours: *counterproductive work behaviour* (Gruys and Sackett 2003), *professional deviant-adaptive behaviours* (Raelin 1994), *workplace deviance* (Bennett and Robinson 2000), *generic work behaviours* (Hunt 1996), or *destructive/hazardous behaviours* (Murphy 1989). These conceptualizations have been based on research conducted using Western samples in Western social and cultural contexts.

Western conceptualizations of job performance in China: Applicability and constraints

Confucian philosophies, especially Ren (仁) (benevolence), Yi (义) (right conduct), Zhong (忠) (loyalty), and Li (礼) (propriety and good manners) have formed the foundation of the Chinese traditional culture, and these philosophies represent behavioural standards in Chinese societies (see reviews by Bond and Hwang 1992; Sha 2000). Specifically, the teachings of the Confucian heritage emphasize the importance of controlling for selfish and greedy behaviours and the importance of spontaneous behaviours that are beyond the explicit role requirements but essential for the society. More than two thousand years ago, Confucius described an ideal commonwealth state, in which:

every man and woman has an appropriate role to play in the family and society. A sense of sharing displaces the effects of selfishness and materialism. A devotion to public duty leaves no room for idleness. Intrigues and conniving for ill gain are unknown. Villains such as thieves and robbers do not exist. The doors to every home need never be blocked and bolted by day or night. These are the characteristics of an ideal work, and commonwealth state (*The Record of Rites* 2004).

In addition to the influence of the traditional culture, the educational systems in Chinese schools, organizations, and society at large are characterized by active disseminations of 'Hao Ren Hao Shi' (好人好事) (good people and good things) and open criticisms of 'Huai Ren Huai Shi' (坏人坏事) (bad people and bad things). President Hu Jintao recently declared the importance of developing an 'advanced socialist culture' at the Tenth National Meeting of the Chinese People's Political Consultative Conference, China's political advisory body. Specifically, President Hu highlighted the importance of 'eight honours' and 'eight shames', and claimed that they are the essence of the socialist value system (*China Daily* 2006). Examples of these honours and shames are the honour of industrious labour, the shame of indolence; the honour of togetherness and cooperation, the shame of profiting at the expense of others; the honour of honesty and keeping one's word, the shame of abandoning morality for profit; the honour of discipline and obedience, the shame of lawlessness and disorder. Accordingly, there has been a nation-wide movement in China to learn and implement this value system.

Taken together, controlling for undesirable behaviours is a common characteristic of ruling classes or governments in any given society, including China. Taking the perspective of convergence theorists we argue that some basic content of CWB identified in the Western workplaces (e.g., 'not to steal from the organization') would also apply in a culturally diverse environment such as China. However, taking the perspective of divergence theorists, people in different social and cultural contexts might have different conceptions about what behaviours constitute CWB. In other words, social and cultural context may shape, to a greater or lesser extent, the specific content of CWB.

Our understanding of the construct of CWB has been primarily led by the literature in North America, with few studies contributed from Europe (e.g., Marcus, Schuler, Quell and Humpfner 2002). There has been some comparative research between Chinese and North American employees on specific incidents of CWB such as absenteeism (e.g., Johns and Xie 1998; Xie and Johns 2000). Other research has considered how negative feedback from co-workers or supervisors impacts employee counterproductive behaviour in China (Kwok, Au and Ho 2005). This research suggests that CWB is an important aspect of job performance in China. It also suggests that certain behaviours (i.e. absenteeism, tardiness, theft) are viewed by Chinese as counterproductive just as they are viewed in the West. Nevertheless, this research has not examined the specific boundary or content of the construct of CWB across cultures.

Study 1 aimed at investigating the content of CWB among mainland Chinese. Consistent with the convergence theorists, we make a general prediction that similarity would exist in some basic content of CWB among North Americans and Chinese. Given the early stage of the cross-cultural research on CWB, we do not formulate specific hypotheses about what items or dimensions might generalize across cultures. Meanwhile, we remain open to the divergence perspective which would predict that Chinese will describe counterproductive work behaviours which are divergent from the Western literature, given the significant differences between North America and China in cultural, economic, social and political environments. Chinese might describe incidents (i.e. behaviours) of a given dimension differently from those reported by Westerners, and they might even report indigenous dimensions of CWB. Thus, we asked the Chinese respondents to describe incidents of CWB, rather than constraining their thoughts with the Western instruments. This indigenous approach facilitated a careful exploration of the convergence and divergence perspectives as well as the Chinese-specific content of CWB.

Study 1

Study 1 serves two purposes. First, it helps identify the content and dimensions of CWB in China using two independent samples of Chinese managers from mainland China. Second, it paves the road for Study 2, as the incidents of CWB reported by the Chinese managers who participated in Study 1 form the indigenous instrument that was later used in Study 2 – the study of the importance of task, OCB and CWB to overall performance ratings in China.

Establishing the content and dimensionality of CWB in China was accomplished using two steps. In the first step a group of Chinese managers was asked to list critical incidents that they considered being CWBs. This step produced a variety of CWB incidents. However, it did not provide the dimensionality of these behaviours. Thus, in the second step a different group of Chinese managers was invited to sort the CWB incidents, derived from the first step, into different categories. Multi-dimensional scaling was used to derive the dimensionality of the Chinese items of CWB. This process is detailed below separately for each step.

Method

Step1: Generating counterproductive work behaviour items in China

Participants for Step 1 were 160 Chinese managers and professionals enrolled in the Executive MBA programmes of two universities located in Guangdong and Sichuan provinces of China; 132 of the participants were male (82.5%). Most of the participants were managers (67%) and professionals (21%), and the remaining were sales-persons (6%) or public servants (6%). The respondents were on average 32.7 years old (SD = 5.62) and had worked at their current jobs for 4 years (SD = 3.60). They had completed an average of 17 years of formal education (SD = 1.74). The participants worked for organizations that represented the various organizational ownerships in China: 45% of the participants worked for state-owned enterprises, 13% for foreign enterprises, 20% for joint ventures and the rest for private firms.

Sample representation has been a challenging issue for research in China, considering the size of the Chinese population and potential variation associated with geographic locations and other contextual factors. In pursuit of a better representation of Chinese managers, we selected the two research sites from Guangdong and Sichuan provinces, because these two provinces represent different levels of economic development and exposure to the Western influences. Guangdong is a coastal province and one of the most developed provinces in China. Most of the Guangdong participants in the study were located in the city Shenzhen, which is the Special Economic Zone (the experimental field for the open door policy and economic reform) in China. Sichuan, on the other hand, is an inland and agricultural province, which had a slower start in the economic reform than Guangdong. The majority of the participants worked in Guangdong or Shenzhen with 22 (14%) participants having studied in either Guangdong or Sichuan on a part-time basis and worked in 10 different provinces across the country.

Procedure for Step 1

Participants were invited to participate in the study on a voluntary basis during the time they were enrolled in the Executive MBA programmes in the respective provinces in China. Participants were presented with a broad definition of counterproductive work behaviour followed by two examples of behaviours. The definition of CWB, taken from Rotundo and Sackett (2002), is 'voluntary behaviour that violates organizational norms and harms the well-being of the organization (p. 69).' This information was presented to the participants in Chinese. The conventional method of back-translation (Brislin, Lonner and Thorndike 1973) was used to translate the definition from English to Chinese.

The participants were then asked to describe five incidents of someone at work engaging in behaviour considered to be CWB. The respondents wrote their responses in Chinese. The 160 respondents generated a total of approximately 800 CWB incidents. A four-step process was followed to analyse the incidents. First, the second author (a native Chinese) reviewed all incidents to ensure that they had clear meaning in the Chinese language and that the incidents referred to employee behaviour. Any incident that was ambiguous or difficult to interpret was removed from further analyses. Second, the researchers reviewed each incident and grouped incidents that were clearly similar but provided by different participants together. For example, incidents like 'fraud organizational statistics' and 'fraud organizational records' were grouped together under 'fraud organizational documents'. After cleaning the 800 incidents, a total of 66 non-repeat behaviours remained. Table 1 presents an English version of these items. A process of back-translation was followed to convert the items from Chinese to English in order to present them in Table 1.

Table 2 presents an overview of the different forms of counterproductive work behaviour that have been reported in the Western literature. A large number of the CWB incidents identified by the Chinese managers (see Table 1) appear to be similar to the CWB incidents reported in the Western literature (Table 2).

Step 1 of the study provides useful insight into the types of behaviours that are perceived to be counterproductive by managers in China. Step 2 was undertaken to determine the dimensionality of the CWB items.

Step 2: Uncovering the dimensionality of counterproductive work behaviour in China

Participants for Step 2 were a different group of 30 Chinese managers enrolled in the MBA programme of a Canadian university. These participants are appropriate for this step because they were all born, raised and worked as managers in China prior to entering the MBA programme and had been studying in Canada for only three to four months when they completed the sorting task. The participants were 47% male, had an average age of 33 years (SD = 3.67), had on average 9.15 (SD = 3.25) years of full-time work experience and 4.19 (SD = 2.47) years experience as a manager. They had worked for various types of Chinese organizations: 40% of the participants worked for state-owned enterprises, 27% for foreign enterprises, 17% for joint ventures and the rest for private firms.

Procedure for Step 2

Participants were invited to participate in this step on a voluntary basis. Participants were presented with a set of instructions in which they were asked to sort the 66 CWB incidents into different categories based on the similarity of the behaviours. The participants were

Table 1.   Study 1: The list of counterproductive work behaviours described by Chinese managers (English version).

Counterproductive Work Behaviour

---

1. Do not protect organizational image in public.	37. Do not complete task on time.
2. Do not pay attention to present the organization well.	38. Do not work hard.
	39. Do not take work responsibility seriously.
3. Destroy organizational interests with others.	40. Talk about colleagues behind their back.
4. Destroy facility.	41. Make small alliances.
5. Destroy organizational reputation.	42. Make or distribute rumours.
6. Not faithful to the organization.	43. Attack colleague by making secretive reports to supervisors.
7. Waste organization's resources.	
8. Fraudulently use organizational documents.	44. Intentionally belittle colleagues.
9. Fraudulently create receipts.	45. Attack others verbally in public.
10. Fraudulently represent statistical figures.	46. Play politics with colleagues.
11. Fraud.	47. Create conflict among colleagues.
12. Leak confidential organizational information.	48. Conflict/fight with colleagues.
13. Use organizational name to cheat others.	49. Cannot control emotion and argue with colleagues.
14. Corruption.	
15. Disobey organizational rules and regulations.	50. Create obstacles for others' work.
16. Deviate from occupational ethics.	51. Bad attitude toward client/customer.
17. Take advantage of imperfect organizational regulations for self.	52. Do not cooperate with others' work.
	53. Low sense of cooperation with others.
18. Take rebate for self.	54. No respect for others.
19. Deviate from contract.	55. Mistreat subordinates.
20. Gain personal benefit through unethical means.	56. Inconsistent behaviour towards management.
21. Openly against organizational leadership.	57. Do not obey superior's work arrangement.
22. Use public facility to make personal gain.	
23. Stealing.	58. Put personal interests above organizational interests.
24. Tell lies.	
25. Sleep during work hours.	59. Complaints that affect work morale negatively.
26. Smoke, eat or make noise in public.	
27. Come to work after drinking alcohol.	60. Inconsistency between what the person says and does.
28. Deviate from dress code.	
29. Do not pay attention to public hygiene.	61. Boast about one's abilities but fail to demonstrate it.
30. Tardiness.	
31. Absence or lateness from work.	62. Take credit for self.
32. Absence without prior report.	63. Deny responsibility.
33. Leaving work station during work time.	64. Say coarse words.
34. Use work time to do things for self.	65. Sexual harassment.
35. Chat during work time.	66. Rudeness.
36. Do not complete assigned tasks.	

---

not given any category labels. The CWB incidents were written on cards in Chinese, and Chinese was the participants' native language. The participants were instructed to read each behaviour carefully and to place it into the category that they believe it belonged to based on the similarity of the behaviours. The instructions stated that they would be likely to create anywhere from 5 to 12 categories. This range was chosen based on a review of prior studies that used a similar procedure and a review of the CWB literature (e.g., Borman and Brush 1993). After each participant completed the sorting task, a research assistant recorded the number of categories that each participant used to sort the CWB incidents and which items were placed in each category. This information served as the basis for the analyses.

Table 2.   A summary of CWB-related dimensions in the Western literature.

Author	Dimension	Behavioural Incident
Katz and Kahn (1978)	Joining/staying with the organization	Low turnover and absenteeism
Murphy (1989)	Destructive or hazardous behaviours	Violating security and safety; destroying equipment, accidents.
	Down-time behaviours	Substance abuse; illegal activities
Campbell (1990)	Maintaining personal discipline	Avoid negative or adverse behaviours (e.g., substance abuse)
Borman and Brush (1993)	Useful personal behaviour	Working within the guidelines and boundaries of the organization
Raelin (1994)	Professional deviant/adaptive	Work-scale (e.g., unethical practices, absenteeism, work-to-rule, bootlegging) Self-scale (e.g., flaunting of external offers, rationalization, alienation, apathy) Career-scale (e.g., premature external search, external performance emphasis)
Robinson and Bennett (1995)	Employee deviance	Property deviance (e.g., damage property) Production deviance (e.g., violate norms about quality or quantity of work) Political deviance (e.g., putting others at personal or political disadvantage) Personal aggression (e.g., aggressive or hostile behaviour towards others)
Hunt (1996)	Generic work behaviours	Adherence to confrontational rules (e.g., follow rules when pressured not to) Industriousness (e.g., find other tasks to work on when finished with regular work) Thoroughness (e.g., keep workplace tidy) Schedule flexibility (e.g., work flexible hours and offer to stay late) Attendance (e.g., late or absent) Off-task behaviour (e.g., use work time to conduct personal affairs) Unruliness (e.g., threaten co-workers, blame others for own mistakes) Theft (e.g., steal) Drug misuse (e.g., drink during work time)
Gruys and Sackett (2003)	Counterproductive work behaviour	Theft and related. Destruction of property Misuse of information. Misuse of time and resources. Unsafe behaviour. Poor attendance. Poor-quality work. Alcohol use. Drug use. Inappropriate verbal actions. Inappropriate physical actions

We analysed these data using multidimensional scaling (MDS). MDS is a useful technique for representing the underlying structure of objects/stimuli from information about the similarity/dissimilarity among the objects (Schiffman, Reynolds and Young 1981). We followed the procedure recommended by Schiffman et al. (1981). The researcher presents the participant with the full set of objects/stimuli and asks the participant to sort them into groups based on their similarity (Schiffman et al. 1981). After each participant completes the sorting task, the researcher prepares a square dissimilarity matrix (66 × 66) in which the cell entries are coded as 1 if the participant sorts the two stimuli into a different group and 0 if the two stimuli are sorted into the same group. This process is repeated for all possible pairs of stimuli, resulting in a square matrix. A separate matrix is computed for each of the 30 Chinese managers. Then, a final matrix is computed across all participants based on the sum of the individual matrices. MDS is applied to the final summed dissimilarity matrix.

Results

The 30 Chinese managers sorted the counterproductive work behaviours into between 5 and 11 categories (M = 7.5). The ALSCAL MDS program was applied to the summed dissimilarity matrix to determine the underlying structure and dimensions of the CWBs. The goodness of fit indices (e.g., stress test and squared correlations) determines the number of dimensions that best fit the data. Solutions for one to six dimensions were produced based on these indices. The squared correlation ranged from .94 for the six-dimension solution to .41 for the one-dimension solution. The stress indexes ranged from .07 for the six-dimension solution to .48 for the one-dimension solution. These indexes were plotted. The index made a considerable drop with the largest drop from the one- to the two-dimension solution and began to level off thereafter. The squared correlation was .76 for the two-dimension solution. Thus, these results suggest that the two-dimension solution provides a good and parsimonious fit with the data. Figure 1 presents the two-dimensional solution from Multidimensional scaling of CWB in China.

A review of the items that have positive loadings on Dimension 1 (Quadrants 1 and 4) reveals that these counterproductive behaviours directly interfere with task completion regardless of whether they are directed at co-workers or the organization. That is, these behaviours (e.g., being absent or late and not cooperating with others' work) impede one's task completion and/or make it difficult for co-workers to perform their jobs and the organization to achieve its goals. In contrast, the items that have negative loadings

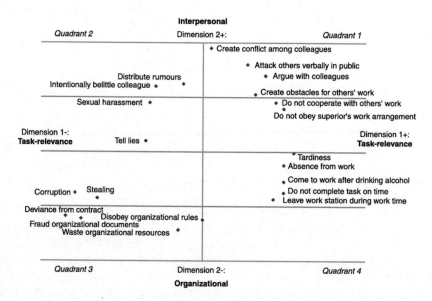

Figure 1.   Two-dimensional solution from multidimensional scaling of counterproductive work behaviours in China.

on Dimension 1 (Quadrants 2 and 3) are also counterproductive but these behaviours do not link directly to one's day-to-day job activities. That is, these behaviours are clearly counterproductive to the interests of co-workers or the organization. However, they do not arise necessarily from the completion of job-related tasks. Examples of items that have very high and negative loadings on Dimension 1 include sexual harassment, theft and corruption. The consequences of these actions are broader than the items that have positive loadings on Dimension 1. Thus, we labelled Dimension 1 as Task-Relevance. A dimension similar to this one was reported in a Western study by Gruys and Sackett (2003).

The items that have positive loadings on Dimension 2 (Quadrants 1 and 2) are all interpersonal and directed towards co-workers or others (e.g., conflict with colleagues, sexual harassment, do not cooperate with others). In contrast, the counterproductive work behaviours that have high and negative loadings on Dimension 2 (Quadrants 3 and 4) are directed towards the organization (e.g., waste organization resources, disobey organization rules, leaves work station during work time, tardiness). Thus, we label Dimension 2 as Interpersonal-Organizational. This dimension was also reported in Gruys and Sackett (2003) and Bennett and Robinson (2000).

Discussion

As the first study of the conceptions of CWB in China, Study 1 provided insightful information concerning the content and dimensions of CWB among Chinese managers. Consistent with convergence theorists, the results suggest that managers in China conceptualize CWB in ways similar to managers from the Western cultures. Specifically, many of the CWBs reported by the Chinese participants are comparable to those reported in the Western literature: conflict, low cooperation, harassment, absenteeism, abuse of organization time, fraud, breaking organization rules, theft and dishonesty. To conclude, the dimensions and utility of the Chinese items are largely consistent with the findings in the Western literature.

Study 1 identified the content and dimensions of counterproductive work behaviour in China using two independent samples of Chinese managers. The results provide a basis for item-level instruments that measure CWB among Chinese managers. Building on the results of Study 1, Study 2 investigates the extent to which a sample of Chinese managers and a comparable sample of Canadian managers value task performance, OCB and CWB when rating overall performance. Thus, the item-level data gathered in Study 1 are validated in Study 2.

Study 2

There has been a general interest among Western researchers in demonstrating that task performance, OCB and CWB are uniquely valued by managers. Thus, a body of Western research examined the unique contribution of these behaviours to ratings of overall job performance, effectiveness and rewards. A majority of this research focused on the importance of task performance and OCB. This research employed a wide range of methodologies: some studies measured relative weights or importance while others measured incremental variance explained by each performance component. Generally, this research reported that task performance and OCB independently contribute to ratings of overall performance. Limited research has considered the relative importance of all three performance dimensions, namely task performance, OCB and CWB to ratings of overall performance. In a within-rater policy-capturing study Rotundo and Sackett (2002) found that all three components were taken into consideration when Western managers rated overall performance, but that managers varied in the weights they gave to each component.

Study 2 investigates the relative importance that Chinese managers place on task performance, OCB and CWB. Consistent with the prior discussion of the importance that Chinese government and organizations have endorsed on controlling for CWB and promoting OCB, we predicted that Chinese managers should share a tendency with North American managers to give significant weights to all three groups of behaviours in ratings of overall performance of their employees.

Consistent with the convergence perspective, China's active participation in globalization, especially her participation in the World Trade Organization, has aroused a nation-wide movement to learn Western technology and philosophy of modern management. During this learning process China has significantly reformed almost every aspect of management, ranging from the national laws and policies for international trade and taxation to various management practices within organizations (see Child 1996). This reform has brought the Chinese managerial practices and philosophies closer to those of the industrialized Western world than ever before. For example, prior to the economic reform, the performance management in Chinese organizations had focused on political ideologies but not on task performance because of the 'iron bowl system' (i.e. a system based on life-time employment and the norm of equality in resource allocation). Over the last two decades, however, Chinese organizations have massively redesigned their human resource management systems to facilitate competition, effectiveness and efficiency. In particular, they reformed the performance management system to reinforce behaviours that directly facilitate organizational effectiveness and efficiency (Chen 2001). This tendency is likely to have increased the similarities between Chinese and Western management practices and to have motivated Chinese managers to endorse values on all categories of behaviour in evaluating employee performance.

Divergence theorists may predict that the cultural differences between China and the West would lead to different weights on task performance, OCB and CWB in performance evaluation. Hofstede's (1991) dimensions of individualism and collectivism have been recognized as the most powerful components of value differences across cultures. Collectivist cultures are characterized by attitudes that favour interdependence, norms that favour embeddedness, and values that favour security, obedience, duty, harmony and personalized relationships. Individualistic cultures are characterized by attitudes that favour independence, and values that favour pleasure, achievement, competition, freedom, autonomy and fairness.

Cross-cultural research has designated Chinese culture as being highly collectivist (Hofstede 1991; Earley 1994; Chen 2001), whereas the North American cultures as being highly individualist. Specifically, the US and Canadian cultures were ranked in 1st and 4th positions respectively on the scale of individualism in Hofstede's (1991) multinational study. Thus it is plausible to predict that Chinese are more likely to engage in and pay attention to workplace behaviours that influence the well-being of their group.

Chen (2001) argued that Chinese have a holistic perspective of management. They tend to believe that all things in the universe (the self, the family, a business unit or a nation) contain competing tendencies that must be balanced and harmonized. Chinese tend to focus on group harmony and shared accomplishment, qualitative and subjective measures, a people orientation, and economic and social concerns in performance management (Chen 2001). Given that OCB is likely to promote shared accomplishment and concerns for social well-being, we predict that Chinese would endorse higher values on OCB than North Americans.

Cross-cultural research on human resource management practices provides support for both the convergence and divergence perspectives. Zhou and Martocchio (2001) compared Chinese and American managers' compensation award decisions using a policy-capturing approach. They found that in comparison with the American managers, the Chinese managers tended to put less emphasis on work performance and more emphasis on the personal needs of the employees when making bonus decisions and on relationship with managers and co-workers when making non-monetary decisions. These results are broadly supportive of the collectivist orientation of the Chinese culture and of the divergence perspective. However, using a sample of employees from mainland China, Chen (1995) found that Chinese respondents demonstrated preferences for individual-based reward allocation, similar to North American counterparts.

The present study attempts to integrate the perspectives of convergence and divergence theorists in exploring the emphasis managers' place on task performance, OCB and CWB when rating overall job performance. Taking a convergence perspective, we predict that Chinese and Canadian managers will share a tendency to give significant weights to all three groups of behaviours in evaluating their subordinate's performance. Taking from the divergence perspective, we predict that Chinese managers will endorse higher values than Canadian managers to OCB in ratings of overall performance.

Hypothesis 1:   Chinese and Canadian managers will independently give significant weight to task performance in ratings of overall performance.

Hypothesis 2:   Chinese and Canadian managers will independently give significant weight to organizational citizenship behaviour in ratings of overall performance.

Hypothesis 3:   Chinese and Canadian managers will independently give significant weight to counterproductive work behaviour in ratings of overall performance.

Hypothesis 4:   Chinese managers will give a higher weight to OCB than Canadian managers in ratings of overall performance.

Policy capturing design

Rating of overall job performance involves managers integrating a wealth of performance-related information into an overall evaluation of the employee. This overall performance rating represents their judgment about how the employee performed. The process of integrating information to make an overall judgment is complex and often not readily observable to outsiders. One approach to obtaining the rater's information processing strategy is known as policy capturing. It involves inferring the weights managers place on different pieces of information from the pattern of their responses to various cues or stimuli (Hobson and Gibson 1983). Applied to the present study, a rater is presented with various descriptions of employees' performance. The independent variables (e.g., task performance, OCB and CWB) are manipulated in the descriptions to reflect different levels of performance. The rater is asked to read each description and to rate the overall performance (dependent variable) of the employee who is described. A regression equation is computed for each rater where the regression coefficients reflect the importance they place on the different stimuli. The end product is a statistical equation or 'captured rating policy' for each rater (Hobson and Gibson 1983).

There are several advantages to the policy capturing approach. It is especially useful when researchers are interested in knowing whether people differ in their judgments (Hobson and Gibson 1983). Furthermore, performance ratings are influenced by raters' perceptions of employees, which are subject to rater errors and biases. Therefore, an approach that presents different raters with the same stimuli permits the researcher to control for factors that are known to bias raters' judgments of employee performance (Hobson, Mendel and Gibson 1981; Zedeck and Kafry 1977).

Method

Job performance survey: Canadian survey

Employee level job performance was presented to managers via hypothetical profiles in which task performance, OCB and CWB were manipulated. The hypothetical job profiles in this study were taken from Rotundo and Sackett (2002) for the job of administrative assistant. A brief review of the steps involved in the development of the profiles is presented in the Appendix. A more detailed review can be found in Rotundo and Sackett (2002).

Job performance survey: Chinese survey

A separate survey was created for the sample of Chinese managers who participated in Study 2. The development of the Chinese version of the survey followed the same three steps as noted above for the Canadian survey. The job was also administrative assistant. A summary of the three steps is presented in the Appendix.

Sample and procedure: Canadian survey

In the Canadian sample a total of 120 executives were invited to participate in the study and a total of 117 completed the survey, yielding a response rate of 97%. Three surveys were not useable (i.e. incomplete responses or random responding). Most respondents were white (79%) with an average age of 40 years (SD = 7.94) and 17 years of work experience (SD = 7.44). Approximately 43% were male and 33% had a master's degree.

The participants were then invited to complete the survey as part of a half-day session on performance management offered through executive programmes at a large Canadian university. The participants were emailed a link to the online survey two weeks prior to the session. A cover letter, which stated that participation was on a voluntary basis and all responses were confidential, served as part of the email, completion of the survey indicated consent to participate. The survey consisted of two sections and required approximately 30 minutes to complete. In the first section subjects were presented with the 32 hypothetical job profiles and asked to rate the overall job performance of the employee depicted within the profile on a five-point Likert scale (1 = low overall performance and 5 = high overall job performance). Information about the tenure and work experience of the hypothetical employees was held constant and included in the introduction of the survey. The second section of the survey requested demographic and background information of the participants (e.g., age, education, race, work experience, gender, occupational title, and prior experience in performance evaluation).

Sample and procedure: Chinese survey

In the Chinese sample a total of 198 executives from three provinces in China volunteered to participate in the study and provided useable complete surveys. This sample is independent from the two samples used in Study 1 and the sample that participated in the development of the Chinese survey. (See Appendix for the information concerning a separate Chinese sample that participated in Step Two of the development of job performance profile.) The participants had an average age of 33.5 years (SD $= 5.68$). Approximately 64.5% were male and 20.2% had a master's degree.

The Chinese participants were managers who enrolled in the Executive and Regular MBA programmes at three Chinese universities located in Shanghai, Sichuan province and Zhejinag province. For the same reason presented in Study 1, we selected the three research sites in pursuit of better representation of Chinese managers. Participation in the study was voluntary. Research assistants at the three universities posted an invitation for participation, along with an introduction of the project and a cover sheet of the questionnaire, in the Executive MBA offices and classrooms. They also presented the objectives and procedures of the project verbally to the potential participants before classes. In the introduction it was clearly specified that the survey should be completed by those who had administrative assistant(s) working for them, and had experience evaluating the performance of their administrative assistant(s). Like the Canadian sample and procedure, the Chinese participants completed a survey that consisted of two sections that required approximately 30 minutes to complete.

Analyses

Two sets of analyses were conducted. First, individual regression equations were computed for each rater to assess the importance of the three performance components to ratings of overall performance. Since the independent variables (i.e. task performance, OCB and CWB) were approximately orthogonal, the standardized regression coefficients are interpreted as weights. Second, independent t-tests were conducted to compare the performance weights between the Canadian and Chinese managers.

Results

Captured rating policy

A regression equation was computed for each participant separately within the Chinese and Canadian samples. Thus, each manager had a set of standardized regression coefficients which represented their weights on task performance, OCB and CWB. The results averaged across participants are presented in Table 3. Hypotheses 1 to 3 predicted that the Chinese and Canadian managers would give significant weights to task performance, OCB and CWB respectively in overall performance ratings. Table 3 shows that on average Chinese and Canadian participants use information about all three performance components when forming overall ratings of employees, thus providing support for Hypotheses 1, 2 and 3. Furthermore, the incremental R^2 provides evidence to suggest that raters in this study took the task seriously when they rated the profiles.

Hypothesis 4 predicted that Chinese managers would place higher weight on OCB than Canadian managers. Independent sample t-tests were run to test whether the mean standardized regression coefficients on OCB were significantly different between the Canadian and Chinese samples. The mean regression weights for OCB were not significantly different between the two samples. Thus, Hypothesis 4 was not supported. However, independent t-tests comparing the mean weights on task and CWB indicated significant differences. More specifically, the mean regression weight on task performance in the Canadian sample was significantly smaller ($p < .01$) than in the Chinese sample [$t(334) = -10.08$], while the mean regression weight on CWB was significantly larger in the Canadian sample [$t(334) = -10.62, p < .01$].

Table 3.   Mean standardized regression coefficients on task performance, organizational citizenship behaviour, and counterproductive work behaviour and multiple R-squared in Study 2.

	China Study 2	Canada Study 2	US[a]
Task			
M	.65	.54	.55
SD	.10	.12	.12
Range	.33 to .82	.24 to .79	.20 to .79
Mean % variance explained	41	32	32
OCB			
M	.22	.24	.20
SD	.11	.12	.09
Range	.00 to .52	−.05 to .55	.01 to .46
Mean % variance explained	6	6	4
CWB			
M	−.43	−.53	−.55
SD	.13	.13	.13
Range	.00 to −.71	−.10 to −.83	−.21 to −.80
Mean % variance explained	19	29	32
Overall job performance[b]			
M	2.52	2.28	2.37
SD	1.18	1.14	1.08
R^2			
M	.63	.65	.67
SD	.10	.09	.09
Range	.41 to .83	.44 to .88	.40 to .87
N	198	114	155

[a]Represents the results for the job of administrative assistant, taken from Rotundo and Sackett (2002);
[b] Represents the mean rating of overall job performance across raters.

Discussion

The results of Study 2 provide clear evidence for the similarities between Chinese and Canadian managers in the relationships between the three performance components and the ratings of overall job performance. Task performance, OCB and CWB formed important domains of job performance for managers from both cultural groups. Moreover, a significant proportion of the respondents from both cultures gave large weights to task performance and CWB (Table 3).

The results yielded from Study 2 are supportive of Hypotheses 1, 2, and 3 about the importance of task performance, OCB and CWB in performance evaluation among Chinese managers. However, inconsistent with our prediction that Chinese managers would place higher importance on OCB in performance evaluation than Canadian managers, the results indicated that Chinese managers placed significantly more weight on task performance than Canadian managers, while Canadian managers placed significantly higher weight on CWB.

The present study was designed to address two research questions: (1) Will Chinese conceptualize the content and dimensions of counterproductive work behaviour similarly to or differently from the conceptualizations reported in the West? (2) Are Chinese and Canadian managers similar or different in the relative importance they endorse on task performance, OCB and CWB in overall performance ratings? The essence of these questions is whether some of the existing knowledge of job performance may generalize across cultural boundaries.

The results of both studies fuel the ongoing debate among the convergence and divergence perspectives. Our study found noticeable similarities between Chinese and Canadian managers in conceptualizations of job performance. The similarities are illustrated in three aspects. First, the Chinese respondents who participated in Study 1 reported many items and dimensions of counterproductive work behaviour that are similar to those found in the Western culture. Second, the Chinese managers from Study 1 sorted the counterproductive work behaviours into categories that produced two dimensions (i.e. task-relevance and interpersonal-organizational) that have also appeared in the Western literature. Third, Study 2 found that task performance, OCB and CWB significantly predicted the ratings of overall job performance for Chinese as well as Canadian managers. Furthermore, the participants in both Chinese and Canadian samples placed high weights on task performance. Considering the significant variation in the cultural, economic, social and political contexts between China and Canada, the identified similarities between Chinese and Canadian managers provide important insights for further research on what constitutes generalizable knowledge of job performance.

Like Canadian managers, the Chinese managers who participated in Study 2 gave the largest weights to task behaviours in performance evaluation. Convergence theorists would argue that when it comes to performance certain work-related behaviours are necessary to perform a job whether you are in one country or another. This might also suggest that the role the traditional culture plays in the performance appraisal process is not as large as that of the social and economic contexts in contemporary China. Having been reformed from a centralized and planned economy to a decentralized and market-oriented economy within 20 years, the speed and magnitude of the social changes that occurred in China are unprecedented. It is possible that the increasingly competitive environment has fuelled organizations and managers to pay much attention to completion of tasks in order to survive and succeed. Future research is needed to further explore how social and cultural contexts might jointly affect managerial conceptions of job performance in China.

The cross-cultural psychology literature has well documented that Chinese tend to share more collectivistic values whereas North Americans tend to hold more individualistic values (Hofstede 1991; Bond 1992). We integrated this literature in developing Hypothesis 4, in which we predicted that Chinese managers would endorse higher values on OCB than Canadian managers. Nevertheless, the research that forms the foundation of our beliefs about the differences between Chinese and North Americans on individualism and collectivism was conducted years ago and prior to the major social, political and economic changes that define contemporary China. Hence, one can't help but wonder if these same cultural differences on individualism and collectivism would emerge today between Chinese and North Americans. This question, however intriguing, is beyond the scope of the present study and requires careful consideration and investigation.

Nevertheless, we measured the cultural values held by the Chinese and Canadian respondents in Study 2 in an exploratory manner and for descriptive purposes using Hofstede's measure. A comparison of the item-level mean scores between the Chinese and Canadian respondents suggests that the Chinese managers who participated in Study 2 are not typically collectivistic, and that they might be even more individualistic than the Canadian respondents in certain respects. For example, the Chinese managers scored higher than the Canadian managers on the typical individualism items such as 'challenging work', 'recognition you deserve', 'freedom to adapt', 'opportunity for advancement' and 'use own skill and ability'. They tied with the Canadian managers in the typical collectivism item such as 'work with people who cooperate'. These results suggest that the lack of support for Hypothesis 4 might be partially due to the individualistic values held by the Chinese respondents. Although these results are inconclusive, they indicate that culture is dynamic and changing. It is possible that Chinese people have generally become more individualistic during the process of industrialization and modernization, which supports the convergence theory. It is also possible that the Chinese managers who participated in Study 2 are particularly individualistic because they are young, well educated, and belong to the leading class of the economic reform. Taken together, the results cast light on the complexity of cross-cultural research on performance management. They call attention to capture the cultural values held by the individual respondents in the tests of culture-related hypotheses.

The Canadian respondents who participated in Study 2 demonstrated very similar rating patterns with the American respondents in Rotundo and Sackett's (2002) study (see Table 3). These results suggest that there might be some typical patterns of responses that North Americans share in evaluating the relative importance of the three components of performance.

Concluding remarks

The present study is among the first investigations of the content and dimensions of counterproductive work behaviour among mainland Chinese. Although our results are preliminary, they provide useful insights on what constitutes CWB in China. Canadian managers who participated in Study 2 gave almost identical and large weights to CWB and task performance, while most Chinese managers gave CWB a lower weight than task performance. The underlying reasons for this variation are likely to be complex. We speculate that economic and cultural contexts might have jointly facilitated the tendency that Chinese respondents gave high weights to task performance and relatively lower weights to CWB. As noted, China's economy is undergoing a critical stage of reform and downsizing to increase profitability and productivity (*People's Daily* 2004). Consistent with the convergence perspective, the pressure of 'produce or perish' has forced Chinese organizations to place a greater emphasis on productivity and task performance than ever before. Meanwhile, in line with the divergence perspective saving face for oneself and that of others is so deeply rooted in the Chinese culture that Chinese often choose not to be critical of others' undesirable behaviours for protecting face and maintaining relationships (see Bond 1992; Chen 2001).

The findings of the study have a number of potential implications for cross-cultural management in performance evaluation. The most obvious is that they shed light on the similarities shared by the Canadian and Chinese managers in their conceptualization of the content of counterproductive work behaviour. Considering the magnitude of the differences in the political, economical and cultural contexts between Canada and China, the identified similarities provide important insights for management. It is possible that certain behaviours such as stealing from organizations, mistreating co-workers, and absence from work are considered as being counterproductive uniformly across cultural boundaries. Should managers strive to reduce CWB, they would be likely to receive support from most employees because the detriments of CWB appear to be commonly recognized in the workplace.

The results of the study suggest that Canadian and Chinese managers assign differential weights to task performance and CWB when rating the overall performance of employees. That is, raters' cultural backgrounds might influence the emphasis they place onto task, OCB or CWB components in evaluating other's performance. In other words, an employee might receive different messages about the extent to which task behaviours are rewarded or CWBs are penalized on the job because of different preferences held by different managers. This raises important questions about the potential inconsistencies that may surface when employees are rated. Our results suggest that the different preferences held by managers are at least partially shaped by their culture. It is important to note that managers are unlikely to be aware of their own preferences, because one's cultural values and their impact on behaviour are not frequently discussed. Therefore, organizations should anticipate and address the potential for evaluation inconsistency. One possible strategy is to facilitate open discussions among managers concerning the potential causes for systematic rating biases inherent in performance evaluation. Another possible strategy is to place more emphasis on objective measures in performance ratings and thus reduce the reliance on subjective evaluations. This potential implication is important not only for multinational corporations, but also for organizations of all sizes, because the labour forces in many countries are becoming more and more culturally diverse.

One limitation of this study is that the data collected in Study 2 were for only one job (i.e. administrative assistant), a job that is low in complexity. This raises questions about whether the pattern of findings reported here would generalize to other jobs. Hence, future research should examine the generalizability of the findings across different jobs and different cultures.

George and Jones (1997) argued that contextual factors, such as industry, technology, and job function, might play an important role in formatting OCB. Organ and Ryan's (1995) meta-analysis, however, found no evidence for the moderating effects of such contextual factors. The results of our study suggest that there are similarities as well as differences in managerial conceptions of performance management cross-culturally. Moreover, what behaviours are attributed to OCB or CWB in a given society are not only led by man-made contextual factors such as cultural values, but also influenced by the physical or natural environments in which the individuals or organizations are embedded. To explore all of the mysteries inherent in performance and behaviours, our field has just started a first step in a journey of a thousand miles.

Acknowledgements

This research was supported by grants to the first and second authors, Maria Rotundo and Jia Lin Xie, Joseph L. Rotman School of Management, University of Toronto, from the Social Sciences and Humanities Research Council of Canada.

References

Bennett, R.J., and Robinson, S.L. (2000), "Development of a Measure of Workplace Deviance," *Journal of Applied Psychology*, 85, 3, 349–360.
Bond, M.H. (1992), *The Psychology of the Chinese People*, Hong Kong: Oxford University Press.
Bond, M.H., and Hwang, K. (1992), "The Social Psychology of Chinese People," in *The Psychology of the Chinese People*, ed. M.H. Bond, Hong Kong: Oxford University Press, pp. 213–231.
Borman, W.C., and Brush, D.H. (1993), "More Progress Toward a Taxonomy of Managerial Performance Requirements," *Human Performance*, 6, 1, 1–21.
Brislin, R. (1993), *Understanding Culture's Influence on Behaviour*, Orlando, FL: Harcourt Brace Jovanovich College Publishers.
Brislin, R.W., Lonner, W., and Thorndike, R.M. (1973), *Cross-cultural Research Methods*, New York: Wiley.
Campbell, J.P. (1990), "Modeling the Performance Prediction Problem in Industrial and Organizational Psychology," in *Handbook of Industrial and Organizational Psychology* (Vol. 1), eds. M.D. Dunnette and L.M. Hough, Palo Alto, CA: Consulting Psychologists Press, pp. 687–732.
Che, H.S., Lin, X.W., Zhang, X.C., and Qiao, Z.H. (2004), "What Managers do before Employee Selection," (original in Chinese), *PKU Business Review*, 4, 68–75.

Chen, C.C. (1995), "New Trends in Rewards Allocation Preferences: A Sino-U.S. Comparison," *Academy of Management Journal*, 38, 2, 408–428.

Chen, M. (2001), *Inside Chinese Business: A Guide for Managers Worldwide*, Boston, MA: Harvard Business School Press.

Child, J. (1996), *Management in China during the Age of Reform*, Cambridge: University of Cambridge Press.

China Daily (2006), "Report of President Hu Jin Tao's speech at the Tenth National Meeting of the Chinese People's Political Consultative Conference", March 11, p. 4.

Cooper, W.H., and Richardson, A.J. (1986), "Unfair Comparisons," *Journal of Applied Psychology*, 71, 2, 179–184.

Earley, P.C. (1994), "Self or Group? Cultural Effects of Training on Self-efficacy and Performance," *Administrative Science Quarterly*, 39, 1, 89–117.

Farh, J., Earley, P.C., and Lin, S. (1997), "Impetus for Action: A Cultural Analysis of Justice and Organizational Citizenship Behaviour in Chinese Society," *Administrative Science Quarterly*, 42, 3, 421–444.

Farh, J., Zhong, C., and Organ, D.W. (2004), "Organizational Citizenship Behaviour in the People's Republic of China," *Organizational Science*, 15, 2, 241–253.

Fleishman, E.A., and Quaintance, M.K. (1984), *Taxonomies of Human Performance*, Orlando, FL: Academic Press.

George, J.M., and Jones, G.R. (1997), "Organizational Spontaneity in Context," *Human Performance*, 10, 153–170.

Gruys, M.L., and Sackett, P.R. (2003), "Investigating the Dimensionality of Counterproductive Work Behaviour," *International Journal of Selection and Assessment*, 11, 1, 30–42.

Hobson, C.J., and Gibson, F.W. (1983), "Policy Capturing as an Approach to Understanding and Improving Performance Appraisal: A Review of the Literature," *Academy of Management Journal*, 8, 4, 640–649.

Hobson, C.J., Mendel, R.M., and Gibson, F.W. (1981), "Clarifying Performance Appraisal Criteria," *Organizational Behaviour and Human Performance*, 28, 164–188.

Hofstede, G. (1991), *Cultures and Organizations: Software of the Mind*, London: McGraw-Hill.

Hunt, S.T. (1996), "Generic Work Behaviour: An Investigation into the Dimensions of Entry-level, Hourly Job Performance," *Personnel Psychology*, 49, 51–83.

Johns, G., and Xie, J.L. (1998), "Perception of Absence from Work: People's Republic of China versus Canada," *Journal of Applied Psychology*, 83, 515–530.

Katz, D., and Kahn, R.L. (1978), *The Social Psychology of Organizations*, New York: Wiley.

Khilji, S.E. (2002), "Modes of Convergence and Divergence: An Integrative View of Multinational Practices in Pakistan," *The International Journal of Human Resource Management*, 13, 2, 232–253.

Kreuger, A.O. (2005), "China and the Global Economic Recovery," keynote address at the American Enterprise Institute Seminar, Washington, DC, 10 January.

Kwok, C., Au, W.T., and Ho, J.M.C. (2005), "Normative Controls and Self-reported Counterproductive Behaviours in the Workplace in China," *Applied Psychology: An International Review*, 54, 4, 456–475.

Landy, F.J., Rastegary, H., Thayer, J., and Colvin, C. (1991), "Time Urgency: The Construct and its Measurement," *Journal of Applied Psychology*, 76, 5, 644–657.

Marcus, B., Schuler, H., Quell, P., and Humpfner, G. (2002), "Measuring Counterproductivity: Development and Initial Validation of a German Self-report Questionnaire," *International Journal of Selection and Assessment*, 10, 1/2, 18–35.

Markus, H.R., and Kitayama, S. (1991), "Culture and the Self: Implications for Cognition, Emotion, and Motivation," *Psychological Review*, 98, 2, 224–253.

McGaughey, S.L., and DeCieri, H. (1999), "Reassessment of Convergence and Divergence Dynamics: Implication for International HRM," *International Journal of Human Resource Management*, 10, 2, 235–250.

Murphy, K.R. (1989), "Dimensions of Job Performance," in *Testing: Applied and Theoretical Perspectives*, eds. R. Dillon and J. Pellingrino, New York: Praeger, pp. 218–247.

Nunnally, J.C. (1978), *Psychometric Theory* (2nd ed.), New York: McGraw Hill.

Organ, D.W., and Ryan, K. (1995), "A Meta-analytic Review of Attitudinal and Dispositional Predictors of Organizational Citizenship Behavior," *Personnel Psychology*, 48, 775–802.

People's Daily Online (2004), "China's SOE Reform on the Right Track and to Make Headway", 30th September, retrieved 30 September 2004 from: http://english.people.com.cn/200409/29/eng20040929_158733.html

Pudelko, M., Fink, G., Carr, C., and Wentges, P. (2006), "Editorial for the Special Section: The Convergence Concept in Cross Cultural Management Research," *International Journal of Cross Cultural Management*, 6, 1, 15–18.

Raelin, J.A. (1994), "Three Scales of Professional Deviance within Organizations," *Journal of Organizational Behaviour*, 15, 483–501.

Robinson, S.L., and Bennett, R.J. (1995), "A Typology of Deviant Workplace Behaviours: A Multidimensional Scaling Study," *Academy of Management Journal*, 38, 2, 555–572.

Rotundo, M., and Sackett, P.R. (2002), "The Relative Importance of Task, Citizenship, and Counterproductive Performance to Global Ratings of Job Performance: A Policy Capturing Approach," *Journal of Applied Psychology*, 87, 1, 66–80.

Schiffman, S.S., Reynolds, M.L., and Young, F.W. (1981), *Introduction to Multidimensional Scaling: Theory, Methods, and Applications*, New York, NY: Academic Press.

Sha, L.X. (2000), "Self and Relationship in the Chinese Culture: A Study of Inter-personal Relationships among Chinese," in *Chinese Psychology in Progress* (in Chinese), eds. H. Chen and K. Leung, Hong Kong: The Chinese University Press, pp. 145–160.

The Record of Rites, Book IX (2004), Multilingual Website of Confucius Publishing, available online at: www.confucius.org

US Department of Labor (1991), *Dictionary of Occupational Titles* (4th ed.), Washington, DC: US Department of Labor.

Vance, C.M. (2006), "Strategic Upstream and Downstream Considerations for Effective Global Performance Management," *International Journal of Cross Cultural Management*, 6, 1, 37–56.

Xie, J.L., and Johns, G. (2000), "Interactive Effects of Absence Culture Salience and Group Cohesiveness: A Multi-level and Cross-level Analysis of Work Absenteeism in the Chinese Context," *Journal of Occupational and Organizational Psychology*, 73, 31–52.

Zedeck, S., and Kafry, D. (1977), "Capturing Rater Policies for Processing Evaluation Data," *Organizational Behaviour and Human Performance*, 18, 269–294.

Zhou, J., and Martocchio, J. (2001), "Chinese and American managers' Compensation Award Decisions: A Comparative Policy-capturing Study," *Personnel Psychology*, 54, 1, 115–145.

Appendix

Steps involved in the development of the profiles in Study 2

Job performance survey: Canadian survey

The development of the hypothetical job performance profiles involved three steps. First, a separate list of behaviours was compiled for each performance component. The behaviours for task performance were taken from the Dictionary of Occupational Titles for the job of administrative assistant (US Department of Labor 1991) and from the extent literature of OCB and CWB. The task items include: answer telephone calls, schedule appointments, compose and type routine correspondence, take dictation, transcribe notes, file correspondence, arrange travel schedule. The OCB items include: help co-workers, inform others before initiating actions that affect them, speak positively about the organization, attend functions that promote the well-being of the organization, make constructive suggestions about processes, and volunteer to serve on committees. The CWB items include: fight with colleagues, spread false rumours, blame others for his/her mistakes, theft, falsify documents, and make unwanted sexual advances.

Second, the behaviours were scaled to ensure that the behaviours that represented each performance component reflected on average comparable levels of performance. This step is important because it confirms that no performance component was manipulated to be stronger than the others. For example, it would be problematic if only high task performance was reflected in the survey (across all profiles) and only low OCB or high CWB and vice versa. It is necessary that the behaviours included in the survey represent comparable levels of all three performance components (when averaged). The equivalent standard deviations on the final pool of items included in the survey for each of task performance, OCB and CWB indicate that this criterion was satisfied. (Descriptive statistics for the pool of task, OCB and CWB behaviours in the final Canadian survey are: task $M = 3.51$, $SD = 1.91$; OCB $M = 3.81$, $SD = 2.21$; CWB $M = 3.38$, $SD = 2.00$.)

Third, the hypothetical profiles were created by randomly sampling one item each from the pool of task performance, OCB and CWB. Thus, the three performance components were uncorrelated (i.e. the correlations between the performance components were 0.01, -0.01, and 0.05). This process resulted in a total of 32 unique hypothetical job profiles. The within-subject analyses (e.g., regression analyses) include three independent variables (i.e. task, OCB and CWB). Thus, 32 unique profiles is a sufficient number to satisfy the recommended profile-to-cue ratio (Nunnally 1978).

Job performance survey: Chinese survey

The same three steps were followed to develop the profiles.

Step One: Profile Development. A list of behaviours was generated separately for task performance, OCB and CWB. For the task performance items, we collected job descriptions for the job of an administrative assistant from four large Chinese organizations, including a state-owned, a foreign enterprise, a joint venture and a government organization. The job descriptions were written in Chinese and were reviewed by subject matter experts for accuracy. These subject matter experts were individuals who were employed in the respective job. They reviewed the task statements to verify that they reflected what their job actually entailed. We then carefully reviewed and compared the contents of the job descriptions. The results of the review process suggest that the tasks performed by administrative assistants are very similar across different Chinese organizations. Moreover, these tasks are highly consistent with those described in the Western research (Rotundo and Sackett 2002). A literature review published in China lends further support to this similarity. In this review the content of an administrative assistant's job includes: answer telephone calls, handle mail, greet visitors, schedule appointments, arrange meetings and business trips, file and draft documents, assist with negotiations and collect information (Che, Lin, Zhang and Qiao 2004). Given that these elements are almost identical with those used in the Canadian survey we decided to adopt the same task items to form the instruments of the task performance for the Chinese survey.

The CWB incidents derived in Study 1 were used to generate a list of behaviours for this performance domain. Hence, these behaviours were already written in the Chinese language and did not require translation. Examples of CWB included in the China survey are: fight with colleagues, gossip about others, spread rumours about colleagues, denies responsibility for actions, theft, falsifies organizational documents, sexual harassment, and attacks colleagues verbally in public. These items are almost identical to those used in the Canadian survey. As noted, research has already considered the content and dimensionality of OCB in China (Farh et al. 1997; 2004). Hence, we included the following OCB items which were common to both the mainland Chinese and Western cultures: assists colleagues in work settings, shows concern about colleagues, enhances superior–subordinate communication, protects organizational image, participates in events organized by the company, improves self by constant learning, makes constructive suggestions about work, and takes tasks beyond one's job responsibility. These behaviours are virtually identical with the items in the Canadian survey.

The purpose of Step Two: Scaling OCB and CWB Items was to scale the behaviours to ensure distributional equivalence (Cooper and Richardson, 1986). Each of the eight behaviours from Step One was modified to reflect high, medium and low levels of performance (e.g., never complains about the organization to co-workers, always participates in events organized by the company), producing a total of 24 behaviours for each performance component.

A total of 90 students enrolled in an Executive MBA programme at a university in the Zhejiang province of China volunteered to complete the survey. This sample of managers is independent of the two samples that participated in Study 1. A total of 19 questionnaires were excluded from the data analysis. These questionnaires were completed by people who either had no prior experience rating administrative assistants or did not complete the questionnaires correctly, Of the participants 80% were male. The participants were on average 29 years old (SD = 2.21), had 17 years of formal education (SD = 1.35), and had worked at their current jobs for 3.3 years (SD = 2.08). A total of 67% of the respondents were managers and 26% were professionals. Of the respondents 52% worked for state-owned enterprises, 25% for foreign enterprises, 13% for joint ventures and the rest for private organizations. Approximately 50% of the respondents worked in Shanghai and Jiangsu province, and the rest worked in 15 different provinces.

In the survey, the managers were provided with the definition of each performance component and asked to read each behavioural statement, then to rate the level of performance it reflected using a seven-point Likert scale (e.g., the Likert scale for task performance was anchored by 1 = low task performance and 7 = high task performance). Item level statistics were computed for each behaviour. The item had to satisfy three criteria in order to be selected for use in the final survey. First, any item with a standard deviation larger than 1.5 was eliminated (Landy, Rastegary, Thayer and Colvin 1991). Second, the aggregate mean and variance for the final set of behaviours had to be similar across performance components. Third, the performance components had to be approximately normally distributed. Items were eliminated until these three conditions were satisfied. The final set of behaviours included 16 items in each performance component. The means and standard deviations on the final set of behavioural items are as follows: task performance M = 3.52, SD = 1.45; OCB M = 3.89, SD = 1.37; CWB M = 3.65, SD = 1.35.

The final step, Instrument Development, involved the creation of the hypothetical profiles. One behaviour was randomly selected without replacement from each set of task performance, OCB and

CWB, producing 16 unique profiles. This step was repeated to obtain another set of 16 profiles, yielding a total of 32 unique profiles satisfying the recommended profile to cue ratio (Nunnally 1978). This procedure resulted in independent performance components. The correlations among the performance components ranged from -0.01 to 0.05. The performance components were randomly ordered within each profile to ensure that primacy or recency effects were not confounded with the importance weights. Chinese names were randomly added to each profile. A few sample profiles are included below.

Example of hypothetical profiles:

Xiao Zhang always makes constructive suggestions about how to improve the organization. She sometimes gossips about others. She often makes errors when scheduling appointments that result in double-booking clients.

Xiao Liu never informs others before initiating actions or changes that may affect them. He is accurate when taking dictation in shorthand or transcribing notes onto a word processor. He occasionally makes unwanted sexual advances toward co-workers.

Xiao Ji never blames others for her mistakes. She composes and types routine correspondence of poor quality containing grammatical errors. She sometimes helps other administrative assistants with their work when they have been absent.

Work and family demands and life stress among Chinese employees: The mediating effect of work–family conflict

Jaepil Choi

Life stress is generally defined as the manifestation of negative psychological reactions to various encounters in life. Due to its negative consequences, both academic researchers and managers have devoted efforts to understanding the factors that cause life stress among employees (Hall and Richter 1988; DeFrank and Ivancevich 1998). It has long been argued that life stress of employees is largely triggered by the work-related factors in the workplace. For instance, Karasek's (1979) job demands–decision latitude model focused on job demands experienced by employees as a key determinant of employee stress (Fox, Dwyer and Ganster 1993; Xie 1996; Schaubroeck and Merritt 1997; Schaubroeck, Lam and Xie 2000). On the other hand, other researchers have suggested that obligations and responsibilities in the family domain can also be the source of life stress among employees (Frone, Russell and Cooper 1992; Williams and Alliger 1994).

In investigating life stress among employees, this study takes on the work–family interface perspective (Edwards and Rothbard 2000). As work and family represent the two key domains of employee life, the complete understanding of employee stress requires that role demands in both domains be considered at the same time. In particular, this study attempts to make contributions to the literature of stress and the work–family interface in three respects. First, since most prior research on life stress focusing on the work–family interface has been performed in Western industrialized nations (e.g., Frone et al. 1992), very little is known about whether or not work and family demands are associated with life stress of employees in developing countries as well. The study reported here examines the effects of work and family demands on Chinese employees' life stress. After a few decades of the active participation of women in economic activities, dramatic changes in family structures, and the more recent market-oriented enterprise reforms, Chinese male and female workers are currently confronting new work and family demands from these respective domains. Therefore, China is an appropriate setting in which to assess the effect of work and family demands on life stress of employees.

Second, this study seeks to compare the relative importance of work and family demands to life stress among Chinese employees. Although demands in both domains are hypothesized to cause employee stress, these demands may have different impacts on stress. Many factors can contribute to such differing effects. For example, an employee's economic level and family situation may determine which domain will put more pressure on the employee. If an organization displays a strong economic efficiency orientation, employees in the organization will be more likely to experience high stress from work demands. However, this study attempts to explain the different impacts of work and family demands on employee stress in terms of characteristics such as societal values. By doing so, this study shows that key stressors of employees may vary at the societal level.

Lastly, this study investigates whether or not the effects of work and family demands on life stress are mediated by work–family conflict. Considering the potential conflict between work demands and family demands (Greenhaus and Beutell 1985; Frone et al. 1992; Edwards and Rothbard 2000), it is reasonable to argue that the influences of work and family demands on life stress arise from the incompatibility of these demands. By examining the potential mediating role of work-family conflict, we seek to specify the processes by which work and family demands cause employee stress in China.

Currently, managers in China are greatly concerned about employee stress in both private and state-owned enterprises (Xie 2002). The examination of the roles of work and family demands, and work–family conflict in determining life stress among Chinese employees can provide companies operating in China with important guidelines in designing and implementing family-friendly policies and work motivation programmes.

Theoretical background and hypotheses

Work demands and life stress among Chinese employees

Work demands are defined as psychological stressors at the workplace, such as the requirements to work fast and hard; having a great deal of work to do; not having enough time; and having conflicting demands (Fox et al. 1993, p. 290). This definition is in line with that of prior research which focused on role overload of employees in terms of the time and energy necessary to finish task requirements (Yang, Chen, Choi and Zou 2000). Of great interest to us is whether or not work demands influence an employee's life stress.

The person-environment (P-E) fit model of stress (French, Caplan and Van Harrison 1982; Edwards 1996) helps us understand how work demands increase life stress among employees. A key argument of the P-E fit model is that demands from environmental spheres can cause life stress in a certain situation. In particular, when job requirements and responsibilities are too heavy to be handled by an employee (i.e. demands–abilities misfit), the employee will be in both negative psychological and physical states (e.g., tension, fatigue and anxiety), which in turn amplify life stress.

Many studies conducted in the Western setting lend support to the argument of the P-E fit model. Chronic exposure to high work demands (Kahn and Byosiere 1992; Williams and Alliger 1994), mental demands involving high concentration on work and problem solving (Schaubroeck and Ganster 1993), and heavy workload (Martin and Wall 1989; Frone et al. 1992; Reynolds 1997) have been found to increase psychological distress of employees. Work demands also have some bearing on the physical state of employees (House, Strecher, Metzner and Robbins 1986). Frone and McFarlin (1989) presented evidence indicating that work overload significantly increases somatic problems, including cardiovascular, gastrointestinal and respiratory symptoms.

Since the Chinese government began implementing economic reform in 1979, many Chinese employees have worked at private firms, joint ventures, and state-owned enterprises around the metropolitan areas and the Special Economic Zones (Entwisle, Henderson, Short, Bouma and Zhai 1995). One of the traditional Chinese values is the emphasis on achieving success in the world and the spread of fame (*li shen yang ming*). An individual who is not successful is criticized as 'incapable' and 'lacking of ambition' (Zuo and Bian 2001). In contemporary China, because this value can be realized through success in the workplace, which not only connotes personal achievement but also contributes to the honour and prosperity of their families (Redding 1993; Yang et al. 2000), many Chinese employees are often willing to engage in extra work in the workplace. Therefore, Chinese employees are highly likely to be susceptible to heavy work demands in the workplace.

In addition, as more Chinese employees work at private, entrepreneurial companies, employment becomes less secure than ever before. Unlike under the traditional 'iron rice bowl', which guaranteed lifetime employment at state-owned enterprises before economic reform (Law, Tse and Zhou 2003), Chinese employees may now lose their jobs involuntarily depending on the economic situation of firms. In particular, one of the objectives of the economic reform during the 1990s was to reduce the number of surplus workers on the state's payroll. In this situation, Chinese employees realize that if their contributions to the firms are not sufficient, they may be considered as redundant workers and will receive various disadvantages in their careers, such as slow promotion, or worse, job loss (Bu and McKeen 2000; Yi and Chien 2002). Therefore, the uncertainty of employment and career success in companies forces them to be more concerned about their work performance and to bear greater workload (Davis 1999).

Altogether, traditional Chinese values lead most Chinese employees to be anxious about achieving success in the workplace. In addition, since 1979, many Chinese employees have been hired by companies which are greatly concerned about economic productivity; they are then expected to meet high work demands. In these circumstances, their increased workload will contribute to the likelihood of suffering from life stress.

The above argument is in line with other studies on life stress among Chinese employees. Using a large sample of Chinese employees who are diverse in terms of the type of occupation and regional locations, Xie (1996, 2002) showed that high work demands yielded a high level of anxiety, psychological depression and psychosomatic health problems. Recently, Schaubroeck and his colleagues (2000) also noted that for Hong Kong employees, work demands increased the level of anxiety and depression. Thus, our first hypothesis is:

Hypothesis 1:   Work demands perceived by Chinese employees will be positively associated with their life stress.

Family demands and life stress among Chinese employees

Family demands have also been identified as a key stressor by the work–family interface researchers (Kopelman, Greenhaus and Connolly 1983; Frone et al. 1992; Rothbard and Edwards 2003). Family demands refer to the time spent, level of commitment to, and responsibilities associated with fulfilling family-related obligations such as the tasks of housekeeping and child-care. The P-E fit model (French et al. 1982; Edwards 1996) described earlier can also be applied readily to the case of the influence of family demands on life stress. Over time, too much attention spent and the physical demands related to taking care of the diverse household work and family-related obligations/responsibilities will affect the psychological and physical well-being of employees (Thomas and Ganster 1995). The harmful consequences of high family demands on employee stress have been confirmed by several studies in the Western setting. For instance, Frone and his colleagues (1992) reported that family demands, such as parental workload, influence employee distress.

Several changes in Chinese society can account for the correlation between family demands and life stress. First, since the Communist Party declared 'women hold up half the sky,' female employment has dramatically increased (Riley 1996). The massive influx of women workers in the workplace requires Chinese men and women to perform new roles in the family domain. However, they could not handle these roles very well (Pimentel 2000). As many women employees are spending a large amount of time in the workplace, they may expect to become involved in less housework. Nevertheless, the actual amount of their housework has not changed much (Bu and McKeen 2000). So the frustration from unmet expectations increases women's life stress caused by family demands. In addition, since housework is not Chinese men's main responsibility, they are less adept at handling family demands, which exacerbates the negative impact of these demands.

Second, the prevalence of adopting egalitarian values in spousal relationships enables husbands and wives to experience conflicts on issues of division of housework and family-related decisions (Lai 1995; Chang 1999). Such spousal conflict contributes to life stress among Chinese employees. Lastly, the one-child-per-family policy, which may have decreased the total amount of child caring, has nevertheless not significantly reduced the role overload for Chinese employees because they now have to do much more per child, and they receive little help from their only children or other sources (Zhang and Farley 1995). The economic reforms also caused a substantial cut in welfare facilities, including day-care centres (Leung 2003). Consequently, the burden of child-care shifted onto the shoulders of the family, thereby aggravating the role overload at home for Chinese employees.

Several relevant empirical studies lend credence to our above reasoning. Lai (1995) indicated that family demands are associated with psychological distress among Chinese employees through family satisfaction. Recently, Xie (2002) also found that too much housework and housing problems significantly predict the level of Chinese employees' stress.

Therefore, we propose the following hypothesis.

Hypothesis 2:   Family demands perceived by Chinese employees will be positively associated with their life stress.

Relative importance of work and family demands to life stress among Chinese employees

As discussed above, role demands in the work and family domains amplify employee stress. Therefore, it is reasonable to raise a subsequent question as to the relative importance of work and family demands to life stress. The meaningful implications of the answer to this question notwithstanding, very few studies have explicitly addressed this issue.

Role salience is a helpful concept in addressing the relative importance of work and family demands. Greenhaus and Beutell (1985) proposed that the amount of pressures on role performance in a particular domain is determined by the extent to which the domain is salient or central to a person's self-conception. An individual is more willing to invest resources to fulfil the obligations of salient domain (Lobel and St. Clair 1992). As a result, deeper involvement in ensuring successful performance of the salient roles is more likely to cause the individual to be mentally drained and physically exhausted, thereby generating stress. It then follows that the relative importance of work and family demands to life stress would be determined by the salience of two domains perceived by the individual.

Although many factors may contribute to the salience of work and family domains, we argue that societal values related to the importance of family and work can have a significant impact. If the values emphasize a particular domain, then that domain will have higher priority than the other domain and thus demands in that domain will increase life stress.

According to Hofstede (2001), people in Western countries such as the US put more values on personal and family time or goals than those in Asian countries such as Japan and Hong Kong. We then expect that the roles in family domain will be more salient than those in the work domain in the West, and therefore, family demands should be more likely to cause life stress than work demands should. A study of Frone and his colleagues (1992) lends support to our argument about the greater importance given to family demands in the US. In their study, the size of effect of family demands on overall depression was larger than that of work demands.

In contrast, Schein (1984) suggested that Eastern societies give greater priority to work than Western societies. In Eastern societies, extra work may be legitimized or even encouraged (Hofstede 2001; Wang, Lawler, Walumbwa and Shi 2004). Thus, the roles in the work domain will be more salient than those in the family domain in the East, and thus, work demands should be more likely to promote life stress than would family demands.

In particular, Redding (1993) has described three values that are well integrated in traditional Chinese societies: family, work and wealth. Hard work and dedication are the primary means to obtaining wealth; family provides the primary motivation for working hard, and thereby accumulating wealth. Chinese work values are congruent with their family values, thereby making it honourable for Chinese individuals to place a priority on work and to sacrifice family time and activities to accommodate work requirements (Yang, Chen, Choi and Zou 2000). In addition, since the Communist Party took power in China, work units (*danwei*) have been an integral part of Chinese communities. To the extent that work domain is central and salient in the life of Chinese employees, work demands should cause more stress than would family demands (Lai 1995; Lin and Lai 1995).

The greater importance of work domain in China has also been suggested by several authors. Lai (1995) argued that due to the centrality of work roles for Chinese employees, work-related stressors may have more importance to psychological distress than family-related stressors. Xie (2002) suggested that job demands have a bigger impact on Chinese employees' stress than family stressors. Therefore, given the work salience and centrality in Chinese society, we propose the following hypothesis.

Hypothesis 3:   The effect of work demands on life stress of Chinese employees will be greater than that of family demands.

The mediating role of work–family conflict

According to the work–family interface perspective, work and family have permeable boundaries and affect each other in various ways (Kanter 1977; Rothbard and Edwards 2003).

Among the several possible linking mechanisms between work and family (Edwards and Rothbard 2000), we focus on work–family conflict and examine its potential mediating role in relationships between work and family demands and life stress. Work–family conflict has been generally defined as a form of inter-role conflict in which work and family role demands are mutually incompatible so that meeting demands in one domain makes it difficult to meet demands in the other.

High work and family demands on Chinese employees will create work–family conflict in several ways (cf. Greenhaus and Beutell 1985; Wharton and Erickson 1993; Williams and Alliger 1994; Doby and Caplan 1995). First, investing time to meet the demands of one domain prevents Chinese employees from finding time to meet the demands of the other domain (i.e. time-based conflict). In particular, the recent rapid growth in the Chinese economy requires employees to spend more time in the workplace. Consequently, Chinese employees are likely to find less time for their family responsibilities. Second, the strain resulting from meeting demands of one domain makes it hard for Chinese employees to concentrate physically and psychologically on performing roles of the other (i.e. strain-based conflict). Third, behavioural habits and styles deeply ingrained in Chinese employees from meeting demands of one domain are often inappropriate in handling demands of the other domain (i.e. behaviour-based conflict). The increasingly prevalent individualistic values and behavioural styles encouraged in many Chinese firms (Chen 1995) are at odds with traditional Chinese values and behavioural styles emphasized at home.

Work–family conflict will affect life stress of Chinese employees. In general, it has been repeatedly found that work–family conflict is negatively associated with an employee's well-being, such as family satisfaction, psychiatric disorders and quality of life (Kopelman et al. 1983; Parasuraman, Greenhaus, Rabinowitz, Bedeian and Mossholder 1989; Williams, Suls, Alliger, Learner and Wan 1991). When Chinese employees undergo work–family conflict for the above reasons, the inter-role conflict limits their experiences, thereby interfering with their ability to function optimally in either role. Failure in dealing with the demands in either domain may hurt their self-conceptions and invite various criticisms from others. In particular, it is known that Chinese are greatly concerned about 'saving face' (*mianzi*) in social encounters (Hu 1944; Earley 1997). When they receive some derogatory social criticisms from others due to the failure in meeting role demands (Zuo and Bian 2001), they lose their 'face'. Under this circumstance, they will experience high levels of life stress.

In addition, as argued by the emotional interference approach (Jackson, Zedeck and Summers 1985), negative emotions or moods result from inter-role conflict between the two domains. Negative emotions such as depression, dissatisfaction and frustration from one domain will spill over to the other domain, and employees will then be likely to be caught in a vicious cycle from the work–family interface. Consequently, the escalated negative emotions will inhibit the role performance of Chinese employees in either domain (i.e. emotion-based conflict: Rothbard 2001) and cause high levels of life stress.

The above discussion suggests that work and family demands will amplify the life stress of Chinese employees through the mediation of work–family conflict. Such a mediation relationship would be one of the mechanisms by which demands of both life domains affect life stress. And, this mediation relationship is in line with previous findings in the work–family interface literature (Parasuraman et al. 1989; Frone et al. 1992). Therefore, we propose:

Hypothesis 4:   The effect of work and family demands on life stress of Chinese employees will be mediated by work-family conflict.

Method

Sample

The data for this study were collected from respondents from various organizations in China. With the support of several managers and the personal network of a Chinese business professor 239 Chinese employees were identified and contacted individually. All of them agreed to participate in this study voluntarily and were fully assured of complete anonymity. About half of the respondents had been recruited from an evening business training programme offered by the Beijing Municipal Bureau of Light Industry (n = 106); the rest of the respondents were identified through the personal relationships of a Chinese professor. They were working at small- to medium-sized companies around the Beijing area, such as a state-owned smelter (n = 36), a state-owned publishing house (n = 27), a collectively owned printing factory (n = 39), and a postal service company (n = 31). The use of employees from a number of companies provided for varying levels of work demands and life stress. A Chinese business professor introduced the study to the respondents in both the training programme and in the companies. Trained assistants administered and collected the completed questionnaires at the training programme classes and work sites.

On the average, the respondents had worked for about 6.5 (s.d. = 6.5) years at their current positions. Among the respondents 75% were below 40 years old, and 79% were female. Married respondents accounted for 68% of the total number of respondents. About 50% worked 40 hours per week. Among the total respondents 20% were at the managerial level, 14% were professionals, while 45% worked as staff members, and the rest were low-level workers. There were less than three dependents in the homes of 75% of the respondents. About 50% of the respondents worked about 20 hours per week to meet their housework commitments.

Measures

Work and family demands in this study were defined in terms of subjective feelings, therefore the participants' subjective experiences in the work and family domains were measured through self-reports. In fact, several authors have argued that people's subjective experiences of work and family demands reflect their objective circumstances well (Staines, Pleck, Shepard and O'Connor 1978; Keith and Schafer 1980; Near, Rice and Hunt 1980).

Three items were used to measure the *work demands* of respondents. On a five-point Likert scale ranging from 1 (very little) to 5 (very much), respondents rated items from Spector's (1975) survey of Organizational Frustration Scale, which measured perceptions of general workload. Coefficient alpha for this scale was .80.

Six items of *family demands* were developed for this study. This measure taps perceptions of family demands in terms of time and energy and role pressure. Respondents indicated the degree of their perceived family demands on a five-point scale from 1 (very little) to 5 (very much). Reliability of this scale was .86.

A *work–family conflict* measure was created on the basis of the literature review (e.g., Kanter 1977; Near et al. 1980; Greenhaus and Beutell 1985; Voydanoff 1987). Four items were rated on a five-point scale ranging from 1 (never) to 5 (often). Of the four items, two items did not specify any direction of the interference; one item represented work-to-family conflict, and the other represented family-to-work conflict. The distribution of the items was done in this way in order to have a general work-to-family conflict index that was not biased toward any particular direction. The scale showed .81 Cronbach's alpha.

Table 1.   Results of factor analysis for independent and dependent variables[a].

Factors and Items	1	2	3	4
1. Family demands				
Energy spent for family responsibilities	**.87**	.11	− .06	− .02
Time for family responsibilities	**.83**	.14	.01	− .04
Effort required for family responsibilities	**.75**	− .00	.07	− .03
Limited time for family responsibilities	**.75**	.15	.31	− .01
Too much family demands	**.72**	.18	.25	.12
Time for relaxation	**.61**	.10	.17	.05
2. Life stress				
Easily gets tired	.06	**.73**	.21	.14
Feeling nervous	.20	**.72**	.05	.05
Trouble breathing or shortness of breath	.10	**.72**	.07	− .09
Spells of dizziness	.19	**.71**	− .04	.08
Trouble getting to sleep	.06	**.68**	− .01	.05
Back pains	− .00	**.68**	.19	.24
Heart pounding	.06	**.58**	.16	− .01
3. Work-family conflict				
Conflict between work and family demands	.01	.07	**.80**	.17
Job situation interferes with family life	.05	.11	**.79**	.08
Insufficient time/energy for both work and family	.32	.22	**.70**	.15
Family situation interferes with job	.38	.12	**.67**	− .06
4. Work demands				
Given too much work to do	.05	.04	.12	**.84**
Too much work responsibility	.14	.17	.16	**.79**
Reasonable work demand (R)	− .11	.05	.00	**.61**
Eigenvalues	3.83	3.53	2.56	1.88

[a] Significant loadings are shown in boldface type.

Life stress was assessed by seven items from the Quality of Employment Survey that measured physical and psychological stress (Quinn and Staines 1979). Each was rated on a four-point scale, ranging from 1 (never) to 4 (often). The coefficient alpha was .83.

The items developed by Western scholars were translated into Chinese using a back-translation method (Brislin 1970) by competent translators to ensure that the final questionnaire items were understandable to Chinese respondents. The items created for this study were directly developed in Chinese by a Chinese member of our research team. As some measures were created for this study, a principal component analysis with varimax rotation was conducted with all the items of work and family demands, work–family conflict, and life stress. As reported in Table 1, it was found that there was no significant cross-loading across multiple factors in all items loaded onto the expected factors.

Control variables

Individual demographic differences are often related to stress. It has been found that men and women are subject to different stressors and react to stressors differently (Jick and Mitz 1985), and thus gender was controlled for. We also controlled for age and marital status, since it is possible that married and older respondents may perceive higher family demands than non-married respondents (Frone et al. 1992). As the structural natures of family domain (e.g., number of dependents and percentage of housework performed) may lead to differences in perceptions of stress symptoms (Jick and Mitz 1985), we controlled for them as well. In addition, we controlled for the number of hours of household work including shopping, cooking cleaning, and other housework. As some evidence suggests that the sources of stress vary systematically among different job levels in an organization (Kahn et al. 1964; Parasuraman and Alutto 1981), job level was included as a control variable. We also controlled for the number of paid working hours and length of tenure.

Results

Descriptive statistics and correlations

Means, standard deviations and correlations are presented in Table 2. Consistent with prior research on work–family conflict, both work and family demands were significantly associated with work–family conflict. In addition, work- and family-demands, and work–family conflict were significantly related to life stress. However, work and family demands did not significantly correlate with each other. Family demands were positively related to age, marital status, number of dependents, household work hours, and percentage of housework, while work demands did not correlate with any control variables. In addition, it was found that the more people dependent on the respondent, the higher work–family conflict and life stress they felt. Older respondents felt higher work–family conflict and life stress, which is consistent with the findings in the study of Lin and Lai (1995), and lower job level employees reported greater life stress. The percentage of housework done was positively associated with the level of life stress. Although Chinese women actively participate in economic activities, their weekly paid working hours were fewer than those of men, which is consistent with Lai's research findings (1995).

Test of hypotheses

The results of hierarchical multiple regression analyses to test the main hypotheses are presented in Table 3. All control variables, including demographic variables and the structural features of work and family domains, were entered at step 1 (Model 1). The block of control variables was not significant, suggesting that those variables did not account for a significant proportion of variance in life stress among Chinese employees. Work and family demands were added at the second step (Model 2). Both work ($\beta = .20$, $p < .01$) and family ($\beta = .29$, $p < .01$) demands were significant predictors of life stress among Chinese employees, even after controlling for the effect of all control variables. Therefore, Hypotheses 1 and 2 are strongly supported.

In order to test Hypothesis 3, which predicts differing importance for work and family demands in determining life stress, we conducted a usefulness analysis (Darlington 1968; Folger and Konovsky 1989). This allowed us to isolate each predictor's unique contribution above and beyond the other predictor's contribution. For this analysis, we first examined the unique contribution of work demands to life stress, beyond family demands. More specifically, we entered all control variables at step 1, and added family demands at step 2 and work demands at step 3. The change in R-square at the third step (adding work demands) isolated the unique contribution of work demands above and beyond family demands. Entering work demands at step 3 increased the square of the multiple correlation coefficient by .04, $p < .05$ ($\Delta F_{1,140} = 6.69$). The unique contribution of family demands apart from work demands was then examined by reversing the order of the second and third steps. Adding family demands at step 3 into a regression equation which already contained all control variables and work demands increased the square of the multiple correlation coefficient by .05, $p < .01$ ($\Delta F_{1,140} = 8.17$). In summary, the unique

Table 2. Correlation matrix of all variables.

Variables	Mean	s.d.	1	2	3	4	5	6	7	8	9	10	11	12
1. Family demands	2.91	.84	(.86)											
2. Work demands	2.86	.86	.10	(.80)										
3. Work-family conflict	2.27	.81	.40****	.29***	(.81)									
4. Life stress	1.97	.65	.31****	.22***	.30***	(.83)								
5. Age	33.62	9.34	.38****	.01	.16*	.14*	—							
6. Sex	1.79	2.44	.06	.04	.03	.09	.05	—						
7. Marriage	.68	.47	.43****	.01	.10	.09	.59***	.09	—					
8. Number of dependents	1.49	1.46	.45****	.02	.16*	.17**	.25***	-.03	.39***	—				
9. House care hours	29.72	33.68	.39****	-.03	.13	.03	.13	.00	.17*	.27***	—			
10. Percentage of housework	.53	.34	.31****	-.08	-.08	.14*	.14*	.06	.13	.20**	.20**	—		
11. Weekly paid working hours	39.22	8.93	.15*	.05	.08	-.10	.11	-.34***	-.02	.14	.09	-.07	—	
12. Number of months in position	76.59	77.65	.15*	.04	.12	.03	.48***	-.03	.26***	-.01	.04	.06	.10	—
13. Job level	2.34	1.03	-.05	-.01	.07	-.16*	.24***	-.04	.20**	.09	-.02	-.16*	-.03	-.04

The reliability coefficients are enclosed in parentheses; *p < .05; ** p < .01; *** p < .001.
The coding scheme was as follows: Sex: 1 = male, 2 = female; Marriage: 0 = Single, Divorced, or Widowed, 1 = Married; Job level: 1 = Workers, 2 = Staff, 3 = Professionals, 4 = Managers.

118 *J. Choi*

Table 3. Results of regression analyses for life stress[a].

Predictors	Model 1	Model 2	Model 3
Step 1: Control variables			
Age	.21	.17	.16
Sex	.03	.00	.00
Marriage	−.05	−.12	−.09
Job level	−.21*	−.17*	−.19*
Number of dependents	.17	.10	.10
House care hours	−.04	−.10	−.10
Number of months in position	−.05	−.06	−.07
Number of weekly paid working hours	−.13	−.17*	−.16*
Percentage of housework performed	.05	.02	.06
Step 2: Family demands and work demands			
Family demands		.29**	.19
Work demands		.20**	.15*
Step 3: Work-family conflict			
Work-family conflict			.20*
F	1.87	3.26***	3.51***
R^2	.11	.20	.23
ΔR^2		.10***	.03*

[a] Regression coefficients are standardized ones; *p < .05; **p < .01; ***p < .001.

contribution of work demands beyond family demands to life stress among Chinese employees ($\Delta R^2 = .04$) was not greater than that of family demands beyond work demands ($\Delta R^2 = .05$). Rather, family demands made a slightly greater contribution to life stress, given the difference in the standardized regression coefficient and the results of the usefulness analysis. Therefore, Hypothesis 3 which predicted that work demands will have a greater effect on life stress than family demands was not supported.

To test Hypothesis 4, we conducted a mediation analysis following the procedure suggested by Baron and Kenny (1986). First, work–family conflict was regressed on work and family demands. For this analysis, all the control variables used in the main analysis were entered at the first step to predict work–family conflict. These control variables as a whole could not predict a significant proportion of variance in work–family conflict ($R^2 = .08$, ns.). After controlling for all control variables, both work and family demands were entered to predict work–family conflict. These two variables as a group predicted a significant proportion of variance in work family conflict ($\Delta R^2 = .29, p < .001$). More specifically, the coefficients on work demands ($\beta = .24, p < .001$) and family demands ($\beta = .49, p < .001$) were highly significant. This result satisfies the first criterion for a mediating effect.

Second, as reported in the result of regression analysis in Table 3, both work and family demands were significantly related to life stress among Chinese employees (Model 2). In Table 3, we added work–family conflict into the regression equation at the third step (Model 3). According to Baron and Kenny (1986), if a predictor which was significant before having a mediator becomes non-significant when the mediating variable is added, the relationship between the predictor and the criterion variable is fully mediated by the mediator. In contrast, if a predictor remains significant after entering a mediator, but the regression coefficient is reduced substantially, we can conclude partial mediation. As reported in Table 3, after adding work–family conflict, family demands became non-significant ($\beta = .19$, ns.). In contrast, work demands were still significant ($\beta = .15, p < .05$), but the magnitude and significance level of a new regression coefficient became smaller than those of the regression coefficient before entering a mediator. Therefore, the result of mediation analyses suggests that while the effect of family demands on life stress of Chinese employees was completely mediated by work–family conflict, the effect of work demands on life stress was only partially mediated by work–family conflict. Overall, Hypothesis 4 is supported.

Discussion

Our study examined the effects of work and family demands on the life stress of Chinese employees. We found that both work and family demands are related to life stress. Contrary to our expectations, it was found that family demands seemed to have a little stronger association with life stress than did work demands. However, the difference was not substantial. Furthermore, this study provided evidence that the effects of work and family demands on life stress were mediated by work–family conflict of Chinese employees.

This study contributes to the stress literature by demonstrating in a developing country that family and work demands are related to employee stress, and that these demands from both domains have a relationship with life stress to a similar extent. This suggests that two major life domains may be two important sources of stressors to employees across diverse contexts. In addition, this study demonstrates that much of the effects of these demands arise from their incompatibility, which shows that previous findings in the literature on the work–family interface can be generalized into other cultural contexts.

Contrary to our expectations that work demands would be more likely to cause life stress among Chinese employees than family demands, the results indicated that the relationship of family demands with life stress is a little stronger than that of work demands or, at least, similar. We speculate that this unexpected finding might be related to the gender composition of our sample which is about 80% female. Although a gender equality policy since the establishment of Communist rule in 1949 has allowed Chinese women to participate actively in the workplace, family care is still regarded as the chief responsibility of women (Lai 1995; Pimentel 2000). Due to the disproportionately heavy responsibilities for household chores assumed by Chinese women, they may experience stress primarily from family demands. As a result, because the majority of our sample would experience high life stress due to high family demands, the relationship between family demands and life stress could be pronounced in this study.

To examine this possibility, we conducted two regression analyses, one for males and one for females (Aiken and West 1991). With the female sample, it was found that family demands were a significant predictor of life stress ($\beta = .32, p < .05$), but work demands were not ($\beta = .06$, ns.) after holding all control variables constant. The reverse pattern was found for the male sample: work demands were a significant predictor of life stress ($\beta = .53, p < .01$), but family demands were not ($\beta = -.03$, ns.) after holding all control variables constant. Taken together, because work demands were not significantly related to life stress among Chinese women who comprise the majority of our sample, the impact of work demands on life stress might be mitigated in this study. In fact, this additional analysis demonstrates that the relative importance of work and family demands varies as a function of gender: for women employees, family demands had a greater influence on life stress than work demands; for men employees, work demands had a stronger impact on life stress than family demands.

The different patterns of the mediating role of work–family conflict in the relationships of work and family demands to life stress are also intriguing. From these different patterns, several speculations can be made. First, as we argued earlier, the centrality of work is widely accepted by Chinese people (Lai 1995; Lin and Lai 1995). Since Chinese employees give low priority to their obligations and responsibilities at the home, the potential interference of role performance in the work domain to the family domain is perceived less seriously by employees. Therefore, to Chinese employees who endorse work centrality, work demands are less likely to interfere with family demands. As a result, work demands can directly cause stress without generating guilt or tension for not performing family responsibilities (i.e. work–family conflict).

If this line of reasoning is correct, then the mediating effect of work–family conflict should be particularly weak among those who strongly endorse work centrality. Although we do not have a direct measure of work centrality, work centrality is likely to be stronger among Chinese men than women (Redding 1993; Yang et al. 2000), since they are the main breadwinners. It then follows that the mediating role of work–family conflict in the relationship between work demands and life stress should be less pronounced among men. To test this reasoning, we performed a mediation analysis only with the male sample. In this analysis, when we added work–family conflict into the regression equation which already contained work and family demands, work–family conflict was only marginally significant ($\beta = .27$, $p < .10$), but work demands were still highly significant ($\beta = .49$, $p < .01$). According to Baron and Kenny (1986), for a third variable to be regarded as a mediator, the variable should be significantly associated with a dependent variable. The marginal significance of work–family conflict and the high significance of work demands even after entering work–family conflict, therefore, signify that the work demands of Chinese men directly yield life stress without causing conflicts with family demands. In summary, the partial mediation of work–family conflict in the relationship between work demands and life stress may result from the centrality of work for Chinese employees. Of course, this speculation deserves further investigation in future research.

Second, two significant predictors among control variables were, interestingly, both work-related variables: job level and number of paid working hours (see Table 3). Although we treated them as control variables, they may also represent work demands to some extent. These two variables were not significantly correlated with work–family conflict (see Table 2). Therefore, work demands reflected by each of these two variables that do not co-vary with work–family conflict were directly related to life stress.

Future research directions

In this study, we focused on the effect of role overload on life stress. Future research could expand to other dimensions of work and family demands, because work and family demands may manifest themselves in factors other than role-related demands. For example, Lai (1995) found that Chinese employees are more vulnerable to interpersonal conflicts in the work and family domains than to role-related demands. Therefore, interpersonal conflict among family members and among coworkers could also affect perceptions of demands.

The difference in relative importance of work and family demands to life stress between men and women, which has been found in an additional analysis, is intriguing. Several studies conducted in the Western setting have found that the key stressors that influence the well-being of men and women have become more similar because of the role convergence between the two genders (Barnett, Marshall and Pleck 1992; Schwartzberg and Dytell 1996). However, this study shows that this trend may not be generalizable in some developing countries where role differentiation between the two genders remains strong. Therefore, future research is needed to capture the varying dynamics of the experience of life stress across the two genders in different societies.

In a related vein, it would be interesting to investigate how the continuing social and economic changes in Chinese society will affect family–work values and relationships. For example, considering the temporal trend of the gradual increase in the percentage of females in the labour force from 43% in 1980 to 45% in 1990 (Joplin, Francesco, Shaffer and Lau 2003) and to 46% in the early 2000s (ACWF 2005), and the continuous growth of the Chinese economy, the number of working women will continue to increase. The improvement of living standards, the one-child-per-family policy, and greater exposure to Western values and practices are all likely to have effects on the workplace and family structures in China. These will definitely affect the extent to which demands in the work and family domains influence life stress. Longitudinal studies can be launched to track changes in demands in both domains and to examine their impacts on stress.

Limitations of the study

This study is not without limitations. First, the highly gender-skewed sample of this study must be assumed to have biased the results. As our additional analysis demonstrated, the relationship between work demands and life stress is stronger among male employees than among female employees. Therefore, the smaller number of male employees than female employees in the sample could have distorted the findings on the relationship between work demands and life stress. This limitation must be taken into account when interpreting the findings of this study. To get a more precise understanding of this relationship, future studies should recruit samples that are balanced in terms of gender composition.

Second, the cross-sectional design of the study prevents the drawing of causal inferences. It is possible that employees who experience high stress may feel that they have too heavy demands from either the work or family domain (Pittman, Solheim and Blanchard 1996). However, given that our findings are consistent with most prior research, the possible problem of reversed causality would not be so serious. Yet, to allay the possibility of reversed causality, future researchers need to consider employing a longitudinal design.

Third, all independent and dependent variables of this study were collected through respondents' self-responses, which may raise the concern about the common methods bias. Some evidence, however, suggests that the bias would not be a serious one. As reported in Table 1, our principal component analysis produced multiple factors consistent with our conceptions of the variables (Podsakoff and Organ 1986). Moreover, two major predictors of life stress, i.e. work and family demands, did not significantly correlate with each other.

Lastly, it is also possible that our significant findings indeed indicate a spurious relationship, meaning that the significant relationships may result from a third variable such as negative affectivity (Brief et al. 1988). Future researchers may want to control for personality traits or dispositional affects that could induce a spurious relationship.

Practical implications

This study has some practical implications for companies operating in China. Given the increasing concern about the dysfunctional consequences of life stress among employees in China (Johns and Xie 1998), Chinese organizations need to implement stress management assistance programmes (cf. Hall and Richter 1988; DeFrank and Ivancevich

1998). First, family issues should be deliberately integrated into human resource management programmes. Since the economic reforms in 1979, many Chinese enterprises have concentrated on the economic aspects of company operations. However, the strong emphasis on economic efficiency should not come to neglect family issues. As the Chinese economy becomes more market-oriented and many foreign firms are entering China, companies in China will confront intensified competition in order to secure high-quality labour. Unless they provide attractive family-friendly programmes such as a flexible work schedule, family leave benefits and child care support programmes (DeFrank and Ivancevich 1998), their employees will experience high stress and will intend to leave the companies.

Chinese companies should work on the reduction of the negative consequences of heavy work demands. Because some of the effects of work demands on life stress are direct, the intervention programme to reduce work demands will be particularly effective in reducing life stress. Karasek's model (1979) provides some clues on how to reduce the negative implication of work demands. The model suggests that high work demands have a motivational potential if employees are allowed to exercise greater job control on the basis of greater decision-making power. Accordingly, Chinese companies need to implement motivation programmes to provide more autonomy to employees. However, it should also be noted that increasing job control alone does not guarantee employees' well-being and health. Only employees who have high confidence in their abilities to cope with stressful situations by having a high level of control (Schaubroeck and Merritt 1997) can use the increased control to reduce their life stress. Therefore, parallel to increasing employees' job control, Chinese organizations need to devote their efforts to training their employees to develop confidence in their task abilities.

Conclusions

This study presents evidence that work and family demands are influential factors that determine to what extent Chinese employees experience life stress. Although it appears that this finding is in line with that of previous studies conducted in the Western setting, there is also some evidence indicating the unique characteristics of Chinese society. Therefore, it is possible that the detailed picture of how work and family demands affect employee stress and how these influences are mediated by work-family conflict may vary across different societies. We hope that the results of this study will motivate further research on this issue in other societies.

Acknowledgements

I would like to thank Chao Chen, Anne Tsui and Heli Wang for their comments and suggestions on the earlier version of the study. This project was supported by a grant from the Research Grants Council of the Hong Kong Special Administration Region, China (DAG05/06.BM35) and a grant from Hong Kong RGC Competitive Earmarked Grants (HKUST 6151/02H).

References

Aiken, L.S., and West, S.G. (1991), *Multiple Regression: Testing and Interpreting Interactions*, Thousand Oaks, CA: Sage.

All-China Women's Federation (ACWF) (2005), "Facts and Data," retrieved 31st October 2005 from: http://www.women.org.cn/womenorg/english/english/fact/mulu.htm

Barnett, R.C., Marshall, N.L., and Pleck, J.H. (1992), "Men's Multiple Roles and Their Relationship to Men's Psychological Distress," *Journal of Marriage and the Family*, 54, 358–367.

Baron, R.M., and Kenny, D.A. (1986), "The Moderator-mediator Variable Distinction in Social Psychological Research: Conceptual, Strategic, and Statistical Considerations," *Journal of Personality and Social Psychology*, 51, 1173–1182.

Brief, A.P., Burke, M.J., George, J.M., Robinson, B.S., and Webster, J. (1988), "Should Negative Affectivity Remain an Unmeasured Variable in the Study of Job Stress?," *Journal of Applied Psychology*, 73, 193–198.

Brislin, R.W. (1970), "Back-translation for Cross-cultural Research," *Journal of Cross-Cultural Psychology*, 1, 185–216.

Bu, N., and McKeen, C.A. (2000), "Work and Family Expectations of the Future Managers and Professionals of Canada and China," *Journal of Managerial Psychology*, 15, 771–794.

Chang, L. (1999), "Gender Role Egalitarian Attitudes in Beijing, Hong Kong, Florida, and Michigan," *Journal of Cross-Cultural Psychology*, 30, 722–741.

Chen, C.C. (1995), "New Trends in Rewards Allocation Preferences: A Sino–U.S. Comparison," *Academy of Management Journal*, 38, 408–428.

Darlington, R.B. (1968), "Multiple Regression in Psychological Research," *Psychological Bulletin*, 79, 161–182.

Davis, D.S. (1999), "Self-employment in Shanghai: A Research Note," *The China Quarterly*, 157, 22–43.

DeFrank, R.S., and Ivancevich, J.M. (1998), "Stress on the Job: An Executive Update," *Academy of Management Executive*, 12, 55–66.

Doby, V.J., and Caplan, R.D. (1995), "Organizational Stress as Threat to Reputation: Effects on Anxiety at Work and at Home," *Academy of Management Journal*, 38, 1105–1123.

Earley, P.C. (1997), *Face, Harmony, & Social Structure: An Analysis of Organizational Behaviour across Cultures*, New York: Oxford University Press.

Edwards, J.R. (1996), "An Examination of Competing Versions of the Person-environment Fit Approach to Stress," *Academy of Management Journal*, 39, 292–339.

Edwards, J.R., and Rothbard, N.P. (2000), "Mechanisms Linking Work and Family: Clarifying the Relationship between Work and Family Constructs," *Academy of Management Review*, 25, 178–199.

Entwisle, B., Henderson, G.E., Short, S.E., Bouma, J., and Zhai, F. (1995), "Gender and Family Businesses in Rural China," *American Sociological Review*, 60, 36–57.

Folger, R., and Konovsky, M.A. (1989), "Effects of Procedural Justice, Distributive Justice, and Reactions to Pay Raise Decisions," *Academy of Management Journal*, 32, 115–130.

Fox, M.L., Dwyer, D.J., and Ganster, D.C. (1993), "Effects of Stressful Job Demands and Control on Physiological and Attitudinal Outcomes in a Hospital Setting," *Academy of Management Journal*, 36, 289–318.

French, J.R.P. Jr., Caplan, R.D., and Van Harrison, R. (1982), *The Mechanisms of Job Stress and Strain*, New York: Wiley.

Frone, M.R., and McFarlin, D.B. (1989), "Chronic Occupational Stressors, Self-focused Attention, and Well-being: Testing a Cybernetic Model of Stress," *Journal of Applied Psychology*, 74, 876–883.

Frone, M.R., Russell, M., and Cooper, M.L. (1992), "Antecedents and Outcomes of Work–Family Conflict: Testing a Model of the Work–Family Interface," *Journal of Applied Psychology*, 77, 65–78.

Greenhaus, J.H., and Beutell, N.J. (1985), "Sources of Conflict between Work and Family Roles," *Academy of Management Review*, 10, 76–88.

Hall, D.T., and Richter, J. (1988), "Balancing Work Life and Home Life: What Can Organizations Do to Help?," *Academy of Management Executive*, 11, 213–223.

Hofstede, G. (2001), *Culture's Consequences: Comparing Values, Behaviours, Institutions, and Organizations across Nations* (2nd ed.), Thousand Oaks, CA: Sage.

House, J.S., Strecher, V., Metzner, H.L., and Robbins, C.A. (1986), "Occupational Stress and Health among Men and Women in the Tecumseh Community Health Study," *Journal of Health and Social Behaviour*, 27, 62–77.

Hu, H.C. (1944), "The Chinese Concepts of 'Face'," *American Anthropologist*, 46, 45–64.

Jackson, S.E., Zedeck, S., and Summers, E. (1985), "Family Life Disruptions: Effects of Job-induced Structural and Emotional Interference," *Academy of Management Journal*, 28, 574–586.

Jick, T.D., and Mitz, L.F. (1985), "Sex Differences in Work Stress," *Academy of Management Review*, 10, 408–420.

Johns, G., and Xie, J.L. (1998), "Perceptions of Absence from Work: People's Republic of China versus Canada," *Journal of Applied Psychology*, 83, 515–530.

Joplin, J.R.W., Francesco, A.M., Shaffer, M.A., and Lau, T. (2003), "The Macro-environment and Work-family Conflict: Development of a Cross Cultural Comparative Framework," *International Journal of Cross-Cultural Management*, 3, 305–328.

Kahn, R.L., and Byosiere, P. (1992), "Stress in Organizations," in *Handbook of Industrial and Organizational Psychology* (2nd ed.), (Vol. 3), eds. M.D. Dunnette and L.M. Hough, Palo Alto, CA: Consulting Psychologists Press, pp. 571–650.

Kahn, R.L., Wolfe, D.M., Quinn, R.P., Snoek, J.R., and Rosenthal, R.A. (1964), *Organizational Stress: Studies in Role Conflict and Ambiguity*, New York: Wiley.

Kanter, R.M. (1977), *Work and Family in the United States: A Critical Review and Agenda for Research and Policy*, New York: Russell Sage Foundation.

Karasek, R.A. (1979), "Job Demands, Job Decision Latitude, and Mental Strain: Implications for Job Redesign," *Administrative Science Quarterly*, 24, 285–310.

Keith, P.M., and Schafer, R.B. (1980), "Role Strain and Depression in Two Job Families," *Family Relations*, 29, 483–488.

Kopelman, R.E., Greenhaus, J.H., and Connolly, T.F. (1983), "A Model of Work, Family, and Interrole Conflict: A Construct Validation Study," *Organizational Behaviour and Human Performance*, 32, 198–215.

Lai, G. (1995), "Work and Family Roles and Psychological Well-being in Urban China," *Journal of Health and Social Behaviour*, 36, 11–37.

Law, K.S., Tse, D.K., and Zhou, N. (2003), "Does Human Resource Management Matter in a Transitional Economy? China as an Example," *Journal of International Business Studies*, 34, 255–265.

Leung, A.S.M. (2003), "Feminism in Transition: Chinese Culture, Ideology and the Development of the Women's Movement in China," *Asia Pacific Journal of Management*, 20, 359–374.

Lin, N., and Lai, G. (1995), "Urban Stress in China," *Social Science and Medicine*, 41, 1131–1145.

Lobel, S.A., and St. Clair, L. (1992), "Effects of Family Responsibilities, Gender, and Career Identity Salience on Performance Outcomes," *Academy of Management Journal*, 35, 1057–1069.

Martin, R., and Wall, T.D. (1989), "Attentional Demand and Cost Responsibility as Stressors in Shopfloor Jobs," *Academy of Management Journal*, 32, 69–86.

Near, J.P., Rice, R.W., and Hunt, R.G. (1980), "The Relationship between Work and Nonwork Domains: A Review of Empirical Research," *Academy of Management Review*, 5, 415–429.

Parasuraman, S., and Alutto, J.A. (1981), "An Examination of the Organizational Antecedents of Stressors at Work," *Academy of Management Journal*, 24, 48–67.

Parasuraman, S., Greenhaus, J.H., Rabinowitz, S., Bedeian, A.G., and Mossholder, K.W. (1989), "Work and Family Variables as Mediators of The Relationship between Wives' Employment and Husbands' Well-being," *Academy of Management Journal*, 32, 185–201.

Pimentel, E.E. (2000), "Just How Do I Love Thee? Marital Relations in Urban China," *Journal of Marriage and the Family*, 62, 32–47.

Pittman, J.F., Solheim, C.A., and Blanchard, D. (1996), "Stress as a Driver of the Allocation of Housework," *Journal of Marriage and the Family*, 58, 456–468.

Podsakoff, P.M., and Organ, D.W. (1986), "Self-reports in Organizational Research: Problems and Prospects," *Journal of Management*, 12, 531–544.

Quinn, R.P., and Staines, G.L. (1979), *The 1977 Quality of Employment Survey*, Ann Arbor, MI: Institute for Social Research, University of Michigan.

Redding, S.G. (1993), *The Spirit of Chinese Capitalism*, New York: Alter de Gruyter.

Reynolds, J.R. (1997), "The Effects of Industrial Employment Conditions on Job-related Distress," *Journal of Health and Social Behaviour*, 38, 105–116.

Riley, N.E. (1996), "Holding Up Half the Economy," *The China Business Review*, Jan/Feb, 22–24.

Rothbard, N.P. (2001), "Enriching or Depleting? The Dynamics of Engagement in Work and Family Roles," *Administrative Science Quarterly*, 46, 655–684.

Rothbard, N.P., and Edwards, J.R. (2003), "Investment in Work and Family Roles: A Test of Identity and Utilitarian Motives," *Personnel Psychology*, 56, 699–730.

Schaubroeck, J., and Ganster, D.C. (1993), "Chronic Demands and Responsivity to Challenge," *Journal of Applied Psychology*, 78, 73–85.

Schaubroeck, J., Lam, S.S.K., and Xie, J.L. (2000), "Collective Efficacy versus Self-efficacy in Coping Responses to Stressors and Control: A Cross-cultural Study," *Journal of Applied Psychology*, 85, 512–525.

Schaubroeck, J., and Merritt, D.E. (1997), "Divergent Effects of Job Control on Coping with Work Stressors: The Key Role of Self-efficacy," *Academy of Management Journal*, 40, 738–754.

Schwartzberg, N.S., and Dytell, R.S. (1996), "Dual-earner Families: The Importance of Work Stress and Family Stress for Psychological Well-being," *Journal of Occupational Health Psychology*, 1, 211–223.

Schein, E.H. (1984), "Culture as an Environmental Context for Careers," *Journal of Occupational Behaviour*, 5, 71–81.

Spector, P.E. (1975), "Relationships of Organizational Frustration with Reported Behavioural Reactions of Employees," *Journal of Applied Psychology*, 60, 635–637.

Staines, G.L., Pleck, J., Shepard, L., and O'Connor, P. (1978), "Wives' Employment Status and Marital Adjustment: Yet Another Look," *Psychology of Women Quarterly*, 3, 90–120.

Thomas, L.T., and Ganster, D.C. (1995), "The Impact of Family-supportive Work Variables on Work–Family Conflict and Strain: A Control Perspective," *Journal of Applied Psychology*, 80, 6–15.

Voydanoff, P. (1987), *Work and Family Life*, Newbury Park, CA: Sage.

Wang, P., Lawler, J.J., Walumbwa, F.O., and Shi, K. (2004), "Work-family Conflict and Job Withdrawal Intentions: The Moderating Effect of Cultural Differences," *International Journal of Stress Management*, 11, 392–412.

Wharton, A.S., and Erickson, R.J. (1993), "Managing Emotions on the Job and at Home: Understanding the Consequences of Multiple Emotional Roles," *Academy of Management Review*, 18, 457–486.

Williams, K.J., and Alliger, G.M. (1994), "Role Stressors, Mood Spillover, and Perceptions of Work–Family Conflict in Employed Parents," *Academy of Management Journal*, 37, 837–866.

Williams, K.J., Suls, J., Alliger, G.M., Learner, S.M., and Wan, C.K. (1991), "Multiple Role Juggling and Daily Mood States in Working Mothers: An Experience Sampling Study," *Journal of Applied Psychology*, 76, 664–674.

Xie, J.L. (1996), "Karasek's Model in the People's Republic of China: Effects of Job Demands, Control, and Individual Differences," *Academy of Management Journal*, 39, 1594–1618.

Xie, J.L. (2002), "Sources and Moderators of Employee Stress in State-owned Enterprises," in *The Management of Enterprises in the People's Republic of China*, eds. A.S. Tsui and C.M. Lau, Norwell, MA: Kluwer Academic Publishers, pp. 299–323.

Yang, N., Chen, C.C., Choi, J., and Zou, Y. (2000), "Sources of Work-family Conflict: A Sino–US Comparison of the Effects of Work and Family Demands," *Academy of Management Journal*, 43, 113–123.

Yi, C., and Chien, W. (2002), "The Linkage between Work and Family: Female's Employment Patterns in Three Chinese Societies," *Journal of Comparative Family Studies*, 33, 451–474.

Zhang, C., and Farley, J.E. (1995), "Gender and the Distribution of Household Work: A Comparison of Self-reports by Female College Faculty in the United States and China," *Journal of Comparative Family Studies*, 26, 195–206.

Zuo, J., and Bian, Y. (2001), "Gendered Resources, Division of Housework, and Perceived Fairness: A Case in Urban China," *Journal of Marriage and the Family*, 63, 1122–1133.

Organizational commitment of Chinese employees in foreign-invested firms

Jos Gamble and Qihai Huang

Introduction

Organizational commitment has been studied extensively in Western management research and remains of substantial importance to managers (Meyer, Stanley, Herscovitch and Topolnytsky 2002). Mowday, Porter and Steers (1982) define it as an attitude in the form of an individual's identification with and involvement in a particular organization. Employee commitment to the organization has been found to relate positively to a variety of desirable work outcomes including employee job satisfaction, motivation and performance and negatively correlated to absenteeism and turnover (Porter, Steers, Mowday and Boulian 1974; Mathieu and Zajac 1990; Kalleberg and Marsden 1995; Meyer et al. 2002; Herrbach, Mignonac and Gatignon 2004). It is argued that individuals who are committed to the organization are less likely to leave their jobs than those who are uncommitted. Individuals who are committed to the organization are reported to perform at a higher level and also tend to stay with the organization, thus decreasing turnover and increasing organizational effectiveness (Porter et al. 1974). Organizational commitment is therefore believed to be critical to organizational effectiveness.

Our knowledge of employee commitment is derived primarily from Western contexts (e.g., Mowday et al. 1982; Meyer et al. 1993). Much less is known of the nexus of relationships between antecedents and organizational commitment in non-Western environments. Until recently, China had low levels of labour turnover, related to the system of lifetime employment in the state sector, known as the 'iron rice bowl' (Warner 1995). With reform and the open door policy, China's economy has integrated extensively into the global economy. Concurrently, with reform and the development of a labour market, labour turnover has increased and become a serious problem for many enterprises. According to one recent study, the nationwide employee turnover rate was 11.3% in 2004, up from 8.3% in 2001 (*The Economist* 2005). Some smaller firms see turnover rates as high as 30% and leading global firms are not immune. According to a survey carried out by Hudson (*South China Morning Post* 2005), turnover rates hover around 40% in some sectors. Some foreign-invested firms, such as Motorola, have responded by consistently paying higher than average wages in order to keep turnover down (*Business Week* 2004).

Job turnover has associated costs. Selection and recruitment consume resources, as can training for new recruits. It can also take time for new employees to reach optimum productivity levels. Retention is much cheaper than recruitment, as the head of accounting firm Ernst and Young in Hong Kong and China suggested (*The Economist* 2005). Similarly, Hudson's chief executive for Asia observed that, 'In China, how to improve retention is becoming the number one thing' (*South China Morning Post* 2005). Thus, retention is now top of the agenda for foreign firms in China. It is a timely point at which to investigate the factors that underlie both labour turnover and retention in China and to explore whether organizational commitment contributes to retention.

National culture has often been proposed to account for the values, beliefs and behaviour of workers in different countries (Hofstede 1984). Thus, Meyer et al. (2002) recommend cross-cultural research to examine relations among the organizational commitment constructs in the context of existing theories of cultural differences. In this study, we seek to understand whether organizational commitment differs between various cultures by exploring the organizational commitment of Chinese employees in a UK invested retailer and its relationship with employees' willingness to stay. This data is compared with the established conclusions from Western contexts.

The contributions of this research are four-fold. First, it examines employees' organizational commitment in the retail sector, an industry that is under-researched. Organizational commitment can function as a mediator in the relationship between HRM practices and service behaviour; for example, the way employees interact with customers in the retail organization (Browning 2006). There is a positive and strong correlation between organizational commitment and job performance for sales employees (Jaramilloa, Mulki and Marshall 2005). Although largely ignored in studies of organizational commitment, the retail sector is of great economic and social significance not only in the developed world but also in developing countries. In particular, the overwhelming focus on China as a global manufacturing base neglects the importance of the service sector in that country. According to Xinhua News Agency (2004), the proportion of China's GDP accounted for by the service sector increased from 21.4% in 1978 to 33.7% in 2002. In the same period, the number of people employed in this sector rose from just 48.9 million to over 210 million. It is estimated that the contribution of this sector to China's GDP will be between 50% and 60% in 2020 (Xinhua News Agency 2004).

As a major component of the service sector, the retail industry is of considerable importance. Some argue that, measured on a purchasing power parity (PPP) basis, by 2004 China had already become the second largest economy in the world after the United States (CIA 2005). Since China's retail sector re-opened to foreign involvement in 1992, it has witnessed a rapid influx of multinational retailers eager to take part in its 'consumer revolution'. By 2005, 40 of the world's 50 top retailers had chain stores in China (*Beijing Review* 2007).

Second, this study investigates the impact of individual components of organizational commitment on willingness to stay with the organization. Meyer and Allen (1991, 1997) point out that commitment-relevant behaviour can best be understood by examining employees' organizational commitment profile. However, little research has been done on this. For example, Meyer et al. (2002) find few studies testing for interactions among the components of the organizational commitment construct.

Third, it investigates further two elements that are considered of key importance in the Chinese context, namely, relationships and 'face', and assesses their role in organizational commitment and their associations with willingness to stay. We focus upon these elements since it appears that Western-based theories of employee behaviour may not sufficiently capture subtle cross-cultural differences (Tsui, Schoonhoven, Meyer, Lau and Milkovich 2004). In the Chinese context, a perspective that ignores interpersonal relations is likely to be inadequate to account for organizational commitment and citizenship behaviour in the organization–employee relationship (Hui, Lee and Rousseau 2004).

The current research also provides new insights by combining survey data with in-depth ethnographic data. Most research on organizational commitment relies solely on data derived from questionnaires. While valuable, such surveys have limitations. In particular they provide little indication of the often subtle and nuanced processes involved either in turnover intentions and willingness to stay or in helping us to understand the bases of organizational commitment.

The following section reviews the literature on organizational commitment and presents insights into some components of organizational commitment derived from the ethnographic fieldwork. We then propose a number of hypotheses and test them using survey data. After discussion of the findings, we draw out implications for both management and theory.

The concept of organizational commitment

Some of the earliest and most influential work on organizational behaviour explored the commitment of an employee to his or her employing organization, usually referred to as organizational commitment (OC) (cf. Meyer et al. 1993). Researchers operate with slightly different definitions of this term. However, the most widely used model is that developed by Meyer and his colleagues (Meyer and Allen 1991; Meyer et al. 1993, 2002). They identified and developed measures of three distinct dimensions in the definition of commitment: affective, continuance and normative. Affective commitment reflects an emotional attachment to, identification with and involvement in the organization. Continuance commitment is based on the perceived costs associated with discontinuing employment in the organization. Finally, normative commitment reflects a sense of obligation on the employee's part to maintain membership in the organization.

Researchers on organizational commitment largely accept the conceptualization and measures of Meyer and Allen (1991) or Mowday et al. (1982) without much critique. They simply either reduce or add some items of scale (e.g., Pitt, Foreman and Bromfield 1995;

Chen and Francesco 2000). The validity of the measurement of organizational commitment developed by Porter et al. (1974) was tested by Yousef (2003) based on two independent samples of about 1000 cases drawn from the United Arab Emirates. Coincidently, Meyer et al. (2002) claim that their model might indeed be applicable in other countries and cultures. Iverson and Buttigieg (1999) point out that recent research has highlighted the problem of conceptual and operational ambiguities in the organizational commitment literature. However, they provide no further clarification and the measures of organizational commitment they adopt are simply selected from Allen and Meyer (1990).

The most widely recognized and earliest conceptualization of organizational commitment is affective commitment developed by Mowday et al. (1982), who defined it as an individual's identification with and involvement in a particular organization. Affective commitment is characterized by three factors: identification – a strong belief in, and acceptance of, the organization's goals and values; involvement – a readiness to exert effort on behalf of the organization; and loyalty – a strong desire to remain a member of the organization. Our research examines the affective dimension of organizational commitment.

The influence of cultural values on organizational commitment

National cultural values inevitably shape the way people interact with one another in social environments, including organizations, because national cultures generate predispositions towards certain behavioural patterns (Child and Markóczy 1993), and different cultures promote unique sets of values, norms and expectations. Cultural values have been demonstrated to affect job satisfaction and organizational commitment in self-managing work teams of American, Filipino, Belgian and Finnish employees (Kirkman and Shapiro 2001). Similarly, in their comparative analysis of affective commitment in Hungary, Italy and the US, Glazer, Daniel and Short (2004) found that the values people endorse are influenced by national culture which, in turn, is likely to influence their organizational commitment. A growing body of research, then, indicates that organizational commitment differs greatly between various cultures (Near 1989).

Anecdotal research evidence suggests that employees in emerging markets might hold values that differ radically from those in developed countries (Kiggundu 1989). Specifically, Banai, Reisel and Probst (2004) raise the issue of the cross-national validity of the affective dimension of organizational commitment; they found that this theory developed in America and West European contexts was not effectively predictive in Hungary.

Drawing on analysis of over 400 cases from an investigation into the impact of culture and work-related values on human resource management policies and practices in seven Taiwan firms, Sparrow and Wu (1998) conclude that national culture-value orientations represent a separate construct to both work values and job satisfaction and organizational commitment. Thus, Meyer et al. (2002) admit that more systematic cross-cultural research is needed, in which relations among the constructs are examined in the context of existing theories of cultural differences. Despite this, it is notable that a recent paper on Chinese employees' organizational commitment claiming a 'cultural perspective' (Yao and Wang 2006), ignores the influences that Chinese culture might have on the construct itself, and simply adopts the scale measurement of the construct developed by Allen and Meyer (1990).

In the Chinese context, key characteristics that are said to affect organizations are respect for hierarchy and the importance of 'face' and relationships (*guanxi*) (Lockett 1988). 'Face' is the respect, pride and dignity of an individual as a consequence of his or her social achievement and the practice of it (Hwang 1987). Sparrow and Wu's (1998) research indicates that Taiwan Chinese have a high preference for collectivism and hierarchical relationships. Lockett (1988) suggests that Western management methods must be adapted to fit better with Chinese conditions and culture. This may apply equally to theoretical constructs applied in research.

Key variables and hypotheses for organizational commitment and intent to leave

Measure development is particularly problematic in comparative research (Davis et al. 1981). Although the dominant Western models reviewed here are not designed as comparative, inevitably they become so when applied to non-Western contexts. In the current research, organizational commitment was measured using its affective dimension rather than other recently identified dimensions of commitment including normative and continuance commitment. The reason for this is that affective commitment has been demonstrated to have the strongest positive correlation with generally desirable work behaviours (Meyer and Allen 1991). It is also consistent with findings presented in a recent meta-analysis concerning organizational commitment (Meyer et al. 2002), which showed affective commitment to be the most reliable predictor of important organizational outcomes, for example, intention to quit, turnover, absenteeism and organizational citizenship behaviour. In addition, affective commitment taps most directly into the psychological attachment in workers' commitment to the organization.

The most widely studied behavioural correlate of organizational commitment is turnover (Meyer and Allen 1991). Turnover often has negative impacts on the organization; for instance, it can significantly raise costs including opportunity costs and those required for the reselection and retraining of new workers. By contrast, employees' willingness to stay indicates their attachment to and desire to remain within the organization (Porter et al. 1974), which is usually a desired outcome for the organization.

In this study, willingness to stay, rather than intent to quit, which has been the focus in much research, is used as an outcome of organizational commitment. Intentions, both intent to quit and willingness to stay, are more directly under the control of individuals than the actual action to quit or stay. Numerous extraneous factors, such as the availability or otherwise of alternative jobs, can interfere with a person's ability to translate intentions into behaviour. Focusing on intentions avoids this complication, by suggesting how individuals might act in an unconstrained environment (Campbell and Campbell 2003). Following Miller and Wheeler (1992), this study utilizes one item to measure the outcome of willingness to stay. As indicated by Cotton and Tuttle (1986), single-item measures of intent to leave were used in most of the studies incorporated in their meta-analysis.

The above analysis leads to the following hypothesis:

Hypothesis 1: Organizational commitment of Chinese employees can significantly predict their willingness to stay.

Chen, Tsui and Farh (2002) argue that some of the items and scale developed by Mowday et al. (1982) in the United States might not be suitable in the Chinese context since they may not be able to capture all the relevant dimensions of organizational commitment. This is because, in China, loyalty to specific persons, such as the supervisor, is said to be more important than commitment to a system (Redding 1990). Based on a survey of 36 companies in Guangzhou and Shanghai, Chen et al. (2002) found that loyalty to supervisor seemed more important than organizational commitment in accounting for employees' performance. Therefore, it is possible that measures of organizational commitment developed in the West may include elements irrelevant to the Chinese context, while elements that are important in this context might be missing.

In order to assess the significance of the key characteristics of Chinese culture relevant to organizations (Lockett 1988), the current research not only examines the construct of organizational commitment as a combined scale of several items, as used in previous research, but also takes one step further and examines the individual components of the concept. Following Mowday et al. (1982), we asked respondents to identify the extent to which they: (a) agree with the company's vision and value; (b) are loyal to the company; and (c) are proud of the company. Actually these three components were included in Porter et al.'s (1974) Organizational Commitment Questionnaire (OCQ). The fifteen items in the OCQ were designed to assess respondents' loyalty and desire to remain with the organization, their belief in and acceptance of the values and goals of the organization and their willingness to put in extra effort to help the organization succeed. Thus, the three questions we asked covered the key aspects of the OCQ.

These items are assumed to measure three different aspects of organizational commitment. On the other hand, they are also meaningful separately since they measure self-reported perceptions of loyalty, pride and belief with regard to the organization a person works for. Organizational commitment-relevant behaviours can best be understood by examining employees' commitment profile (Meyer and Allen 1991, 1997). Furthermore, it is important to question what needs or values are relevant for the development of commitment (Meyer and Allen 1991). Werther (1988) suggests that to be loyal, people must share in a common vision of what the organization is and what it might be. If that vision offers the promise of benefits for the individual, commitment may grow out of the perception and expectation of a common fate, creating a shared destiny between the employee and organization. Thus they are less likely to have intent to leave. However, there is little detailed empirical research on values or needs that are important for the development of organizational commitment. Our in-depth ethnographic data provide insights into several aspects of organizational commitment of Chinese employees in the retail sector.

One author, a native Chinese speaker, spent three months in a Beijing warehouse store owned by the UK multinational retail firm, 'StoreCo', conducting both participant and non-participant research. 'StoreCo' is one of the world's largest home improvement retailers. By 2006, with its mainland China subsidiary operating 51 stores in 23 cities it had become that country's third largest foreign retailer and its largest home improvement chain store. Ethnographic research, which enables the capture of elusive, ambiguous and tacit aspects of research settings with rich and thick data (Linstead 1997), is particularly rare in the Chinese context. The researcher was given unfettered access to observe and talk with both employees and customers. Such an approach allows the researcher to accrue some of the trust due someone with 'insider status', an important factor in a society where contact making is highly personalized (Gamble 2003a, pp. xx–xxii). During the three months daily fieldwork, the researcher developed relationships with employees from every level in the store's hierarchy and was treated as a staff member. In addition to daily encounters and observation, more than one hundred open-ended and semi-structured interviews were conducted with store employees, including managers, team leaders, supervisors, and junior level staff from various departments. Many employees were interviewed on more than one occasion. Observations were also made of everyday activities in the store, including interactions between employees and between employees and customers.

Benson, Debroux, Yuasa and Zhu (2000) find that in most of the cases in their study, company values and missions were not clearly defined. Our fieldwork suggested that 'belief in company's vision and values', one of the most frequently asked or tested questions in the organizational commitment research and organizational commitment questionnaire, is problematic.

First, a company's vision and values can be abstract concepts to employees. They may not know what the company's vision and values are but still answer the question, based on their limited understanding, or even misunderstanding, of them. 'StoreCo's' mission states: 'We will be the best at giving people the inspiration, confidence and solutions to create homes to be proud of' (Employees' Handbook 2002, p. 4). It is not easy for employees to understand how to give customers inspiration and confidence. Dalton and Austen (1995) argue that employee commitment to the company can be increased by teaching employees certain values. During our fieldwork, the firm provided induction training to new employees with the company's culture including its history and mission as essential content (see also Gamble 2006b). Additionally, a large poster carrying the mission statement had been on the wall next to the store's escalator since the store opened. However, during the ethnographic research not a single employee encountered by the researcher appeared to know that this was the firm's mission statement.

Second, a company's vision and values can have many aspects, which may not all be relevant to employees' organizational commitment. 'StoreCo' lists several values, which include: striving to be better, customer driven, can do attitude, mutual respect (huxiang zunzhong) and down-to-earth (Employees' Handbook 2002, p. 4). Among the five aspects, only mutual respect for people seems directly relevant to employees' interest, in that it includes respect between employees and respect by customers toward employees. This contrasts to the four other values which are either customer or firm oriented. Notably, employees tended to focus upon and remember only this value as the only one that was relevant to their own particular interest.

Third, the values may not be internally consistent within themselves. The above mentioned five values might not seem inconsistent. However, in practice, each employee's views were based on their own understanding or experience of the values and these could be contradictory. For instance, the values of 'customer-driven' and 'down-to-earth' can be contradictory. Customer-driven is a key value to the company and most employees understood it to mean putting customers' interest first. However, this conflicts with the business aim of profit maximization and specifically cost control, the most important element of the value 'down-to-earth' according to the store's training officer.

The layers of the return procedure, in particular for faulty goods made this contradiction overt. Ordinary employees have limited scope to decide whether a customer can return a product. Indeed, to reduce store costs they are encouraged not to accept returns. Accordingly, employees were either taught or learned by themselves how to put off customers' return demands by ensuring that they went through several departments and levels of employees. In practice, the customer cannot usually complete the procedures in one visit to the store. Employees joked that this way of dealing with returns and complaints was designed to 'wear out' the customer. By such a procedure, a customer often had to return to the store several times and deal with various different employees. Often the outcome was that customers lost patience and gave up their quest and complied with the store's arrangement. On the other hand, some customers lost their temper and vented anger on employees. It can be questioned then, to what extent the companies' rhetorical values are relevant for the development of employees' organizational commitment (Meyer and Allen 1991) and willingness to stay when they conflict with and are undermined by actual procedures.

Moreover, the value of being customer-driven can result in mistreatment of employees by 'difficult' customers. Many employees encountered unreasonable customers, but they had to repress their feelings and not argue when faced with rude or even violent customers (see also Gamble 2007). Accordingly, some felt themselves to be 'servants', a lower status to their masters, the customers. Many employees acknowledged that this was a key reason they did not like to work in retail stores.

Similar findings of the unimportance of company values to Chinese employees' commitment have been reported in other research (e.g., Taylor 2001; Cooke 2004). In a large, foreign owned toy factory in China, Cooke (2004) found that employees could be compliant with corporate culture rather than committed to it, although there is a strong espoused culture in the company. While most workers she interviewed stated that the management of the company was good and fair towards workers, they did not show enthusiasm or commitment to the company's goals other than complying with instructions. Similarly, Taylor's (2001) study of Japanese multinationals in China also suggests a general lack of collective belief among workers in any form of association with the company beyond the wage–labour exchange.

As pointed out earlier, cultural differences can have an effect on the concept of organizational commitment. This can be reflected in the way that people in different cultures may have different understanding of organizations. Based on a survey of Chinese and Western employees of organizations in Hong Kong, Wheaton (1999) found that Chinese and Westerners defined the organization differently and this influenced the way they felt their attachment to the firm. Chinese and Western participants were committed to different constituencies within the organization. Westerners viewed interpersonal relationships as a means to an end, with the organization being the object of commitment. Meanwhile, Chinese committed to interpersonal networks and saw these relationships as the primary organization–member engagement. Similarly, Redding (1990) found earlier that Chinese are more loyal to individuals than to a system.

Some researchers have paid attention to the role of relationships between employees in an organization, namely, social capital, and the extent to which this is important to develop effective organizations (e.g., Nahapiet and Ghoshal 1998; Cohen and Prusak 2001). Conflict with superiors has been shown to hinder empowered employees to develop or maintain high levels of organizational commitment (Janssen 2004). Reliance upon *guanxi*, dyadic, particularistic relationships, are widely reported to be a pervasive feature in Chinese society (Huang, Nichols and Friedman 2003). Interpersonal relationships between subordinates and their superiors are seen as one of the most important characteristics of traditional Chinese organizations (Hui et al. 2004). It is often claimed that interpersonal relationships can be correlated with organizational outcomes. Furthermore, it has been shown that supervisory support has a more positive effect on organizational commitment than peer employee support (Yoon, Baker and Ko 1994). In a similar vein, Chen et al. (2002) suggest that employees' relationship with their supervisor was more strongly associated with performance than organizational commitment.

In their study of organizational citizenship behaviour and organizational commitment, Hui et al. (2004) analyze data from 605 matched cases of employees and their immediate supervisors in a Chinese steel conglomerate. They conclude that organizational citizenship behaviour and affective commitment can be construed as a form of reciprocity to a specific person, the supervisor, rather than to the work organization. Perceived organizational support does not activate Chinese employees' citizenship behaviours, whereas personal relationships with supervisors do. In this fieldwork and earlier research, conducted by one of the authors, on the same firm (Gamble 2003b, 2006a), two of the most frequently stated reasons why employees interviewed would like to work for the company were that the company has good personal relationships and a harmonious environment and that it is a leading multinational firm. The former motive is consistent with the question of 'how do you rank the relationship between subordinate and superior'. The latter factor is indicative of employees' perception that employment in a large multinational provides them not only with good prospects of job security, but also pride or 'face'.

Chinese people are frequently reported to be concerned with 'face' (Hwang 1987), and to be extremely conscious of how they appear to others. In popular perceptions, foreign-invested firms are desirable employers. The expectation is that a foreign firm, and especially a Western multinational, when compared to local firms, will provide better pay, conditions, training and promotion prospects (Gamble 2003b). Working for a FIE brings 'face'. Thus we might anticipate that those working for a UK subsidiary are likely to be proud. Equally, we can expect that employees are less likely to quit a company in which they take pride.

Therefore, the following hypotheses are proposed:

Hypothesis 2: Belief in the company's values is not significantly correlated with willingness to stay.

Hypothesis 3: Professed loyalty to the organization cannot predict willingness to stay.

Hypothesis 4: Pride in working for the company is significantly correlated with willingness to stay.

Hypothesis 5: Good relationships between subordinates and superiors can significantly predict employees' willingness to stay.

Another important dimension relevant to this research is the aftermath of labour reform in China. These reforms have steadily dismantled the 'iron rice bowl', and signalled the end of lifetime employment status for workers. The reforms push workers into a labour market which remains poorly developed, in particular in terms of the social security system. Without a secure job, workers feel their fate to be uncertain (Cook and Maurer-Fazio 1999). Employees are likely to regard job security as extremely important to avoid such uncertainties in a rapidly changing society. Accordingly,

Hypothesis 6: The perception of job security positively and significantly increases employees' willingness to stay.

Method and results

Data were collected from stores owned by the above-mentioned UK multinational retail firm in China. A survey-based questionnaire was completed by a cross-section of employees at four stores (two in Shanghai and one each in Beijing and Shenzhen respectively). The questionnaire is based partly upon the United Kingdom Department of Employment's Workplace Employee Relations Survey; as such it is a well-tested and robust research instrument. Specific questions and translations were discussed with several Chinese colleagues to ensure their comprehensibility and applicability in the Chinese context. Additionally, both authors are Chinese speakers, one being a native speaker. We also had the final Chinese text back-translated to English by another bilingual research assistant to ensure translation equivalence (Mullen 1995).

Respondents may be tempted to give the socially desirable response rather than describe what they actually think, believe or do. To reduce the possibility of social desirability bias (Arnold and Feldman 1981), the questionnaire stated clearly that it was for research purposes only and that all responses would be kept confidential. Completed questionnaires were returned either via mailbox or to a designated place in the department where respondents worked. There was no evidence that respondents were biased towards a 'desired response' because of worries over confidentiality. In fact, some respondents expressed concern that top management would not hear their voice. 'Please report my discontent answers to the management!' commented one employee on their questionnaire.

Response rates were high at over 90% since the firm's personnel department sanctioned the survey. The sample for analysis consists of 394 employees, representing about 45% of the total employees in these four stores. The majority (58%) of the sample were aged between 22 and 27. More than two thirds of respondents were single and 69% were male. Commensurate with the firm's relatively short history in China, most (82%) employees had tenure of less than two years with the company. Two thirds of them had education not higher than senior higher school.

The organizational commitment measure consisted of three items similar to the organizational commitment scale developed by Mowday et al. (1982) as explained earlier. The items were 'I agree with company's opinion and value,' 'I have loyalty to my company' and 'I am proud to tell others that I work for this company.' The job security variable was measured by the respondents' rating of the extent, 'I feel secure for my job in this company'.

All the above survey measures were assessed with five-point Likert scales, with anchors ranging from 'very strongly disagree' (1) to 'very strongly agree' (5). The relationship question asked respondents to rate the relationship between superiors and subordinates, ranging from 'very bad' (1) to 'very good' (5).

The variable of willingness to stay was measured by asking the respondent if he or she was willing to stay with the company within the next three years. It was coded 1 for yes, and 0 for no and 'don't know'. Age, education and tenure were measured by cohort number of years respectively. Gender was coded 1 for male and 0 for female. Marital status was coded 1 for married and 0 for single.

Table 1 contains descriptive statistics of the variables, including the main demographic characteristics of the sample, the means, SDs of the other variables, and the valid numbers of cases. It is worth pointing out that the loyalty variable has the highest mean among the three items, which is 4.21 (the other two are 3.96 and 4.01 respectively), approaching the highest possible score of 5, indicating most respondents saw themselves as 'loyal' or 'very loyal' to their company.

The three-item measure of organizational commitment is internally consistent with coefficient alpha = .81 (see Table 2). Table 2 also contains the scale alpha if a particular item is deleted. It shows that the exclusion of the belief item would only slightly reduce the

Table 1. Descriptive statistics.

Variable	Mean	SD
How long have you worked for this firm?	NA	NA
Your age	NA	NA
Your education	NA	NA
Prior work experience in sales or service	NA	NA
Marital status	NA	NA
I feel secure for my job in the firm	3.64	0.861
How would you describe the relationship between manager and workers	3.80	0.780
I agree with the firm's opinion and goals	3.96	0.771
I have loyalty to my firm	4.21	0.756
I am proud to tell others I work for this firm	4.01	0.905
Three-item organizational commitment	12.18	2.089
Willing to stay three years	NA	NA

Table 2a.   Reliability analysis – scale alpha.

	Mean	*SD*	*Cases*
1. Value	3.9609	.7723	384.0
2. Loyal	4.2135	.7587	384.0
3. Proud	4.0052	.9083	384.0

Table 2b.   Item total statistics.

	Scale mean if item deleted	*Scale variance if item deleted*	*Corrected item total correlation*	*Alpha if item deleted*
Belief	8.2188	2.3593	.5927	.8126
Loyal	7.9661	2.2364	.6829	.7289
Proud	8.1745	1.7632	.7353	.6705

Reliability coefficients: 3 items; Alpha = .8132; Standardized item alpha = .8142.

reliability of the scale. If the loyalty item is excluded, the reliability decreases to 0.7289, which is above the usually accepted value of 0.7 (Nunnally 1978), while the exclusion of the proud item would detract substantially from reliability of the scale (0.6705).

A factor analysis was conducted on the commitment items to assess unidimensionality. As Table 3 shows, only one factor emerges from the factor analysis, with an eigenvalue of 2.191, accounting for 73.026% of the variation in the data. In this sense, it can be said that the three items tap into one unidimensional construct and thus can be combined to produce a single score measurement of organizational commitment.

To test our hypotheses, we used logistic regression. Table 4 is the correlation matrix of the variables.

We ran two regressions. First, we regressed willingness to stay on the organizational commitment scale, the demographic variables, the relationship between superior and subordinate and job security variables. Second, we treated the three items of organizational commitment, namely, belief, loyalty and pride, as separate variables and regressed the willingness to stay variable on these three variables, together with the demographic variables, and the relationship and job security variables.

To assess if there was a problem of multicollinearity, we performed a regression diagnostic test in advance. The variance inflation factors (VIF) for the variables in the first model are between 1.046 and 1.732 and the VIF for the variables in the second model range from 1.067 to 2.529. Our VIF values are much lower than the recommended cut-off threshold of 10 (Hair et al. 1998) suggesting the absence of multicollinearity in the data.

Table 3.   Factor analysis – total variance explained.

	Initial eigenvalues			*Extraction sums of squared loadings*		
Component	*Total*	*Variance %*	*Cumulative %*	*Total*	*Variance %*	*Cumulative %*
1.	2.191	73.026	73.026	2.191	73.026	73.026
2.	.515	17.165	90.191			
3.	.294	9.809	100.000			

Extraction method: Principal component analysis.

Table 4.   Variable correlation matrix.

	1	2	3	4	5	6	7	8	9	10	11	12
1. How long have you worked for this company?	1											
2. Age	.147**											
3. Educational level	−.032	−.013										
4. Marital status	.137**	.450**	−.101*									
5. Do you have previous experience in the sales or service sectors?	−.146***	0.107***	−.018	131**								
6. I feel my job, in this company, is secure	−.173***	.028	−.155**	.028	.027							
7. I agree with the company's goals and values	−.150***	.048	−.033	.083	−.041	.491**						
8. I feel loyal to the company	−.137***	.012	−.050	.111**	.046	.458***	.504**					
9. I am proud to tell others I work for this company	−.161**	.080	−.105*	.047	.015	.549***	.581**	.695**				
10. How would you describe the relationship between managers and workers?	.081	.092	.074	.032	.008	.443**	.376**	.322**	.460**			
11. Three-item organizational commitment scale	−.176**	.058	−.078	.091	.012	.592**	.806**	.852**	.902**	.458**		
12. Do you intend to be working for this company in three years time?	−.091	.071	−.082	.068	.087	.417**	.356**	.346**	.475**	.374**	.466**	

**Correlation is significant at the 0.01 level (2-tailed); *Correlation is significant at the 0.05 level (2-tailed).

Table 5. Summary of the regression results.

Models	Model 1 OC Scale				Model 2 The three components			
Independent variables	Coef	Wald	Sig	Exp	Coef	Wald	Sig	Exp
Tenure	-0.021	0.022	0.882	0.979	-0.017	0.014	0.906	0.983
Age	0.029	0.022	0.881	1.029	0.009	0.002	0.964	1.009
Education level	-0.100	0.325	0.569	0.904	-0.075	0.174	0.677	0.928
Marital status	0.295	0.743	0.389	1.344	0.312	0.806	0.369	1.366
Job security	0.633	9.837	0.002**	1.884	0.614	8.943	0.003**	1.848
Relationship	0.570	8.126	0.004**	1.769	0.553	7.493	0.006**	1.738
Three-item OC scale	0.452	21.857	0.000**	1.571				
Belief in company values					0.349	2.278	0.131	1.471
Loyalty to the company					0.223	0.778	0.378	1.250
Pride working for the company					0.714	9.130	0.003**	2.043
Constant	-8.797	40.566	0.000	0.000	-8.383	34.843	0.000	0.000
-2 log likelihood		463.183 to 344.659				463.183 to 343.131		
Model Chi-square		118.524 p = .000				120.052 p = .000		
Improvement in prediction		69 to 78.3%				69 to 80.2%		
Hosmer and Lemeshow Test		χ^2 2.528 df 8 sig 0.960				χ^2 5.1120 df 8 sig 0.745		
Cox and Snell R^2		0.272				0.275		
Nagelkerke R^2		0.382				0.387		
n		374				374		

**Significant at the 0.01 level (2-tailed).

The results of the logistic regressions are presented in Table 5. The regressions have model chi-squares that are significant and the improvement in prediction level (prediction improved from 69% to 78.3% and 69% to 80.2%) indicates good fit for both models. The Hosmer and Lemeshow tests (p = 0.960 and 0.745) reveal no difference in the actual and predicted dependent values. The fit for model 2 (three components) is better than for model 1 (organizational commitment scale). This is indicated by the improvement in prediction level (accuracy 80.2% for model 2 and 78.3% for model 1) and the −2 log likelihood statistic. The Cox and Snell and Nagelkerke R square measures confirm the slightly better fit for model 2.

In model 1, organizational commitment is statistically significant in predicting the outcome of willingness to stay. Therefore Hypothesis 1 is supported. Job security and relationship variables contribute significantly to the prediction of willingness to stay (p = 0.002 and 0.004 respectively). Consequently, both Hypotheses 5 and 6 are supported in model 1.

Again in model 2, the relationship and job security variables significantly affect willingness to stay (p = 0.003 and 0.006 respectively). In other words, those who considered their job secure were more likely to be willing to stay with the company. In addition, those who reported a good relationship between superior and subordinate were also significantly more likely to declare their intent to stay with the company. These results once again confirm Hypotheses 5 and 6.

Among the three items of the organizational commitment, only the pride variable contributes significantly to the prediction of willingness to stay (p = 0.003) as shown in model 2. The statistic indicates that if employees felt proud of working for the company, they were significantly more likely to be willing to stay. Therefore, Hypothesis 4 is supported. The other two items of the organizational commitment scale, belief and loyalty, have no significant (p = 0.131 and p = 0.378 correspondingly) impact on the outcome of willingness to stay. In other words, neither of them seems an important factor in predicting willingness to stay, and thus Hypotheses 2 and 3 are also accepted.

Discussion

Some researchers have suggested that demographic features of employees are related with their intent to leave. However, Meyer et al. (2002) demonstrate that demographic variables play a relatively minor role in the development of organizational commitment, regardless of its form, and accordingly in intent to leave. Our finding is consistent with their conclusion. This finding is not surprising given the existence of a huge pool of surplus labour in the Chinese market. Most retail sector jobs do not require high level educational qualifications: much of the population can do the job and competition in such a labour market is fierce. While the economic reforms provide many people with unprecedented opportunity and choice, others face the threat of unemployment and income uncertainty. In earlier interview-based research on the same firm, one of the authors found that job security was important to and significantly associated with employees' desire to remain in the company (Gamble 2006a). The quantitative data in this study confirms the finding that as the security of the socialist 'iron rice bowl' has withered, multinationals such as this large UK firm constitute a life-raft of stability.

We assumed that organizational commitment in our sample would predict significantly the organizational outcome, willingness to stay, as suggested by the literature. Such a hypothesis was supported in our survey data analysis by using logistic regression. This finding lends support to suggestions that organizational commitment is a global predictor

(Campbell and Campbell 2003) and claims that the organizational commitment construct is valid across nations and cultures (Meyer et al. 2002).

However, this conclusion should be treated with caution and further investigation of organizational commitment is needed. As Meyer and Allen (1991) point out, researchers need to examine employees' commitment profiles and determine what needs or values are relevant for the development of commitment. Our analysis of the three items attempted this by exploring further the effect of the individual elements of organizational commitment on willingness to stay. Our further analysis suggested that employees' belief in the company's values and their loyalty to the company were not associated with willingness to stay. In contrast, the feeling of pride of working with the company predicts significantly the organizational outcome willingness to stay. Thus two of the three components do not appear consistent with organizational commitment in terms of predicting willingness to stay.

Professed loyalty to the organization may be no more than rhetoric to Chinese employees, who are loyal to interpersonal networks instead. Company values may not be so important or relevant to them, on the other hand. The unimportance of loyalty and belief items in organizational commitment was indicated by little change in alpha values if the two items are deleted as pointed out earlier (see also Table 4).

The above has discussed why loyalty and belief in company values might not help much to improve employees' attachment to the company and consequent willingness to stay. It is worth noting that Pitt et al. (1995) use a four-item organizational commitment scale developed by Hunt, Chonok and Wood (1985), without taking loyalty and belief questions into account. Our findings lend support to their decision to omit these two questions. It is believed that several techniques can be used to induce organizational commitment in Western firms, one of which is to create a company culture by emphasizing company values and shared mission (Benson et al. 2000). However, most research begs the question of what the organization's vision and value are. To build organizational commitment, organizations should first understand whether loyalty and values are relevant to organizational commitment, as argued above.

As pointed out earlier, cultural differences can affect the concept of organizational commitment. This can be reflected in that people in different cultures may have different understandings of organization (Wheaton 1999). Accordingly, people can have their own perceptions and expectations of organizational values and their relevance to themselves. As found in the earlier analysis, if organizational values are irrelevant to employees, they cannot make employees feel attached to the organization and willing to stay. Not surprisingly, professed loyalty to the organization becomes simply rhetoric and cannot predict employees' willingness to stay.

It is easier to understand the other three findings of the survey data analysis, that is, the significant effect of pride, job security and relationship between management and workers on willingness to stay. The two concepts of pride and relationship are the most important elements to Chinese culture relevant to organization (Lockett 1988). Organizational citizenship behaviour and affective commitment can be construed as a form of reciprocity to a specific person, the supervisor, rather than to the Chinese work organization (Hui et al. 2004). Not surprisingly, employees would like to stay with firms that provide them with a good working environment. Equally, employees are willing to work for firms of which they proud and which bring them 'face'. Meanwhile job security is a major concern to many Chinese employees whose society is in transition. If firms like this UK multinational can give them a life-raft of stability, most will grasp it firmly.

Management implications

What is the organization to employees? The perception of organization is the relationship between the organization and employees as understood by the employees, of which the relationship between management and employees is a crucial part. Iverson and Buttigieg (1999) suggest that line managers may have their own misguided assumptions about what motivates employees and how to manage them. Thus employees' understanding of organization and accordingly their organizational commitment are likely to be at least as strongly associated with and affected by how HR policy is implemented and who implements it as they are by the stated policies and values.

Benson et al. (2000) suggest that in Western firms, several techniques are used to induce organizational commitment. One approach is to create a company culture by emphasizing company values and shared mission. This could be applied in the West as well as China, although the organization's vision and value must be relevant to the interests of employees so that they can help generate employees' attachment and organizational commitment. To help ensure positive outcomes in terms of building organizational commitment, management should perhaps consider the dimensions that are important to employees as suggested in our analysis: the sense of job security, good relationships between management and workers and the pride of employees. Employees are willing to stay with and contribute more to organizations of which they are proud. Pride is the deeper dimension of employee satisfaction and commitment and loyalty is a manifestation of pride.

The adaptation of Western and Japanese methods in ways that recognize the Chinese context has the potential to develop a management model which could resolve some of the problems attributed to cultural factors (Lockett 1988). For instance, managers need to gauge the nature and implications of context specific values and historical practices among the local workforce in order to develop employee organizational attachment (Banai et al. 2004).

Limitations of the research

One possible limitation of our research is that it was conducted in a relatively newly established company, with its first store opened in 1999. Accordingly, its employees were young and new, both in terms of age and tenure. Organizational commitment together with willingness to stay may develop over time. To date, most research conducted to investigate the development and consequences of commitment has been cross-sectional and correlational (Meyer et al. 2002); longitudinal research is warranted.

Another possible limitation is the measure of the items that we analyse as individual variables. Most research on organizational commitment uses several items to measure the construct. Likewise, scale measure of an individual variable, for example, loyalty, by using both positively and negatively worded items may help to improve its reliability. However, in their assessment of the British Organizational Commitment Scale, Peccei and Guest (1993, p. 22) conclude 'that there is nothing to be gained by retaining these [negatively worded] items in the scale', a conclusion supported by Mathews and Shepherd (2002).

Implications for theory

The findings have implications for other transitional economies, which have similar situations to China, and particularly those in transition from state-planned labour systems to an uncertain labour market, in which social capital plays an important role (Huang 2002). It has been suggested that employees in developing economies might hold values that are quite different to those in developed countries (Kiggundu 1989). Banai et al. (2004) thus suggest the need to consider a pattern of cross-national differences for work-related organizational commitment.

In our research, two key elements of organizational commitment, loyalty to organization and belief in organizational values, are not associated with employees' willingness to stay. This finding is different from research conducted in the West. On the other hand, factors that are relevant to the Chinese context: job security, pride and relationship between superior and subordinate, predict well employees' willingness to stay. This finding indicates the importance of national context. More generally, since transition is a path-dependent transformation (Stark 1992), the findings highlight the necessity in researching China and other transitional economies to take into account their specific context and characteristics when developing and designing research agendas and methodological strategies. Similarly, some researchers criticize the cross-national validity of the affective dimension of organizational commitment developed in the West (e.g., Banai et al. 2004). Research into the multidimensional structure of organizational commitment should remain sensitive to the special characteristics of the researched sample group, including national traits attributable to cultural factors (Wang 2004). Chen and Francesco (2003) suggest that for Chinese employees affective commitment might reflect more an emotional attachment to specific people within the organization, rather than to the organization itself. It is necessary to develop organizational commitment constructs and measurements that can be helpful to understand and develop employees' attachment to their organizations in their context.

With regard to further research on this topic in China, it will be interesting to explore whether the organizational commitment of employees in state-owned and non-state owned enterprises has similar impacts on organizational outcomes, for example, willingness to stay. Chiu (2002) suggests that there are systematic differences between state and non-state firms' workers in terms of organizational commitment. However, his research focused only on workers in the manufacturing sector in Shanghai. Similarly, a survey conducted in seven industrial companies in Guangdong province indicates that SOE and FIE employees have the same level of affective commitment and normative commitment (Wang 2004). However, the labour process in sales-orientated employment has some specific features that distinguish it from industrial work (Smith 1997). It remains interesting, then, to compare different ownership in the retail sector. There is also scope to explore whether organizational commitment varies in subsidiaries of multinationals of different national origin.

Individuals who are committed to the organization can perform at a higher level, thus increasing organizational effectiveness (Porter et al. 1974). Research has suggested that organizational commitment functions as a complete mediator in the relationship between HRM practices and service behaviour in the retail organization (Browning 2006). Particularly, for sales employees there is a positive and strong correlation between organizational commitment and job performance (Jaramilloa et al. 2005). It will be interesting to investigate if this construct can predict Chinese employees' performance. Equally, we need to consider the above mentioned cultural elements and how they might influence performance.

Conclusion

In this study, we sought to understand whether organizational commitment differs between various cultures by exploring the organizational commitment of local employees in the

Chinese subsidiary stores of a UK multinational retailer and its relationship with employees' willingness to stay. It was found that loyalty to organization and belief in company values, dimensions believed to be important in Western contexts, were not associated with employees' willingness to stay. By contrast, factors seen as more important and relevant to the Chinese context, feeling proud of working for the company, good relationships between management and employees, and job security were good predictors of employees' willingness to stay.

It can be concluded that when applying theories developed in the West to China, context-specific cultural and institutional characteristics need be considered. Equally, for expatriate managers of Chinese workers, it is valuable to recognize the significant role that such context-specific features might play in developing an effective management model. Our analysis suggested that dimensions which are important to these employees include: the sense of job security, good relationships between management and workers, and the pride of employees. The findings here can also have implications for other non-Western economies and in particular other transitional economies which, like China, are in transition from a state planned labour system to an uncertain labour market.

Acknowledgements
This study is a result of research sponsored by the ESRC/AHRC under its Cultures of Consumption Programme award number RES-143-25-0028 for the project 'Multinational Retailers in the Asia Pacific'.

References
Allen, N.J., and Meyer, J.P. (1990), "The Measurement and Antecedents of Affective, Continuance, and Normative Commitment to the Organization," *Journal of Occupational Psychology*, 63, 1–18.
Arnold, H.J., and Feldman, D.C. (1981), "Social Desirability Response Bias in Self-report Choice Situations," *Academy of Management Journal*, 24, 2, 377–385.
Banai, M., Reisel, W.D., and Probst, T.M. (2004), "A Managerial and Personal Control Model: Predictions of Work Alienation and Organizational Commitment in Hungary," *Journal of International Management*, 10, 3, 375–392.
Beijing Review (2007), "Are M&As Suffocating Chinese Business?," accessed on 20 March 2008 from: http://www.bjreview.com.cn/expert/txt/2007-06/04/content_65184.htm.
Benson, J., Debroux, P., Yuasa, M., and Zhu, Y. (2000), "Flexibility and Labour Management: Chinese Manufacturing Enterprises in the 1990s," *International Journal of Human Resource Management*, 11, 2, 183–196.
Browning, V. (2006), "The Relationship between HRM Practices and Service Behaviour in South African Service Organizations," *International Journal of Human Resource Management*, 17, 7, 1321–1338.
Business Week (2004), "Is China Running out of Workers?", 25 October.
Campbell, D.J., and Campbell, K.M. (2003), "Global Versus Facet Predictors of Intention to Quit: Differences in a Sample of Male and Female Singaporean Managers and Non-managers," *International Journal of Human Resource Management*, 14, 7, 1152–1177.
Chen, Z.X., and Francesco, A.M. (2000), "Employee Demography, Organizational Commitment, and Turnover Intentions in China: Do Cultural Differences Matter?," *Human Relations*, 53, 6, 869–687.
Chen, Z.X., and Francesco, A.M. (2003), "The Relationship between the Three Components of Commitment and Employee Performance in China," *Journal of Vocational Behavior*, 62, 3, 490–510.
Chen, Z.X., Tsui, A.S., and Farh, J.L. (2002), "Loyalty to Supervisor vs. Organizational Commitment: Relationships to Employee Performance in China," *Journal of Occupational and Organizational Psychology*, 75, 3, 339–356.
Child, J., and Markóczy, L. (1993), "Host-country Managerial Behaviour and Learning in Chinese and Hungarian Joint Ventures," *Journal of Management Studies*, 30, 4, 611–631.
Chiu, W.C.K. (2002), "Do Types of Economic Ownership Matter in Getting Employees to Commit? An Exploratory Study in the People's Republic of China," *International Journal of Human Resource Management*, 13, 6, 865–882.
CIA (2005), *The World Fact Book: China*, retrieved 1 November 2005, from: http://www.cia.gov/cia/publications/factbook/geos/ch.html#Econ

Cohen, D., and Prusak, L. (2001), *In Good Company: How Social Capital Makes Organizations Work*, Boston, MA: Harvard Business School Press.

Cook, S., and Maurer-Fazio, M. (1999), "Introduction," *Journal of Development Studies*, 35, 3, special issue, 1–15.

Cooke, F.L. (2004), "Foreign Firms in China: Modelling HRM in a Toy Manufacturing Corporation," *Human Resource Management Journal*, 14, 3, 31–52.

Cotton, J.L., and Tuttle, J.M. (1986), "Employee Turnover: A Meta-analysis and Review with Implications for Research," *Academy of Management Review*, 11, 1, 55–70.

Dalton, T., and Austen, G. (1995), *Operating Successfully in China: Lessons from Leading Australian Companies*, Melbourne: International Market Assessment.

Davis, H.L., Douglas, S.P., and Silk, A.J. (1981), "Measure Unreliability: A Hidden Threat to Cross-national Marketing Research?," *Journal of Marketing*, 45, 98–109.

Employees' Handbook (2002) Unpublished company document.

Gamble, J. (2003a), *Shanghai in Transition: Changing Perspectives and Social Contours of a Chinese Metropolis*, London: RoutledgeCurzon.

Gamble, J. (2003b), "Transferring Human Resource Practices from the United Kingdom to China: The Limits and Potential for Convergence," *International Journal of Human Resource Management*, 14, 3, 369–387.

Gamble, J. (2006a), "Introducing Western-style HRM Practices to China: Shopfloor Perceptions in a British Multinational," *Journal of World Business*, 41, 4, 328–343.

Gamble, J. (2006b), "Multinational Retailers in China: Proliferating 'McJobs' or Developing Skills?," *Journal of Management Studies*, 43, 7, 1463–1490.

Gamble, J. (2007), "The Rhetoric of the Consumer and Customer Control in China," *Work, Employment & Society*, 21, 1, 7–25.

Glazer, S., Daniel, S.C., and Short, K.M. (2004), "A Study of the Relationship between Organizational Commitment and Human Values in Four Countries," *Human Relations*, 57, 3, 323–345.

Hair, J., Andersen, R., Tatham, R., and Black, W. (1998), *Multivariate Data Analysis*, Upper Saddle River, NJ: Prentice Hall.

Herrbach, O., Mignonac, K., and Gatignon, A.L. (2004), "Exploring the Role of Perceived External Prestige on Managers' Turnover Intentions," *International Journal of Human Resource Management*, 15, 8, 1390–1407.

Hofstede, G. (1984), *Culture's Consequences: International Differences in Work-related Values*, London: Sage (abridged edition).

Huang, Q. (2002), "Social Capital and China's Private Enterprise Start-ups: An Examination with Special Reference to the IT Sector," unpublished PhD thesis, University of Bristol.

Huang, Q., Nichols, T., and Friedman, A. (2003), *Social Capital in the West and China*, MMU working paper WP03/03.

Hui, C., Lee, C., and Rousseau, D.M. (2004), "Employment Relationships in China: Do Workers Relate to the Organization or to People?," *Organization Science*, 15, 2, 232–240.

Hunt, S.D., Chonok, L.B., and Wood, V.R. (1985), "Organizational Commitment in Marketing," *Journal of Marketing*, 49, 1, 112–126.

Hwang, K.K. (1987), "Face and Favor: The Chinese Power Game," *American Journal of Sociology*, 92, 4, 944–974.

Iverson, R.D., and Buttigieg, D.M. (1999), "Affective, Normative and Continuance Commitment: Can the 'Right Kind' of Commitment Be Managed?," *Journal of Management Studies*, 36, 3, 307–334.

Janssen, O. (2004), "The Barrier Effect of Conflict with Superiors in the Relationship between Employee Empowerment and Organizational Commitment," *Work and Stress*, 18, 1, 56–65.

Jaramilloa, F., Mulki, J.P., and Marshall, G.W. (2005), "A Meta-analysis of the Relationship between Organizational Commitment and Salesperson Job Performance: 25 Years of Research," *Journal of Business Research*, 58, 705–714.

Kalleberg, A.L., and Marsden, P.V. (1995), "Organizational Commitment and Job Performance in the US Labor Force," in *Research in the Sociology of Work* (Vol. 5), eds. R.L. Simpson and I.H. Simpson, Greenwich, CT: JAI, pp. 235–257.

Kiggundu, M.N. (1989), *Managing Organizations in Developing Countries: An Operational and Strategic Approach*, West Hartford, CT: Kumarian Press.

Kirkman, B.L., and Shapiro, D.L. (2001), "The Impact of Cultural Values on Job Satisfaction and Organizational Commitment in Self-managing Work Teams: The Mediating Role of Employee Resistance," *Academy of Management Journal*, 44, 3, 557–569.

Linstead, S. (1997), "The Social Anthropology of Management," *British Journal of Management*, 8, 85–98.

Lockett, M. (1988), "Culture and the Problems of Chinese Management," *Organization Studies*, 9, 4, 475–496.

Mathews, B.P., and Shepherd, J.L. (2002), "Dimensionality of Cook and Wall's (1980), British Organizational Commitment Scale Revisited," *Journal of Occupational and Organizational Psychology*, 75, 369–375.

Mathieu, J.E., and Zajac, D.M. (1990), "A Review and Meta-analysis of the Antecedents, Correlates and Consequences of Organizational Commitment," *Psychological Bulletin*, 108, 171–194.

Meyer, J.P., and Allen, N.J. (1991), "A Three-component Conceptualisation of Organisational Commitment," *Human Resource Management Review*, 1, 1, 61–90.

Meyer, J.P., and Allen, N.J. (1997), *Commitment in the Workplace: Theory, Research, and Application*, Thousand Oaks, CA: Sage Publications.

Meyer, J.P., Allen, N.J., and Smith, C.A. (1993), "Commitment on Organizations and Occupations: Extension and Test of a Three-Component Conceptualization," *Journal of Applied Psychology*, 78, 531–551.

Meyer, J.P., Stanley, D.J., Herscovitch, L., and Topolnytsky, L. (2002), "Affective, Continuance, and Normative Commitment to the Organization: A Meta-analysis of Antecedents, Correlates, and Consequences," *Journal of Vocational Behavior*, 61, 1, 20–52.

Miller, J., and Wheeler, K. (1992), "Unravelling the Mysteries of Gender Differences in Intentions to Leave the Organization," *Journal of Organizational Behavior*, 13, 5, 465–478.

Mowday, R.T., Porter, L.W., and Steers, R.M. (1982), *Employee–organization Linkages: The Psychology of Commitment, Absenteeism, and Turnover*, New York: Academic Press.

Mullen, M.R. (1995), "Diagnosing Measurement Equivalence in Cross-national Research," *Journal of International Business Studies*, 26, 3, 573–596.

Nahapiet, J., and Ghoshal, S. (1998), "Social Capital, Intellectual Capital and the Organizational Advantage," *Academy of Management Review*, 23, 2, 242–266.

Near, J.P. (1989), "Organizational Commitment among Japanese and US Workers," *Organization Studies*, 10, 3, 281–300.

Nunnally, J.C. (1978), *Psychometric Theory* (2nd ed.), New York: McGraw-Hill.

Peccei, R., and Guest, D. (1993), "The Dimensionality and Stability of Organisational Commitment,". Discussion Paper Number 149, London: Centre for Economic Performance, London School of Economics.

Pitt, L.F., Foreman, S.K., and Bromfield, D. (1995), "Organizational Commitment and Service Delivery: Evidence from an Industrial Setting in the UK," *International Journal of Human Resource Management*, 6, 2, 369–390.

Porter, L.W., Steers, R.M., Mowday, R.T., and Boulian, P.V. (1974), "Organizational Commitment, Job Satisfaction, and Turnover among Psychiatric Technicians," *Journal of Applied Psychology*, 59, 5, 603–609.

Redding, S.G. (1990), *The Spirit of Chinese Capitalism*, Berlin: Walter de Gruyter.

Smith, V. (1997), "New Forms of Work Organization," *Annual Review of Sociology*, 23, 315–339.

South China Morning Post (2005), "More Cheer for Job Seekers," 6 August.

Sparrow, P., and Wu, P.C. (1998), "Does National Culture Really Matter? Predicting HRM Preferences of Taiwanese Employees," *Employee Relations*, 20, 1, 26–56.

Stark, D. (1992), "Path Dependence and Privatisation Strategies in East Central Europe," *East European Politics and Societies*, 6, 1, 17–55.

Taylor, B. (2001), "The Management of Labour in Japanese Manufacturing Plants in China," *International Journal of Human Resource Management*, 12, 4, 601–620.

The *Economist* (2005), "China's People Problem," April 16, pp. 53–54.

Tsui, A.S., Schoonhoven, C.B., Meyer, M.W., Lau, C.M., and Milkovich, G.T. (2004), "Organization and Management in the Midst of Societal Transformation: The People's Republic of China," *Organization Science*, 15, 2, 133–144.

Wang, Y. (2004), "Observations on the Organizational Commitment of Chinese Employees: Comparative Studies of State-owned Enterprises and Foreign-invested Enterprises," *International Journal of Human Resource Management*, 15, 4/5, 649–669.

Warner, M. (1995), *The Management of Human Resources in Chinese Industry*, London: Macmillan.

Werther, W.B. Jr. (1988), "Loyalty at Work," *Business Horizons*, 31, 2, 28–35.

Wheaton, A. (1999), "The Generation of Organizational Commitment in a Cross-cultural Context," *Asia Pacific Business Review*, 6, 11, 73–103.

Xinhua News Agency (2004), "China Will Double the Contribution of the Service Sector to its Economy in 15 Years," 8 January.

Yao, X., and Wang, L. (2006), "The Predictability of Normative Organizational Commitment for Turnover in Chinese Companies: A Cultural Perspective," *International Journal of Human Resource Management*, 17, 6, 1058–1075.

Yoon, J., Baker, M., and Ko, J. (1994), "Interpersonal Attachment and Organisational Commitment: Subgroup Hypothesis Revisited," *Human Relations*, 47, 3, 329–351.

Yousef, D.A. (2003), "Validating the Dimensionality of Porter et al.'s Measurement of Organizational Commitment in a Non-western Culture Setting," *International Journal of Human Resource Management*, 14, 6, 1067–1079.

Emotional bonds with supervisor and co-workers: Relationship to organizational commitment in China's foreign-invested companies

Yingyan Wang

Introduction

In societies where personal relationships are the basic unit of social structure, employees are more likely to conceptualize their employment as a relationship with specific organization members (Hui, Lee and Rousseau 2004). For example, compared with Westerners, Chinese have a stronger sense of responsibility and obligation toward those who have close relationships with them (Wong, Wong and Ngo 2002). The studies of loyalty to a supervisor and supervisor–subordinate relationship (Law, Wong, Wang and Wang 2000) have shed light on the practice of human resource management in Chinese companies. However, the linkage with significant others in the Chinese context has not been thoroughly examined. In a society where personal relationships are emphasized in the social life of individuals, pleasant relationships with other kinds of close members such as co-workers might also play an important role in ameliorating relationships in the workplace. Thus far, the influence of the linkage between an employee and co-workers has not yet received sufficient attention.

Furthermore, although the emotion-focused aspect in the workplace has received great attention among scholars, most research has only focused on the emotional bond in an organization as a whole, without paying sufficient attention to particular constituencies within the organization. For example, the theory of organizational commitment has examined the dimension of affective commitment, which is an emotion-focused commitment to the organization (Dvir, Kass and Shamir 2004). As some researchers have critically noted, the large body of literature on emotional attachment to organization is in contrast with the scarcity of research associated with commitment to particular elements. It was not until recently that the research on commitment to supervisor has begun (Chen, Tsui and Farh 2002). More research is needed in the aspects of clarifying and presenting the role of emotional attachment with particular constituencies within an organization. Also, the theory should be able to account for how the emotion-focused aspects with organization members and the organization as a whole are related.

Consequently, the present study aims to address three research questions. First, what are emotional bonds with supervisor and co-workers in the Chinese context? Second, given that organizational commitment has been regarded widely as a multi-dimensional concept, what are the relationships between emotional bonds with supervisors and co-workers, and different dimensions of organizational commitment? Third, considering the concerns of high turnover rates in foreign-invested enterprises in China, what are the practical implications for human resource management in light of the role played by emotional bonds with supervisors and co-workers? The theoretical framework guiding this study will draw upon research on emotion-oriented aspects in the organizational context and studies on the recognition of organizational commitment in China.

Emotional bonds with supervisor and co-workers in the Chinese context

Among the different foci of commitment, the elements of supervisor and co-workers may take on special meaning and importance because of the unique characteristics of the relationship-oriented Chinese society (Chen et al 2002). For example, Chinese managers put more emphasis on relationship with co-workers when making non-monetary decisions, whereas more emphasis is put on relationship with managers when making non-monetary award decisions (Zhou and Martocchio 2001). Recent research concerning relationships with supervisors was conducted in terms of two different approaches. One is a cognitive approach, which focuses on the perception, intuition and reasoning of how employees conceptualize their relationships with supervisors. Applying a cognitive approach, commitment to supervisor has been found to be an important predictor of both employees' performance and organizational citizenship behaviour in Chinese joint ventures (Wong et al. 2002). The other is to examine the supervisor–subordinate relationship in terms of behaviour approach. For example, the study of building and maintaining good interpersonal connection with a supervisor, and measuring the connection by individualized behaviour and activities (Law et al. 2000) falls into such a category. In contrast to the cognitive and behaviour perspectives, the present research examines the relationship with supervisor in an emotional perspective. Emotional perspective has been applied in leadership theory, such as the examination of the emotional recognition ability and positive affectivity (Rubin, Munz and Bommer 2005) of the leaders, while the role played by the emotional bond an employee has with a supervisor has not been examined.

It has been argued that interactions with superiors contribute significantly to perceived social support at work in the Western context (Kirmeyer and Lin 1987). The importance of the emotional bond with a supervisor might be explained in light of traditional Chinese culture and contemporary Chinese socio-economical conditions. As suggested by some scholars, the important status of a superior is ingrained in the Chinese culture, which has its roots in Confucianism (Farh and Cheng 2000). The attachment to the supervisor arises out of respect to a prescribed social norm, which supposes that inferiors should maintain loyalty to an authority figure. Relevant to this point is the argument by Chen et al. (2002), which considers that sensitivity to social roles and their accompanied obligations remain major characteristics of the contemporary Chinese, although some of the sacred ties valued by traditional Chinese culture have been transformed, for example, the minister-to-the-ruler tie is replaced by the subordinate-to-the-leader tie.

In contrast to the relative emphasis on the relationship between supervisors and subordinates, peer relations have received less attention (Kirmeyer and Lin 1987) and often are downplayed by managers as irrelevant, distracting or unproductive (Bramel and Friend 1987). However, some evidence has shown that supportive relationships among co-workers may have important and positive performance-related consequences for organizations (Shah and Jehn 1993) and may prompt employees to share knowledge (Reagans and McEvily 2003). Individuals with emotional bonds are more motivated to be of assistance to one another (Bacharach, Bamberger and Vashdi 2005). Relationships with co-workers are argued to be associated with burnout (Leiter and Maslach, 1988) and turnover behaviour (Leonard and Levine 2006). Impression management motives were also found to be related to citizenship behaviours directed toward co-workers but not to the organization per se (Finkelstein 2006).

The meaning of emotional bonds with co-workers might share some common ground with the emotional bond with a supervisor, in that an individual is encouraged to form pleasant interpersonal relationships, valued by a traditional social norm, with co-workers. However, in many foreign-invested enterprises in China, the emotional bonds with co-workers might arise from individual networks established by guest workers from the same hometown. In many cases, a number of migrant workers move from their hometown to find new jobs together with their families or friends. In the highly concentrated industrial districts such as middle-sized cities in south China, it is common to see large numbers of workers from local districts waiting at the company entrance, hoping to be interviewed (Wang 2004). Those workers are usually interdependent among themselves within their own networks. Furthermore, the strong emotional tie is addressed in traditional Chinese culture. In the workplace, employees may treat their co-workers as their own brothers and sisters and have concern for each other very much in the private domain, which is atypical of Western society.

Hypotheses

Although researchers have found that in the Chinese context, commitment to supervisor, co-workers and organization are expressed as different foci, there has been no empirical research focusing on examining the impacts of emotional attachment to the supervisor and coworkers on organizational commitment. According to Wang (2004), the construct of organizational commitment in the Chinese context is composed of a five-dimension model, i.e. affective commitment, active continuance commitment, passive continuance commitment, normative commitment and value commitment, which is different from a widely acknowledged three-dimensional theory proposed by Meyer and Allen (1991). The five-dimension organizational commitment model has been extended from a transposition of Western methodology to a Chinese context and reflects more Chinese characteristics. Considering that the present study of emotional bonds with a supervisor or coworkers is conducted in the Chinese context, it is appropriate to apply a model of organizational commitment which is correspondent with the Chinese characteristics.

Unlike Western culture, Chinese culture fosters a strong vertical link between supervisor and subordinate (Redding 1990). Leaders are likely to be involved personally with their subordinates. Also, commitment to the supervisor has been found to be likely to influence organization-relevant outcomes, such as organizational citizenship behaviour (Cheng, Jiang and Riley 2003). Since the employees are often tied to the organization through regular interaction with their supervisor, the individual bonds with a supervisor are likely to affect the way that these employees become emotionally involved with the organization to which they belong. In China especially, the vertical link between supervisor and subordinate is more likely to be emotional and supportive, rather than rational and logical. Consequently, a strong emotional bond with a supervisor will be more likely to influence employees in their degree of emotional attachment to the organization than factors based purely on reason. In contrast, a weak emotional bond with a supervisor will be less likely to make the employees feel affectivity toward the organization.

Traditional Chinese culture supports norms of reciprocity and emphasizes harmony and stability in the workplace (Fryxell, Dooley and Li 2004). For over two millennia Confucianism has represented official state philosophy in China, in which the self exists wholly in and through social roles on relational ties, and located within networks, such as those of established friendships (Snell and Tseng 2003). However, it is hard to imagine that the way in which employees interact with co-workers would affect their emotional attachment to the organization because interactions with co-workers do not necessarily imply affective involvement with the organization. To a great extent, interpersonal relationships with co-workers continue because of the common interests among the employees, whereas the interests among employees might not be in congruence with those of the organization. Therefore, as a result, it is not envisaged that the emotional bonds with co-workers would have any impact on the affective commitment to the organization. Considering the emotional bonds with a supervisor and co-workers, only the former might affect affective commitment to an organization.

Hypothesis 1: A stronger emotional bond with a supervisor is more likely to help to increase an employee's affective commitment to the organization.

The impact of emotional bonds with a supervisor and co-workers on normative commitment can be examined in terms of the meaning of social norms in traditional Chinese culture. Normative commitment originates from the social norm, and the meaning of normative commitment refers to the obligation or the sense of responsibility in remaining with an organization. It is widely known that in Chinese society, the sense of obligation and responsibility are highly valued in traditional Chinese thinking. People who are more likely to develop normative commitment are those who are in favour of such kinds of social norms that value obligation and responsibility toward others. The emotional bonds with a supervisor can work to improve the loyalty toward the supervisor, and by the same token can be transformed to loyalty toward the organization. Therefore, for employees who have an emotional bond with their supervisors, they are more likely to develop and maintain normative commitment toward the organization. In contrast, for those who do not have strong emotional bonds with their supervisors, they are less likely to develop and maintain normative commitment toward the organization.

Hypothesis 2a: A stronger emotional bond with a supervisor is more likely to help to increase an employee's normative commitment to the organization.

In a similar way, emotional bonds with co-workers also increase employees' loyalty and responsibilities to their co-workers. In the workplace, employees are motivated to cooperate with their co-workers to complete the work when there are strong emotional bonds among them. Responsibilities toward other co-workers to complete work might be able to assist the employees to improve their responsibilities towards the organization as a whole. Therefore, it is highly likely that the more an employee feels emotional bonding with co-workers, the more likely that he or she will feel normatively committed towards the organization. In contrast, when the employee has weak emotional bonds with co-workers, he or she is less likely to develop and maintain normative commitment toward an organization.

Hypothesis 2b: Stronger emotional bonds with co-workers are more likely to increase employees' normative commitment to the organization.

Active continuance commitment is a specific characteristic that has emerged in empirical studies in the Chinese context, which has also been named as the ideal commitment (Ling, Zhang and Fang 2001). It is more related to the active motivation associated with working. It is possible that for individuals who are especially interested in seeking active opportunities, in the current Chinese context, the active continuance commitment becomes a specific dimension. In many Western studies, the recognition of the cost associated with leaving or staying with the organization is regarded as equal to that of the active motivation that might encourage employees to stay. In China, people who are in close relationships with leaders are more likely to acquire promotion opportunities. The ability to maintain a good relationship with the leader can substantially affect an individual's success in the workplace. While a strong emotional bond with a supervisor implies that an individual is loyal to his supervisor, he will be more likely to have more opportunities to enjoy better conditions compared to other employees. Having an emotional tie with a supervisor, therefore, can affect an employee's active continuance dimension of organizational commitment. For employees who have strong emotional bonds with their supervisors, they are more likely to feel active continuance commitment toward the organization. In contrast, for those who have weak emotional bonds with their supervisor, they are less likely to feel active continuance commitment toward the organization.

Hypothesis 3a: A stronger emotional bond with a supervisor is more likely help to increase an employee's active continuance commitment to the organization.

With respect to the influence of emotional bond with co-workers on the development of active continuance commitment, similar to the way the impact of emotional bond with a supervisor was examined, it is also necessary to examine how the emotional bond might function in assisting the individual to acquire more success. It is very likely that strong emotional bonds with coworkers may help the individual to acquire more support from his co-workers. Individuals with strong emotional bonds with co-workers are those who have the ability to maintain and develop good relationships with co-workers. In the Chinese context, since the ability to maintain and develop good relationships with others is highly valued, it is also likely that individuals who are specialized in developing and maintaining good relationships with co-workers are more likely to be selected as a group leader, thus increasing the opportunities for promotion. Therefore, it can be argued from the above statement that employees with emotional bonds with co-workers are more likely to have active continuance dimension of organizational commitment.

Hypothesis 3b: Stronger emotional bonds with co-workers are more likely to increase employees' active continuance commitment to the organization.

The impact on passive continuance commitment, of emotional bonds between supervisory and lower-level employees, should be analysed in terms of the reality of foreign-invested enterprises considering that, in China, the comparative levels of continuance commitment are different in state-owned enterprises and foreign-invested enterprises (Wang 2004). Employees with a high level of passive continuance commitment recognize the costs associated with leaving the organization or have to stay with the company due to a lack of other job opportunities. As a point of difference from state-owned companies, people working in foreign-invested companies have more latitude in deciding their own jobs because their place of permanent residence is not necessarily of any great consequence to them. People are not loathe to quit their job if they do not want to continue working in a foreign-invested company, although in rare cases illicit companies do not permit the employees to quit freely. In general, passive continuance commitment in foreign-invested companies is not high.

An emotional bond with a supervisor may have a significant impact on the active continuance commitment in that employees might feel there are more future advancement prospects, whereas research does not conclusively show that an emotional bond with a supervisor has an effect on the passive continuance commitment to the organization. It is generally more likely for employees to feel positive about their future because of the emotional bond with a supervisor. Therefore, it can be argued that employees' emotional bonding with a supervisor is not related to passive continuance commitment to the organization.

In contrast, the relationships of emotional bonds with co-workers and passive continuance commitment are varied. Many guest workers working in the same company come from the same hometowns because people like to move to a new place together with their friends to find a job. Thus, there is usually a close network among guest workers often with people from the same hometown forming small inside cliques. Once an individual has developed a very good relationship and maintains emotional ties with his co-workers, he would be unwilling to lose the emotional ties with his co-workers, because the ties are more than a mere relationship in the workplace. Employees would also get substantial spiritual support from their co-workers even outside the work domain. Therefore, considering the unwillingness to change and the cost of losing the emotional ties with co-workers, it would be reasonable to expect that people with an emotional bond with co-workers can be characterized by a higher level of passive continuance commitment.

Hypothesis 4: Stronger emotional bonds with co-workers are more likely to increase employees' passive continuance commitment to the organization.

Finally, value commitment represents a unique dimension in the Chinese context, referring to an employee's feeling of value congruence with the organization and a willingness to exert considerable effort on behalf of the organization. The relationship between emotional bond with a supervisor and value commitment can be examined in terms of the value congruence with the supervisor and the organization. It can be speculated that employees perceive the value and goal of the organization through their interaction with the supervisor. When there is a positive emotionality between an employee and the supervisor, the employee is more likely to interact with his supervisor actively. In addition, the act of interacting is more likely to facilitate the value congruence between an employee and the organization. As a result, those employees who feel strong emotional ties with their supervisor are more likely to understand the value and goals of the organization, thereby developing value commitment to the organization.

In contrast, emotional ties with co-workers do not play a role in promoting the value congruence between the employees and the organization. Employees are more likely to help each other when they are in good relationships but they are less likely to work in a manner which is aligned to the organization's standpoints and philosophies. For instance, workers in good relationships cooperate when dealing with poor conditions that might be provided by the company. Furthermore, good relationships with co-workers might promote an informal productive network outside the formal domain of the organization, in the dimensions which are not related to the organization. Therefore, it is hard to imagine that the emotional ties with co-workers would affect the value dimension of organizational commitment.

Hypothesis 5: A stronger emotional bond with a supervisor is more likely to increase an employee's value commitment to the organization.

Method

Participants

A survey was recently conducted in Guangdong province, the first district to launch reform and become receptive to new modes of operation at the end of the 1970s. Questionnaires and in-person interviews were used in the present study. First, the twenty biggest foreign-invested companies in Guangdong province were selected, and telephone enquiries were made to the top managers in each company to see if they were willing to cooperate with this form of research of organizational commitment. Although details of individual questionnaires were not allowed to be divulged to the company, the final summary reports of the organizational commitment level of each company could be submitted. When the research policy was explained, four of the companies contacted were willing to cooperate. There were two Japanese-Chinese joint ventures, one Hong Kong company and one Taiwanese company, in the air-conditioning, paper, steel and automobile industries respectively. There were almost 6000 employees in total working for the four companies. Of the 1262 questionnaires randomly distributed 1160 were collected. The questionnaires were distributed in envelopes, and, in order to maintain secrecy, participants were asked to seal the envelopes before handing them in. It had been indicated on the questionnaire that the study was for research only and no individual information would be disclosed. After collecting the questionnaires, five employees from each company were selected randomly to be interviewed. The questions included how long they planned to stay at their current company, how they got along with their co-workers and the nature of their relationships with their supervisors.

Since this study is targeted at the rank-and-file employees, the questionnaires were distributed among typical employees, who were mostly working under the supervision of local Chinese superiors. Considering that many studies have examined demographic variables, in which it has been suggested that demography affects organizational commitment, it is important to take demographic features into account in this sample. One remarkable feature of foreign-invested industrial companies on the Southeast China coast is that more female workers than male are hired as rank-and-file employees, while their supervisors are in most cases males. As can be seen in the present study, all four companies hired at least 65% female employees. Also, young people in their 20s and 30s are more likely to work as guest labourers, and switch jobs frequently. In the present study, over 90% of the employees of the four companies were under 30, and the tenures of over 80% of the employees were less than five years.

Organizational commitment

Organizational commitment was measured using Wang's (2004) scale. According to Wang (2004), there were five items from the OCQ, ten items from Ling et al.'s scales, which were originally in Chinese, and three items of normative commitment.

Two bilingualists were asked to translate the eight English items first and then compare their translations in order to get a standard Chinese translation of the eight items. All the items were measured with a five-point scale with anchors labelled 1 = disagree; 2 = moderately disagree; 3 = neither agree nor disagree; 4 = moderately agree; 5 = agree.

An exploratory principal components analysis with varimax rotation of the 18 items yielded five factors, which presented the five-dimension organizational commitment model in the Chinese context. The five factors accounted for 61% of the total variance. The first factor contains three items of affective commitment with loadings of greater than .60. A sample question was 'I am extremely glad that I chose this company to work for over others I was considering at the time I joined'. Next three items were used to measure normative commitment with loadings greater than .50. A sample item was 'I consider it my obligation to work for the same company all the while'. Passive continuance commitment was measured by three items with loadings greater than .60. A sample item was 'I work for the company because I cannot find a better one'. Then, there were five items in measuring active continuance commitment with loadings greater than .60. A sample item was 'I work for the company because it provides me with many OJB training opportunities'. Finally, value commitment was measured by four items with loadings greater than .70. A sample question was 'I am willing to put in a great deal of effort beyond that normally expected in order to help this company to be successful'. Cronbach's alpha coefficients were .73 for the affective commitment subscale, .61 for the normative commitment subscale, .64 for the passive continuance commitment subscale, .80 for the active continuance commitment subscale and .81 for the value commitment subscale.

Furthermore, covariance structural analysis was used to confirm the structure of the model. Consistent with Wang (2004), the model of five dimensions shows a good level of fit (GFI = .96; CFI = .94).

Antecedent variables

Emotional bond with supervisor was measured by the item of 'I am feeling emotional attachment to my supervisor', using a five-point scale with anchors labelled 1 = disagree; 2 = moderately disagree; 3 = neither agree nor disagree; 4 = moderately agree; 5 = agree.

Similarly, *emotional bond with co-workers* was measured by the item of 'I am feeling emotional attachment to my co-workers', using a the same five-point scale.

Control variables

From the earliest stages of the study on organizational commitment, demographic factors have received considerable attention. Some studies have shown that age, tenure (Reilly and Orsak 1991; Hackett, Bycio and Hausdorf 1994) and gender (Alvi and Ahmed 1987) are related to organizational commitment, although there remains some controversy regarding the extent to which differing demographic variables might influence organizational commitment within different samples. In addition, considering the possibility that employees with different job roles and status might come from differing sectors of the population, such that manual and non-managerial workers are more likely to work as temporary guest workers in foreign-invested companies, job roles and status were also considered to be important control variables in the present study. Therefore, five demographic variables in total were included as control variables, namely: gender, age, tenure, job role and status.

Results

Correlations

Means, standard deviations and correlations of all the variables in the present study are shown in Table 1. The general rule of thumb implies that the correlations of the data should not exceed .75 considering the risk of multicollinearity (Tsui, Ashford, St. Clair and Xin 1995). Since the highest correlation in the present sample was between affective commitment and active continuance commitment at $r = .615$, it does not present a serious multicollinearity problem.

Consistent with Hypotheses 1, 2a, 3a and 5, emotional bond with a supervisor is positively related to: affective commitment ($r = .394$, $p < .01$); normative commitment ($r = .280$, $p < .01$); active continuance commitment ($r = .362$, $p < .01$); and value commitment ($r = .266$, $p < .01$). Furthermore, emotional bonds with co-workers are also related to: normative commitment ($r = .082$, $p < .01$); active continuance commitment ($r = .072$, $p < .05$); and passive continuance commitment ($r = .165$, $p < .01$), which are consistent with Hypotheses 2b, 3b and 4.

Hierarchical multiple regression analyses

Two-step hierarchical multiple regressions were conducted to determine whether emotional bonds with supervisor and co-workers have any impact on each sub-dimension of organizational commitment. In the first step, the five control variables (gender, age, tenure, job role and status) were entered. In the second step, two variables of emotional bonds with supervisor and co-workers were entered. The results of hierarchical multiple regression analyses are shown in Table 2. First, for the regressions on each sub-dimension of organizational commitment, the significance of the ANOVAs reached the $p < .01$ level. After entering emotional bonds with supervisor and co-workers, the variances indicated show some improvement compared with the models in the first step. Second, as shown in model 2, the emotional bonds with supervisor have a positive impact on affective commitment ($\beta = .372$, $p < .01$), while emotional bonds with co-workers are not positively correlated to affective commitment ($\beta = .041$), which means that Hypothesis 1 is supported. Third, as shown in model 4, the emotional bonds with a supervisor have a positive impact on normative commitment ($\beta = .257$, $p < .01$), also emotional bonds with co-workers are positively correlated to normative commitment ($\beta = .058$, $p < .05$), which means that Hypotheses 2a and 2b are supported. Next, as shown in model 6, the emotional bond with a supervisor has a positive impact on active continuance commitment ($\beta = .313$, $p < .01$), and emotional bonds with co-workers are positively correlated to active continuance commitment ($\beta = .054$, $p < .05$), which means that Hypotheses 3a and 3b are supported. Furthermore, as shown in model 8, the emotional bonds with supervisor have no impact on passive continuance commitment ($\beta = -.020$), while emotional bonds with co-workers are positively correlated to passive continuance commitment ($\beta = .163$, $p < .05$), which means that Hypothesis 4 is supported. Lastly, as shown in model 10, the emotional bonds with supervisor have a positive impact on value commitment ($\beta = .254$, $p < .01$), while emotional bonds with co-workers are not positively correlated to value commitment ($\beta = -.041$), which indicates that Hypothesis 5 is supported.

Table 1. Means, standard deviation and inter-correlations among study variables (n = 1160).

	Mean	SD	1	2	3	4	5	6	7	8	9	10	11
1. Affective commitment	2.973	1.002											
2. Normative commitment	2.159	0.920	.528**										
3. Active continuance commitment	2.347	0.955	.615**	.516**									
4. Passive continuance commitment	2.340	0.998	.126**	.286**	.157**								
5. Value commitment	4.444	0.710	.469**	.268**	.364**	−.027							
6. Emotional bond with supervisor	2.740	1.378	.394**	.280**	.362**	.019	.266**						
7. Emotional bonds with co-workers	2.505	1.423	.071*	.082**	.072*	.165**	−.023	.078**					
8. Gender [a]	0.789	0.408	−.200**	−.171**	−.253**	−.149**	−.086**	−.142**	.007				
9. Age [b]	1.761	0.615	.036	.111**	.125**	.149**	.040	.081**	−.017	−.325**			
10. Tenure [c]	2.123	0.974	.080**	.157**	.128**	.176**	.077**	.090**	.023	−.256**	.466**		
11. Job role [d]	0.170	0.376	.045	.039	.143**	.087**	.028	.137**	−.035	−.182**	.254**	.216**	
12. Status [e]	0.136	0.343	.077**	.067*	.158**	.007	.122**	.163**	−.054	−.139**	.257**	.365**	.242**

Notes: *p. < .05; **p < .01; [a] male = 0, female = 1; [b] under 19 = 1, 20–29 = 2, 30–39 = 3, 40–49 = 4, 50–59 = 5, over 60 = 6; [c] under 1 yr = 1, 1–3 years = 2, 3–5 years = 3, 5–10 years = 4, 10–15 years = 5, over 10 years = 6; [d] manual workers = 0, non-manual works = 1; [e] non-managerial = 1, managerial = 1.

Table 2. Hierarchical multiple regression analyses (n = 1160).

	Affective commitment		Normative commitment		Active continuance commitment		Passive continuance commitment		Value commitment	
	Model 1	Model 2	Model 3	Model 4	Model 5	Model 6	Model 7	Model 8	Model 9	Model 10
Control variables										
Gender	−.202**	−.161**	−.138**	−.110**	−.221**	−.186**	−.096**	−.099**	−.073*	−.044
Age	.060	−.055	015	.019	−.001	.004	.061	.064	−.024	−.022
Tenure	.037	.034	.116**	.112**	.018	.014	.145**	.135**	.033	.035
Job role	.003	−.029	−.016	−.038	.074*	.048	.043	.049	−.013	−.037
Status	.050	.005	.005	−.024	.103**	.067*	−.086**	−.073*	.109**	.073*
Emotional bonds										
with supervisor		.372**		.257**		.313**		−.020		.254**
with co-workers		.041		.058*		.054*		.163**		−.041
F	10.922**	36.456**	10.416**	20.765**	21.485**	37.159**	12.723**	13.993**	4.886**	14.723**
Df	1159	1159	1159	1159	1159	1159	1159	1159	1159	1159
ΔR^2		.140		.069		.099		.026		.061
R^2	.041	.181	.043	.112	.085	.184	.052	.078	.021	.082

Notes: *p. < .05; **p < .01; the coefficients shown here are standardized regression coefficients.

Discussion

The research questions revisited

Three research questions have been addressed here. First, the meanings of the emotional bonds with supervisor and co-workers have been discussed in the Chinese context. Second, the relationships between emotional bonds with supervisor and co-workers and different dimensions of organizational commitment have been examined in accordance with the features of foreign-invested companies in China. The results indicate that emotional bonds with both supervisor and co-workers were related to normative commitment and active continuance commitment. Furthermore, emotional bonding with co-workers accounts for passive continuance commitment, while an emotional bond with a supervisor is associated with affective and value commitment. Lastly, based on the theoretical findings concerning the relationships between emotional bonds with supervisor and co-workers and different dimensions of organizational commitment, more practical implications might be discussed regarding the problem of high turnover rates in foreign-invested companies in China.

Implications

From the theoretical point of view, the present study extends the understanding of foreign-invested enterprises in China with an emotion-focused perspective, confirming that emotional bonds with a supervisor and co-workers contribute differently to sub-dimensions of organizational commitment. Practical and theoretical implications may be derived from the results of the present study. First, the findings of this research provide confirmative evidence that emotional bonds among various organizational members have different impacts on the way in which individuals create and visualize their relationships with the organization. The results promote an understanding of relational perspective in the Chinese context, in that, not only may a relationship with one's supervisor anchor the relationship with the organization hand-in-hand with one's willingness to contribute to it (Hui et al 2004), a relationship with one's co-workers may also anchor the relationship with the organization, along with one's willingness to stay with the organization. Emotional bonds with one's supervisor play an important role in motivating employees to work at their utmost, whereas emotional bonds with co-workers have more impact on maintaining a stable workforce. Employees' emotional bonds with organizational members take on paramount importance to Chinese employees, indicating that interpersonal relationships are an essential component of Chinese social structure (Hui et al. 2004).

Furthermore, the present study of emotional bonds with supervisor and among co-workers has contributed to the understanding of emotion in the organizational context. As critiqued by Callahan (2000), much research on organizational phenomena has focused on the rational side of functions, issues and components of organizational life, resulting in the removal of emotional elements from our understanding of organizational phenomena. The present research attempts to focus on positive emotion in the organizational context, linking the interpersonal emotional bonds with the psychological relationship with the organization as a whole. The results enable a deeper insight into the conceptual framework regarding the mechanism of how emotional aspects at an individual level function to link with the cognitional and attitudinal aspects at a meso level.

Owing to the rapid growth of internationalization of Chinese firms, IHRM in the Chinese context has been attracting more academic and practical interest in recent years (Shore, Eagle and Jedel 1993; Yan and Gray 1994; Leung, Smith, Wang and Sun 1996; Lu and Bjorkman 1997; Calantone and Zhao 2000; Child and Yan 2003; Shen and Edwards 2004).

Also, the research on organizational commitment has received considerable attention in the field of human resource management for several decades. A critical reason is that study in the field has been found to be related to individuals' behaviour, such as turnover and self-rated performance. With that in mind, there are some practical implications that could be associated with the results of the present research. The understanding of the emotional bonds with supervisor and co-workers revolve around the issue of hiring and managing relations in foreign-invested companies in China, identified as being a major challenge for foreign companies in China (HR Magazine 2006).

China has become one of the most attractive destinations for foreign direct investment in the world (Qiu 2005) through its open door policy inviting foreign investors to operate in the country through joint venture, licensing, counter-trade, wholly-owned operations, and cooperative development of resources (Davidson 1987). However, China has a severe shortage of local management talent, and this limits the speed with which an MNC can localize its management personnel for its China operations (Pucik 1984; Li and Tsui 2002). Foreign-invested companies in China suffered a high employee turnover rate of 14% in 2005 (*Kanan Monthly* 2006). Turnover rates among low-skilled workers are frequently in the range of 30 to 40% annually – and sometimes rise above 100% (Beamish 2006). In addition, the average tenure for 25- to 35-year-olds – the age group targeted most by multinational companies – fell from an average of three to five years in 2004 to just one to two years in 2005 (HR Magazine 2006). It has been argued that organizational commitment is closely related to organizational withdrawal behaviours. Normative commitment has been found to be the most important predictor of employees' job changing behaviours in the Chinese context (Yao and Wang 2006). The present study implies that the fostering of emotional bonds with other organizational members would be an effective method to improve normative commitment, thereby affecting employees' turnover intention. Since cultural and value differences may affect important attitudinal and behavioural variables of employees (Walumbwa and Lawler 2003; Lu and Lee 2005), it is especially important for foreign top-level managers dispatched from mother companies to understand the importance of emotional workplace bonds in China, and develop effective HRM practice in order to build on strong emotional bonds among the company members.

So far, affective commitment has been most intensively examined by researchers, identified as a powerful factor in affecting employees' attendance at work, in-role job performance and organizational citizenship behaviour. Emotional bonds with the supervisor are more important in affecting employee's affective commitment than those with co-workers, as can be seen from the present study. The contribution of the emotional bond with a supervisor helps to foster affective commitment, and therefore, it would be reasonable to assume that employees with high levels of emotional bonds with their supervisors will be less likely to leave the company and will have a heightened feeling of identification with the company.

Moreover, emotional bonds with supervisor and co-workers both help to increase active continuance commitment. The active continuance commitment encompasses the desire to work for the company associated with some HRM practice, such as OJB training and promotion. The results imply that people with a high level of emotional bonds with both supervisor and their co-workers are more likely to feel the desire to work for the company based upon their satisfaction with some HRM practice. Many foreign-invested companies have realized the importance of providing more training opportunities and an enhanced promotion plan that might suit the requirements of local employees. However, it can be inferred from the present study that in a society which emphasizes interpersonal relationships, particular focus should also be paid to the maintenance of a pleasant and healthy working atmosphere, aimed at facilitating emotional bonds among people in the workplace. The maintenance of a pleasant and healthy working atmosphere can help indirectly to increase the effect of HRM practice. Therefore, the emphasis is directed toward the effective combination of pleasant emotional bonds inside the company, which is also referred to as harmony and guanxi, and HRM practice of individual skill training and promotion policy.

Furthermore, emotional bonds among co-workers might help to increase passive continuance commitment, which might be associated greatly with employee's psychological well-being. The thought that staying with the company because there is a lack of other choices might work negatively – both psychologically and emotionally. However, emotional bonds with co-workers might help employees to feel less indifference to the organization and to be more actively involved in internal communication with other employees. Also, the association of value commitment and emotional bonds with a supervisor implies that the link between employees and their supervisor is critical in order to motivate employees to do their best for the company. More informal communication opportunities, such as an office party or office sports meeting, which might help to increase the communication between employees and their supervisor or co-workers, are also helpful in creating emotional bonds inside the company.

Limitations and future research

It should be noted that in the present study, assessments of the relationships between employees and their co-workers or supervisor are subject to the condition that they stay in the same company. The original personal relationships change when the supervisor or co-workers leave the original company. Therefore, the hypotheses only hold while the supervisor and co-workers remain with the same organization.

Furthermore, while this research has produced interesting results, it is important to remember that the research is completed against a cultural background which values interpersonal relationship highly. To what extent these results will generalize across organizations and the participant population is a question that remains to be explored. Also, the restriction of cross-sectional data prevents the inference of causality. A longitudinal design is required to infer causality that exists between emotional bonds and organizational commitment. In addition, the restriction of the current sample to foreign-invested companies limits the degree of generalization of the present findings. Research might be extended to different types of ownership, such as state-owned companies, and individual firms.

It is intriguing to examine the problem of emotional bonds in terms of their impact on behaviour consequences, such as organizational citizenship behaviour and in-role or extra-role performance. It is highly possible that the interaction between the emotional bonds with supervisors and peers will moderate the relationship between organizational commitment and important behavioural variables. Further research is needed into such aspects.

Conclusions

Throughout this study, the current understanding of the possible antecedents of differing dimensions of organizational commitment in terms of the emotional bonds with supervisor and co-workers is extended. Hypotheses are suggested in light of the emotion-focused aspects with significant others that are related with five sub-dimensions of organizational commitment, given that previous study has revealed that a five-component model fits the construct of organizational commitment of Chinese employees best (Wang 2004). After analysis with hierarchical multiple regression analysis, emotional bonds with supervisor and co-workers have been found to contribute differently to sub-dimensions of organizational commitment. The key findings are that emotional bonds with both supervisor and co-workers are related to normative commitment and active continuance commitment. Furthermore, emotional bonding with co-workers accounts for passive continuance commitment, while an emotional bond with a supervisor is associated with affective and value commitment. Consequently, all the original hypotheses are supported by the analysis. By focusing on the positive emotion in the organizational context, the present study links the interpersonal emotional bonds with the psychological relationship those individuals have with the organization as a whole.

It can be inferred from the results that management should recognize the importance of the emotional bonds with a supervisor and co-workers while contemplating the appropriate measures required to improve the level of organizational commitment. Practical implications for human resource management in Chinese foreign-invested enterprises are discussed. It is suggested that, although the emotional bonds with co-workers have been under-emphasized by management for a long period, the improvement of emotional bonds with both supervisor and co-workers would be an effective way to resolve the major challenge of the problem of high turnover rates of local employees for Chinese foreign-invested enterprises.

Alvi, S.A., and Ahmed, S.W. (1987), "Assessing Organizational Commitment in a Developing Country: Pakistan, a Case Study," *Human Relations*, 40, 267–280.
Bacharach, S.B., Bamberger, P.A., and Vashdi, D. (2005), "Diversity and Homophily at Work: Supportive Relations among White and African-American Peers," *Academy of Management Journal*, 48, 4, 619–644.
Beamish, P.W. (2006), "The High Cost of Cheap Chinese Labor," *Harvard Business Review*, 84, 6, 23.
Bramel, D., and Friend, R. (1987), "The Work Group and its Vicissitudes in Social and Industrial Psychology," *Journal of Applied Behavioural Science*, 23, 233–253.
Calantone, R.J., and Zhao, Y.S. (2000), "Joint Ventures in China: A Comparative Study of Japanese, Korean, and U.S. Partners," *Journal of International Marketing*, 9, 1, 1–23.
Callahan, J.L. (2000), "Emotion Management and Organizational Functions: A Case Study of Patterns in a Not-for-Profit Organization," *Human Resource Development Quarterly*, 11, 3, 245–267.
Chen, Z.X., Tsui, A.S., and Farh, J. (2002), "Loyalty to Supervisor vs. Organizational Commitment: Relationships to Employee Performance in China," *Journal of Occupational and Organizational Psychology*, 75, 339–356.
Cheng, B.S., Jiang, D.Y., and Riley, J.H. (2003), "Organizational Commitment, Supervisory Commitment, and Employee Outcomes in the Chinese Context: Proximal Hypothesis or Global Hypothesis?," *Journal of Organizational Behaviour*, 24, 313–334.
Child, J., and Yan, Y. (2003), "Predicting the Performance of International Joint Ventures: An Investigation in China," *Journal of Management Studies*, 40, 2, 283–320.
Davidson, W.H. (1987), "Creating and Managing Joint Ventures in China," *California Management Review*, 29, 4, 77–94.
Dvir, T., Kass, N., and Shamir, B. (2004), "The Emotional Bond: Vision and Organizational Commitment among High-tech Employees," *Journal of Organizational Change Management*, 17, 2, 126–143.
Farh, J.L., and Cheng, B.S. (2000), "A Cultural Analysis of Paternalistic Leadership in Chinese Organizations," in *Management and Organizations in the Chinese Context*, eds. J.T. Li, A.S. Tsui and E. Welson, London: MacMillan, pp. 84–130.
Finkelstein, M.A. (2006), "Dispositional Predictors of Organizational Citizenship Behaviour: Motives, Motive Fulfilment, and Role Identity," *Social Behaviour and Personality: An International Journal*, 34, 6, 603–616.
Fryxell, G.E., Dooley, R.S., and Li, W. (2004), "The Role of Trustworthiness in Maintaining Employee Commitment During Restructuring in China," *Asia Pacific Journal of Management*, 21, 515–533.
Hackett, R.D., Bycio, P., and Hausdorf, P.A. (1994), "Further Assessments of Meyer and Allen's (1991), Three-component Model of Organizational Commitment," *Journal of Applied Psychology*, 79, 1, 15–23.
HR Magazine (2006), "Companies in China Struggle to Keep Staff," 16th October.

Hui, C., Lee, C., and Rousseau, D.M. (2004), "Employment Relationships in China: Do Workers Relate to the Organization or to People," *Organization Science*, 15, 2, 232–240.

Kanan Monthly (2006), "The Reason for High Turnover Rates in Japanese-invested Enterprises in China,". (original in Japanese), 25th June, 39.

Kirmeyer, S.L., and Lin, T. (1987), "Social Support: Its Relationship to Observed Communication with Peers and Superiors," *Academy of Management Journal*, 30, 1, 138–151.

Law, K.S., Wong, C., Wang, D., and Wang, L. (2000), "Effect of Supervisor-subordinate Guanxi on Supervisory Decisions in China: An Empirical Investigation," *International Journal of Human Resource Management*, 11, 4, 751–765.

Leiter, M.P., and Maslach, C. (1988), "The Impact of Interpersonal Environment on Burnout and Organizational Commitment," *Journal of Organizational Behaviour*, 9, 297–308.

Leonard, J.S., and Levine, D.I. (2006), "The Effect of Diversity on Turnover: A Large Case Study," *Industrial and Labor Relations Review*, 59, 547–572.

Leung, K., Smith, P.B., Wang, Z., and Sun, H. (1996), "Job Satisfaction in Joint Ventures Hotels in China: An Organizational Justice Analysis," *Journal of International Business Studies*, 27, 5, 947–962.

Li, J., and Tsui, A.S. (2002), "A Citation Analysis of Management and Organization Research in the Chinese Context: 1984–1999," *Asia Pacific Journal of Management*, 19, 87–107.

Ling, W., Zhang, Z., and Fang, L. (2001), "A Study of the Organizational Commitment of Chinese Employees/ Zhong-guo zhi gong zu zhi cheng nuo yan jiu," *Social Sciences in China/ Zhongguo Shehui Kexue* (original in Chinese), 128, 2, 90–102.

Lu, L., and Lee, Y. (2005), "The Effect of Culture on the Management Style and Performance of International Joint Ventures in China: The Perspective of Foreign Parent Firms," *International Journal of Management*, 22, 3, 452–462.

Lu, Y., and Björkman, I. (1997), "HRM Practices in China-Western Joint Ventures: MNC Standardization versus Localization," *International Journal of Human Resource Management*, 8, 5, 614–628.

Meyer, J.P., and Allen, N.J. (1991), "A Three-component Conceptualization of Organizational Commitment," *Human Resource Management Review*, 1, 61–89.

Pucik, V. (1984), "The International Management of Human Resources," in *Strategic HRM*, eds. C.J. Fombrun, N.M. Tichy and M.A. Devana, New York: Wiley, pp. 403–419.

Qiu, Y. (2005), "Problems of Managing Joint Ventures in China's Interior: Evidence from Shaanxi," *Advanced Management Journal*, 70, 3, 46–57.

Reagans, R., and McEvily, B. (2003), "Network Structure and Knowledge Transfer: The Effects of Cohesion and Range," *Administrative Science Quarterly*, 48, 240–267.

Redding, S.G. (1990), *The Spirit of Chinese Capitalism*, New York: Walter de Gruyter.

Reilly, N.P., and Orsak, C.L. (1991), "A Career Stage Analysis of Career and Organizational Commitment in Nursing," *Journal of Vocational Behaviour*, 39, 311–330.

Rubin, R.S., Munz, D.C., and Bommer, W.H. (2005), "Leading from within: The Effects of Emotion Recognition and Personality on Transformational Leadership Behaviour," *Academy of Management Journal*, 48, 5, 845–858.

Shah, P.P., and Jehn, K.A. (1993), "Do Friends Perform Better than Acquaintances? The Interaction of Friendship, Conflict and Task," *Group Decision and Negotiation*, 2, 149–165.

Shen, J., and Edwards, V. (2004), "Recruitment and Selection in Chinese MNEs," *International Journal of Human Resource Management*, 15, 4/5, 814–835.

Shore, L.M., Eagle, B.W., and Jedel, M.J. (1993), "China–United States Joint Ventures: A Typological Model of a Goal Congruence and Cultural Understanding and their Importance for Effective Human Resource Management," *International Journal of Human Resource Management*, 4, 1, 67–83.

Snell, R.S., and Tseng, C.S. (2003), "Images of the Virtuous Employee in China's Transitional Economy," *Asia Pacific Journal of Management*, 20, 3, 307–332.

Tsui, A.S., Ashford, S.J., St. Clair, L., and Xin, K.R. (1995), "Dealing with Discrepant Expectations: Response Strategies and Managerial Effectiveness," *Academy of Management Journal*, 38, 1515–1543.

Walumbwa, F.O., and Lawler, J.J. (2003), "Building Effective Organizations: Transformational Leadership, Collectivist Orientation, Work-related Attitudes and Withdrawal Behaviours in Three Emerging Economies," *International Journal of Human Resource Management*, 14, 7, 1083–1101.

Wang, Y. (2004), "Observations on the Organizational Commitment of Chinese Employees: Comparative Studies of State-owned Enterprises and Foreign-invested Enterprises," *International Journal of Human Resource Management*, 15, 4/5, 649–669.

Wong, Y., Wong, C., and Ngo, H. (2002), "Loyalty to Supervisor and Trust in Supervisor of Workers in Chinese Joint Ventures: a Test of Two Competing Models," *International Journal of Human Resource Management*, 13, 6, 883–900.

Yan, A., and Gray, B. (1994), "Bargaining Power, Management Control and Performance in United States–China Joint Ventures: A Comparative Case Study," *Academy of Management Journal*, 37, 6, 1478–1517.

Yao, X., and Wang, L. (2006), "The Predictability of Normative Organizational Commitment for Turnover in Chinese Companies: A Cultural Perspective," *International Journal of Human Resource Management*, 17, 6, 1058–1075.

Zhou, J., and Martocchio, J.J. (2001), "Chinese and American Managers' Compensation Award Decisions: A Comparative Policy-capturing Study," *Personnel Psychology*, 54, 1, 115–145.

The effect of organizational psychological contract violation on managers' exit, voice, loyalty and neglect in the Chinese context

Steven X. Si, Feng Wei and Yi Li

China, the world's largest transitional economy, is faced with the problems posed by trying to bring into its historic and lingering culture of government control of the economy, culture, organization, a mindset necessary to function efficiently in the competitive world of market economics. In some respects, China has derived great benefits from its recent past: its diligent workers still accept comparatively low wages, and in many respects, strong government control has allowed for major efficiencies in infrastructure modernization projects. Thus, China has, over the last two decades, consistently maintained one of the highest rates of economic growth in the world, and its economy has now become one of the driving forces in the development of the global economy as a whole (Robert 2005). Chinese enterprises and Western firms both recognize that such growth, coupled with the fact that China holds 20% of the world's population, must surely make the country a prime target market; however, a number of human resource issues, such as the need to continually improve human resource quality and human resource management effectiveness, have now become increasingly important and problematic factors in sustaining the country's economic growth. In a market of such potential, failure simply cannot be allowed to become an option; therefore, business people, academicians, and all companies, Chinese and foreign, wishing to do business in China, must engage in thorough examinations of cultural and human dynamics to successfully conduct and manage business within the country.

To date, however, Western understanding of the intricacies of the workings of the Chinese market has not been strong. While the investigation of firms that have operated in mature American or Asian economies can provide some insights, this information is not necessarily uniformly applicable in transitional economies such as China's (Boyacigillar and Adler 1991; Si and Bruton 1999, 2003, 2005; Si and Hitt 2004). The weakness of our understanding may be a key factor related to the high levels of managerial and employee dissatisfaction currently found in China. Our pilot study of Chinese human resource management found that in recent years, while managers' salaries and benefits have been steadily increasing in China, the level of satisfaction of managers with their firms has not been growing commensurately; meanwhile, the level of satisfaction of Chinese firms with the achievements of their HRM in matters of attracting, training and retaining high-quality employees and managers indicates that there is much room for improvement (Sturges and Guest 2004).

Prior evaluations of such dissatisfaction in China have focused almost exclusively on financial criteria rather than on key human resource management issues in the Chinese context. On the one hand, such a focus is understandable: financial issues are intrinsically quantifiable and thus can be easily measured. On the other hand, even financial issues themselves must ultimately be evaluated in terms of not only rising expectations but also the dissatisfaction that may occur when current Chinese salaries are compared to those in developed capitalist economies: in other words, even in what would seem to be the most easily quantifiable aspects of job satisfaction, the process of evaluation must necessarily involve cultural and human issues that are far more difficult to define and gauge. Worldwide, scholarly investigations have already revealed that such issues are fundamental to employee satisfaction, not only in emerging economies but also in developed economies. It is therefore unreasonable to assume or to hope that such issues will be somehow less important in a rapidly modernizing third-world nation trying to adjust to the requirements of a demand economy when that nation's history of prior industrialization has occurred almost entirely within the context of half a century of command economy. Any attempt at dealing with the problem of current employee dissatisfaction in the Chinese economy, especially at the managerial level, in terms that will allow for rational solutions by HRM systems, simply cannot afford to overlook the human and cultural issues involved in increasing manager satisfaction.

While other problems arising from the possible clash of western and eastern cultural values may be deeper, the problems and tensions involved in shifting from a command to a demand economy are far more immediate. After all, Western firms partnering with Chinese firms can go a long way toward resolving clashes between eastern and western values by hiring, training and retaining good local Chinese managers, people whose deep knowledge of both traditions enable them to mediate between the two. Ensuring high levels of job satisfaction for Chinese managers can thus be seen as the key to enabling such firms to create the synergies necessary for achieving their own objectives: or, to repeat a familiar refrain, the current lack of knowledge about Chinese HRM practices may be a key factor causing performance problems for firms within the country.

It should be noted from the start of this investigation that there exists no readily available 'off-the-shelf' solution to the current problems of manager satisfaction in China. Chinese HRM styles and practices from the tradition of the command economy did not evolve in an environment of rapidly shifting economic models and goals with high labour and management mobility. Traditionally, Chinese firms were very much like extended families. People were hired for life, and, in the old command economy, Chinese managers were very much involved in promoting the outside interests of employees, often at company expense – for instance, managers would arrange wedding ceremonies, often using company trucks to take workers and guests to and from the celebrations. There was of course little possibility that such practices or orientations could survive for long after the beginnings of the shift toward a market-driven economy; but there remains the problem of dealing effectively with attitudes and expectations that were engendered by fifty years of the command economy's structures and attitudes, and their effects on current attitudes toward the workplace. The most readily identifiable icon and linchpin of the command economy era was the commitment to lifetime employment: when the Chinese state declared that mandatory lifetime employment policies had ended, the basic structures of Chinese business, and the attitudes of the Chinese people towards employment had to change, no matter how unwillingly, in fundamental ways.

Today in China, most companies increasingly need to manage their people in a loose business environment of high general turnover rates. Layoffs have become widespread and have brought with them unfamiliar pressures; the spectre of unemployment and sudden reductions in the quality of life have become the heaviest loads that many managers and employees have to bear, and for which there are no easy solutions. The problems resulting from the constant uncertainly of employment prospects include great reductions in employee job satisfaction, loyalty and work performance, as well as increases in hostile behaviour. Ironically, however, the readiness of companies to lay people off has triggered a strong enough tendency for employees to move on under their own steam that many companies are now suffering from undesirably high rates of voluntary turnover, generally symptomatic of low employee morale and loyalty. Additionally, the fast pace of modern lifestyles has made individuals' values change dramatically from traditional bedrock values. In modern China, the number of people accepting short and temporary contract relationships and opting to take their chances on free and random employment is increasing. There are of course some more or less traditional farmers who take temporary construction work in the coastal cities and then leave for the interior to help with the rice planting or harvest; but it is also true that a great number of educated and upwardly-mobile individuals have taken a liking to adopting a succession of varied life styles; such people, often possessing exactly the type of modern education so necessary to management, do not always want to set up a fixed, long-term contract relationship with any organization (or even with a spouse).

Companies operating in China are thus experiencing increasing pressures in matters pertaining to attracting, retaining and promoting valuable human resources; the creation of long-term employment relationships and an enduring organizational culture is no longer something that occurs spontaneously or can be taken for granted. In the literature, the psychological contract has become one of hottest issues for interpreting the above phenomenon in the past decade or so (e.g., Rousseau and McLean Parks 1993; Robinson, Kraatz and Rousseau 1994; Robinson and Morrison 1995; Robinson 1996; Turnley and Feldman 1998 1999, 2000; Chun Rousseau and Lee 2004; Dabos and Rousseau 2004; Raja, Johns and Ntalanis 2004). Such studies have tended to attack the problem from two perspectives. First, some studies have focused mainly on psychological contracts between organizations and general employees; since only a few of these studies have focused at all on the effects of psychological contracts on managers, they have not shed much light on this aspect of the problem. Second, other studies have taken psychological contract violations as integral parts of the overall analysis of psychological contract structure in behavioural terms; such studies have empirically examined managers' exit, voice, loyalty and neglect (EVLN) to explore specific effects of organizational contract violations in the Chinese context.

Theoretical background and hypotheses

The organization–manager psychological contract

Modern organizations cannot succeed unless the people they employ agree to contribute to their mission and survival. In the realities of the business world, workers and employers need to agree on the contributions that workers are expected to make to the firm, and vice versa. Understanding and effectively managing psychological contracts can help firms thrive (Rousseau 2004).

In the literature, the classical perspective focused on the original psychological contract as the subjective perception by both the employee and the organization of their mutual obligations to each other. Later on, a number of scholars described the psychological contract as a kind of unwritten contract with implicit obligations and expectations between workers and employers, or described the psychological contract as an employee's subjective perception of obligations in his or her relationships with the employing organization (e.g., Argyris 1960; Levinson et al. 1962; Schein 1965; Kotter 1973; Rusbult, Farrell, Rogers and Mainouss 1988; Farrell 1983; Rousseau and McLean Parks 1993; Rousseau and Tijoriwala 1996, 1998; Taylor, Knox, Napier and Mayrhofer 2002; Rousseau and Shperling 2003; Rousseau 2004; Ho 2005).

More recently, scholars have reported that the psychological contract between an employee and an organization exists in a two-dimensional structure. These are: (1) the transactional contracts and the relational contract (Rousseau and McLean Parks 1993; Robinson, Kraatz and Rousseau 1994; Tsui, Pearce, Porter and Tripoli 1997; Millward and Hopkins 1998); and (2) implicit and explicit contracts (Kickul and Lester 2001, 2004). Simultaneously, some researchers have argued that the psychological contract between an employee and an organization has a three-dimensional structure: (1) the transactional dimension; (2) the relational dimension; and (3) the team-player dimension (Rousseau and Tijoriwala 1996). There are, however, obvious and distinct differences between managers and general employees: as a manager is obviously in a more powerful position than a general employee, a manager must take on higher responsibilities, obligations, expectations and requirements. Hence, the current study argues that besides the general organization–employee psychological contract, there also exists a separate psychological contract between an organization and its managers. The organization–manager psychological contracts should motivate a manager to fulfil commitments made to a firm, but can only do so when a manager is confident that the firm will reciprocate and fulfil its end of the bargain. In the current reality of Chinese business, mutual organizational and managerial commitments are a highly topical issue, as no clear understanding of what the commitments are or how they can be fulfilled exist. While in many cases managers believe that they work hard to fulfil the commitments they have made to their firms, and vice versa, there are still many cases in which either the managers or the firms or both feel short-changed. In the current study, we attempt to explore this issue and the relevant relationships in the Chinese business environment. We hypothesize that:

Hypothesis 1:   In China, the organization–manager psychological contract consists of a three-dimension structure including a transactional psychological contract, a relational psychological contract and a managerial psychological contract.

Hypothesis 1a: In China, an organization's psychological contract with a manager consists of a three-dimension structure including a transactional psychological contract, a relational psychological contract and a managerial psychological contract.

Hypothesis 1b: In China, a manager's psychological contract with an organization
consists of a three-dimension structure including a transactional
psychological contract, a relational psychological contract and a
managerial psychological contract.

The organization–manager psychological contract and EVLN model

In an organization's psychological contract with a manager or the manager's
psychological contract with the organization, either side can have a major effect on the
benefits derived from their mutual relationship. Additionally, either side can also affect
the ability of an organization to attract and retain high quality managers. In 1983 Farrel
proposed a model describing managers' EVLN. For purposes of simplification, this study
will refer to this as the EVLN model. In this model, voice and loyalty are considered as
constructive in organizational development, as managers use both to try to establish and
maintain satisfactory employment relationships. On the other hand, exit and neglect are
considered destructive behavioural responses, as managers generally use them only after
they have decided that their relationships with their companies are not worth maintaining.

In many cases, the psychological contract can be understood as passive organizational
behaviours which can have positive or negative effects on the managerial behaviours. In this
study, we argue that the substitution of a psychological contract for the old trust relationship
can lead to reductions of managers' voice and loyalty, and at the same time lead to increases
in exits and neglect. According to traditional Chinese culture, a firm, which was generally
family run, had such strong trust among its members that it seldom needed a contract to
control them. Even today, many Chinese firms prefer to base their internal relationships on
trust and a feeling of mutual dependency among their managers; the belief is that such a
style will reduce managers' uncertainty and maintain a healthy exchange relationship
between firms and managers to achieve desired goals for both the firms and their managers
(Si, Ahlstrom and Huo 2001). The idea of the psychological contract has come as an entirely
new concept learned from Western human resource management; it was perceived from the
start as foreign, and interacted in largely negative ways with the mutual trust-based
relationships native to Chinese culture. To be sure, such trust-based relationships largely
excluded outsiders, and made Chinese business resemble cliques – modern business, with
its needs to hire specialists from other regions, and to conduct business with strangers,
seems to demand the use of contracts, both written and implicit.

Prior research on the relationship between the psychological contract and
employees' behavioural responses revealed similar findings. For instance, scholars
(e.g., Robinson and Rousseau 1994; Robinson and Morrison 1995; Robinson 1996)
reported that an employee's perception of the psychological contract is positively
related to passive employee behaviours; the resultant high turnover rate can lead to a
low work performance and low organizational citizenship behaviour. Guzzo, Noonan
and Elron (1994) indicated that the advent of the psychological contract was positively
related to low job satisfaction and high turnover rates. Turnley and Feldman (1998)
found that the psychological contract led to low job satisfaction, low organizational
commitment, low on-the-job performance and organizational citizenship behaviours and
high turnover rates. Turnley and Feldman (1999) further investigated and found that the
psychological contract is positively related to employees' exit and neglect and
negatively related to employees' voice and loyalty. The current study assumes these
findings can also be applied to examine managers' EVLN based on the following
reasons. (1) Researchers (e.g., Si 1990) reported that the concept of employees in China

could be split to include two different classes, managers and workers, and that the differences between the two classes were so great that studies might have to be carried out on the two groups separately. (2) Managers and workers do, however, both share the same underlying culture and so their behaviours are largely affected by the same political system. (3) Managers and workers have both had similar poor experiences in the past, and so they all must currently prioritize their economic goals with a view towards obtaining the best outcome in the future. Based on the above reasons, we hypothesize that:

Hypothesis 2:   In China, an organization's psychological contract will be positively related to an increase of managers' exits.

Hypothesis 3:   In China, an organization's psychological contract will be positively related to a reduction of managers' voice.

Hypothesis 4:   In China, an organization's psychological contract will be positively related to an increase of managers' neglect.

Hypothesis 5:   In China, an organization's psychological contract will be positively related to a reduction of managers' loyalty.

Method

Subjects

The sample consisted of 626 entry and middle-level managers from various companies located in five Chinese cities (Shanghai, Suzhou, Chongqing, Yinchuan and Putian) with approximately equivalent demographics. MBA students were given instructions by their professors in the classroom on how to gather data. These MBA students issued and collected the surveys from the managers throughout their companies, as well as from HR managers. All the surveys were accompanied by uniform instructions and evaluated according to strict testing procedures.

Managers responded to the questionnaires at their companies' locations in China. All participants were promised anonymity and no specific sensitive information was requested. Many of our selected questionnaire items were selected from earlier questionnaires designed by Western scholars; these were then translated into the native languages of the respondents at the bilingual faculty at Pennsylvania State University. Back translations and successive revisions were conducted by native language speakers of the two different language versions of the questionnaires.

Usable questionnaires were returned by 524 managers for a response rate of 87%; no major differences were found in response rates across cities.

Variables

The organization–manager psychological contract

The organization–manager psychological contract included the organization's perceived obligations and managers' perceived obligations. Although the larger study included a variety of measures, we examined a single popular management questionnaire instrument for this study. Specifically, the measure comprised 24 items addressing the typical dimensions of the employment relationship studied in previous research (e.g., Robinson et al. 1994; Rousseau and Tijoriwala 1998; Turnley and Feldman 2000; Guest and Conway 2002). Both the organization's perceived obligations and the managers' perceived obligations were examined by a multi-item measure developed for this study.

The organization's perceived obligations were examined through a category including 12 items ($\alpha = .81$): promotion, pay raises, salary, training, reasonable requirement, job security, comfortable context, career development, communication, delegation, trust and feedback on job performance. In this study, managers were asked to rate each of these items based on the extent to which they believed their organizations were committed to provide them on a five-point scale (1 = not at all and 5 = very highly). The managers' perceived obligations were also examined through a category with the following items ($\alpha = .88$): obeying rules, maintaining the organization's image in a positive manner, willingness to accept a transfer, loyalty, commitment to organizational culture, long-term service, volunteering to do non-required tasks on the job, promoting subordinates, helping subordinates make progress, providing subordinates with career development, evaluation, dealing with complaints. The managers were also asked to rate each of these items based on the extent to which they felt committed to fulfilling their obligations to the organizations on a five-point scale (1 = not at all and 5 = very highly).

Psychological contract violations

Managers' perceptions of psychological contract violations were measured with the same items used in measuring the overall psychological contract. Respondents were asked to rate how well the organization had achieved each aspect of its obligations based on a five-point scale (1 = very well achieved to 5 = very poorly achieved). All variables were measured by a five-point Likert scale (1 = definitely would not react in this way to 5 = definitely would react in this way). Exit was measured with four items ($\alpha = .84$) similar to those used in Rusbult et al. (1988). A sample exit item is: 'I would think about quitting my job.' Voice was measured with four-items ($\alpha = .70$) adapted from Rusbult et al. (1988). A sample voice item is: 'I would talk to my supervisor to try to change working conditions or policies that were negatively affecting me.' Loyalty was measured with four items ($\alpha = .77$) accepted from Rusbult et al. (1988). A sample loyalty item is: 'I would hang in there and wait for the problem to go away.' Neglect was measured with four items ($\alpha = .81$) from Rusbult et al. (1988). A sample neglect item is: 'I would put less effort into my job.'

Measure model (Lisrel analysis)

The hypotheses were tested by structural equation modelling (SEM) with a Lisrel 8.2 version. Resulting from an evolution of multi-equation modelling developed principally in econometrics and merged with the principles of measurement from psychology and sociology, SEM has emerged as an integral tool in both managerial and academic research. SEM can also be used as a means of estimating other multivariate models (e.g., regression). In general, SEM techniques are distinguished by two characteristics: (1) estimation of multiple and interrelated dependence relationships, and (2) the ability to represent unobserved concepts in these relationships and account for measurement error in the estimation process. In this study, we followed the two-step procedure suggested by Hair, Anderson, Tatham and Black (1998) to test the hypothesized relationships. First, we analyzed the factor structure of the scales in two parts: (1) we examined the factor structure of organization–manager psychological contract and psychological contract violation to examine the discriminate validity of the two constructs; and (2) we examined the factor structure of all the variables in the study, seeking a basis for the structural relationship among the variables. After confirming the factor structures, we formed composite variables for each construct from their respective items and used those composites as single indicators of their respective factors.

Results

The structural equation modelling analyses of the respondents surveyed are reported in Tables 1–3. The means, standard deviations and correlations for the study variables are presented in Table 1. All the correlations were in the expected directions, indicating preliminary support for the hypothesized relationships. The structural equation modelling analysis of 24 items representing organization–manager psychological contract, 12 of which measured perception of the organization's obligations and psychological contract violation and the other 12 of which measured perception of managers' obligations, showed that the three-dimension model provided the best fit for the data.

The fit statistics for a model of an organization's obligations were as follows: chi-square (χ^2), 101.75 with 51 degrees of freedom; comparative fit index (CFI), 0.93; root-mean-square error of approximation (RMSEA), 0.062. All the factor loadings were also significant ($p < .05$). In order to provide a stringent test of our hypotheses, we examined three alternative models (a one-factor model, a two-factor model and a four-factor model) by comparing them with our hypothesized three-dimension model, the results of which are presented in Table 2.

As shown in Table 3 the fit statistics for perceived managers' obligations model were as follows: chi-square (χ^2), 82.30 with 51 degrees of freedom; comparative fit index (CFI), 0.97; root-mean-square error of approximation (RMSEA), 0.049. All the factor loadings were also significant ($p < .05$). We examined three alternative models (a one-factor model, a two-factor model and a four-factor model) by comparing them with our hypothesized three-dimension model, the results of which are presented in Table 3.

Table 1. Means, standard deviations and correlations.

Variable	mean	s.d.	1	2	3	4	5	6
Exit	1.85	1.27						
Voice	3.34	1.23	−.213***					
Loyalty	3.27	1.20	−.592***	.412***				
Neglect	1.62	1.01	.506***	−.324***	−.468***			
Managerial psychological contract violation	3.31	1.24	.325***	−.260***	.163***	−.341***		
Relational psychological contract violation	2.42	1.08	−.056	.058	−.112*	.067	.000	
Transactional psychological contract violation	2.57	0.94	.100*	−.103*	−.027	−.080	.000	.000

*p < .05, **p < .01, ***p < .001.

Table 2. Results of organization's obligations model comparisons.

	χ^2	df	χ^2/df	P	GFI	AGFI	CFI	RMSEA
One-factor model	269.98	54	5.00	0.00	0.85	0.78	0.76	0.13
Two-factor model	141.12	53	2.66	0.00	0.92	0.88	0.89	0.081
Three-factor model	101.75	51	2	0.00	0.94	0.90	0.93	0.062
Four-factor model	116.00	48	2.42	0.00	0.93	0.89	0.91	0.075

Table 3.   Results of managers' obligations model comparisons.

	X^2	df	χ^2/df	P	GFI	AGFI	CFI	RMSEA
One-factor model	459.93	54	8.51	0.00	0.77	0.67	0.76	0.17
Two-factor model	213.76	53	4.02	0.00	0.88	0.82	0.90	0.11
Three-factor model	82.30	51	1.61	0.004	0.95	0.92	0.97	0.049
Four-factor model	95.40	48	1.99	0.00	0.94	0.90	0.96	0.062

The results in Table 2 and Table 3 show that the three-dimension model provided the best fit; thereby reinforcing our hypotheses that the three-factor model of an organization's perceived obligations was the best fitting model.

The current study examined the fit of the hypothesized model (Figure 1). The results indicated: $\chi^2 = 487.30$, df $= 6$, CFI $= 0.30$, RMSEA $= 0.40$, which showed that the hypothesized model needed to be revised. Thus, with the suggestions for revision of the model, changes that would permit a one-to-one correlation between the independent and the dependent, and at the same time eliminate the paths without significant effects (including the paths from relational psychological contract violation to exit, voice and loyalty, and from transactional psychological contract violation to neglect), we revised the model. The statistics of the revised model were as follows: $\chi2 = 9.86$, df $= 5$, CFI $= 0.99$, RMSEA $= 0.044$, which showed that the revised model fitted the data very well and could be accepted. We used this model to test the hypothesized relationships (see Figure 2).

As shown in Figure 2, both managerial psychological contract violation and transactional psychological contract violation were positively related to exit and negatively related to voice; managerial psychological contract violation was negatively related to loyalty; managerial psychological contract violation was positively related to neglect; and relational psychological contract violation was negatively related to neglect. The results partially supported Hypothesis 2, 3, 4, and 5.

This study's results provide valuable information to clarify the relationships among the organization–manager contract, the organization–manager psychological contract,

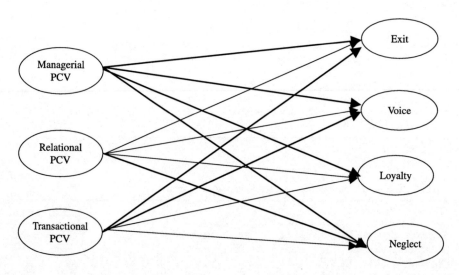

Figure 1.   Hypothesized model.

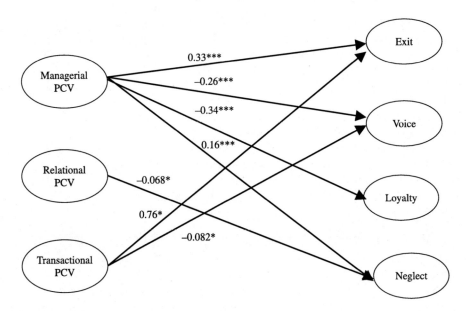

Figure 2.   Results from structural equation modelling.
*p < .05;**p < .01;***p < .001.

and organization–manager psychological contract violations; the results also provide valuable information and measurement means for interpreting managers' EVLN behaviour. The validity and reliability of the measurement model for the organization–manager psychological contract were tested and supported: all three dimensions demonstrated acceptable means, standard deviations, and internal consistency reliabilities. In addition, confirmatory factor analyses provided support for the existence of an underlying three-dimension structure in the basic organization psychological contract (a structure including a transactional psychological contract, a relational psychological contract and a managerial psychological contract). The current study also revealed partial support for our hypotheses that organization–manager psychological contract violation has significant influence on managers' EVLN behaviour in the Chinese context.

Discussion and implications

This study attempted to extend Turnley and Feldman (1999)'s findings from general employees to managers. In addition, it examined the organization–manager psychological contract violation's possible positive effects on exit and neglect as well as its possible negative effects on manager voice and loyalty in the Chinese context.

The hypothesized effects of organizations' transactional psychological contract violation on managers in China lead to some valuable discussions: while the transactional psychological contract is an organization's basic promises to managers involving managers' fundamental demands, the fulfilment of the contract will not necessarily result in loyalty, though the violation of the contract may lead to disappointment and a resultant willingness to leave if the use of voice does not work. In general, Chinese managers will not react to contract violations in passive ways because they have a great sense of self-discipline and high expectations for their future development. That most Chinese managers would tend to use positive ways of expressing their dissatisfactions is at least in part attributable to the ancient traditional Chinese culture (Rowley, Benson and Warner 2004). Most Chinese have a higher level of collectivism than do their counterparts in the West, whose cultures have higher levels of individualism (Earley 1989; Si and Cullen 1998; Parnell 2005). In general, people in a more collectivistic culture are much more likely try to maintain smooth interpersonal relations, evaluate individual behaviour based on the group norm, and use positive ways to express their dissatisfactions (Hofstede 1980; Mente and Boyd 1989; Ralston, Gustafson, Cheung and Terpstra 1993).

This study also found that an organization's relational psychological contract violation had no significant influences on the managers' behaviours except neglect in China. It might be because the managers are not very sensitive to the fulfilment or violation of employment relationship. In the business reality, they care more about self-realization (managerial psychological contract) and their interest (transactional psychological contract). This result may be a reflection of the current psychology and value system of managers in the Chinese context.

In addition, this investigation found that transactional psychological contract violations will lead to reductions in managers' neglect. This finding is strikingly different from finding from previous research focusing on general employees, and strongly suggests that managers may have a different psychology from that of general employees, a psychology that leads managers to exhibit very different responses. Specifically, when a manager's social relationship is unbalanced, that manager is most likely to try to improve the relationship actively by working harder (reduction of neglect) and is most unlikely to use destructive approaches (e.g., neglect) to obtain psychological balance. This finding is not consistent with our hypotheses and future study will have to explore the logic behind such behaviour.

This study developed measurements of the organization–manager psychological contract with three dimensions that could be utilized effectively for further study of the organization–manager psychological contract in the Chinese context. Second, the study provided empirical findings to yield explanations of the relationships between organization–manager psychological contract violations and managers' EVLN behaviours in the Chinese context. These findings should be useful for both managers and scholars to understand better the above relationships in the largest transitional economy in the world.

There are some limitations with this piece of research. First, we collected raw data from managers but did not try to get comparative samples for this study that could conceivably have revealed possible common method biases. Second, there generally exists a time lag between a manager's perceptions of psychological contract violations and resultant changes in that manager's behaviour; since the two events do not always occur simultaneously, a longitudinal study needs to be conducted in the future. In addition, other factors mediating and moderating the above relationships also need to be tested in the future for better explanations of managers' behaviour in response to perceived psychological contract violations.

Conclusion

This study examined, in the Chinese context, the organization–manager psychological contract violation's possible positive effects on exit and neglect as well as its possible negative effects on manager voice and loyalty.

Our findings provide valuable information to clarify the relationships among organization–manager, organization–manager psychological contract and organization–manager psychological contract violation and also provide valuable information and methods of measuring to aid in interpreting managers' EVLN behaviour. This study finds that Chinese managers tend to place their heaviest emphasis on the managerial psychological contract and the transactional psychological contract. This study also finds that organizational psychological contract violations of either or both the managerial psychological contract and the transactional psychological contract will increase managers' tendencies towards destructive behaviour and decrease managers' tendencies toward constructive behaviour.

This study contributes to the literature by drawing attention to the effect of organizations' transactional psychological contract violation on managers in the Chinese context. The findings also provided valuable information for a number of foreign companies that seek effective human resource management in China and other emerging economies in the world.

Acknowledgements

The authors would like to thank all of the people who provided data for this research project. The assistance of John Cullen, Gary Johns, Michael Poole and Malcolm Warner on an earlier draft is also greatly appreciated.

References

Argyris, C.P. (1960), *Understanding Organizational Behaviour*, Homewood, IL: Dorsey Press.

Boyacigillar, N.A., and Adler, N.J. (1991), "The Parochial Dinosaur: Organizational Science in a Global Context," *Academy of Management Review*, 16, 2, 262–290.

Dabos, G.E., and Rousseau, D.M. (2004), "Mutuality, and Reciprocity in the Psychological Contracts of Employees, and Employers," *Journal of Applied Psychology*, 89, 1, 52–72.

De Mente, B.L. (1989), *Chinese Etiquette and Ethics in Business*, Lincolnwood, IL: NTC Publishing Group.

Earley, P.C. (1989), "Social Loafing and Collectivism: A Comparison of the United States, and the People's Republic of China," *Administrative Science Quarterly*, 34, 565–581.

Farrell, D. (1983), "Exit, Voice, Loyalty, and Neglect as Responses to Job Dissatisfaction: A Multidimensional Scaling Study," *Academy of Management Journal*, 26, 596–607.

Guest, E.D., and Conway, N. (2002), "Communicating the Psychological Contract: An Employer Perspective," *Human Resource Management Journal*, 12, 2, 22–38.

Guzzo, R.A., Noonan, K.A., and Elron, E. (1994), "Expatriate Managers and the Psychological Contract," *Journal of Applied Psychology*, 79, 617–626.

Hair, J., Anderson, R., Tatham, R., and Black, W. (1998), *Multivariate Data Analysis*, Englewood Cliffs, NJ: Prentice Hall.

Ho, V.T. (2005), "Social Influence on Evaluation of Psychological Contract Fulfilment," *Academy of Management Review*, 30, 1, 113.

Hofstede, G. (1980), *Culture's Consequences: International Differences in Work Related Values*, Beverly Hills, CA: Sage Publications.

Hui, C., Rousseau, D.M., and Lee, C. (2004), "Psychological Contract and Organizational Citizenship Behaviour in China: Investigating Generalizability and Instrumentality," *Journal of Applied Psychology*, 89, 2, 311–321.

Kickul, J., and Lester, S.W. (2001), "Broken Promises: Equity Sensitivity as a Moderator between Psychological Contract Breach and Employee Attitudes and Behaviour," *Journal of Business and Psychology*, 16, 191–217.

Kickul, J., Lester, S.W., and Belgio, E. (2004), "Attitudinal and Behavioural Outcomes of Psychological Contract Breach: A Cross Culture Comparison of the United States and Hong Kong Chinese," *International Journal of Cross-cultural Management*, 4, 2, 229–252.

Kotter, J.P. (1973), "The Psychological Contract," *California Management Review*, 15, 91–99.

Levinson, H., Price, C.R., Munden, K.J., Mandl, H.J., and Solley, C.M. (1962), *Men, Management, and Mental Health*, Cambridge, MA: Harvard University Press.

Millward, L.J., and Hopkins, L.J. (1998), "Psychological Contracts, Organizational and Job Commitment," *Journal of Applied Social Psychology*, 28, 16, 1530–1556.

Parnell, M.F. (2005), "Chinese Business Guanxi: An Organization or Non-organization?" *Journal of Organizational Transformation and Social Change*, 2, 1, 29–45.

Raja, U., Johns, G., and Ntalanis, F. (2004), "The Impact of Personality on Psychological Contract," *Academy of Management Journal*, 47, 3, 350–367.

Ralston, D.A., Gustafson, D.J., Cheung, F.M., and Terpstra, R.H. (1993), "Differences in Managerial Values: A Study of U.S., Hong Kong, and PRC Managers," *Journal of International Business Studies*, 24, 2, 249–276.

Robert, T. (2005), "China's Human Resource Management Strategies: The Role of Enterprise and Government," *Asian Business & Management*, 4, 5–21.

Robinson, S.L. (1996), "Trust and Breach of the Psychological Contract," *Administrative Science Quarterly*, 41, 574–599.

Robinson, S.L., Kraatz, M.S., and Rousseau, D.M. (1994), "Changing Obligations and the Psychological Contract: A Longitudinal Study," *Academy of Management Journal*, 37, 137–152.

Robinson, S.L., and Morrison, E.W. (1995), "Organizational Citizenship Behaviour: A Psychological Contract Perspective," *Journal of Organizational Behaviour*, 16, 289–298.

Robinson, S.L., and Rousseau, D.M. (1994), "Violating the Psychological Contract: Not the Exception but the Norm," *Journal of Organizational Behaviour*, 15, 245–259.

Rousseau, D.M. (2004), "Research Edge: Psychological Contracts in the Workplace: Understanding the Ties that Motivate," *The Academy of Management Executive*, 18, 1, 120–127.

Rousseau, D.M., and McLean Parks, J.M. (1993), "The Contracts of Individuals and Organizations," *Research in Organizational Behaviour*, 15, 1–43.

Rousseau, D.M., and Shperling, Z. (2003), "Pieces of the Action: Ownership and the Changing Employment Relationship," *Academy of Management Review*, 28, 4, 553–570.

Rousseau, D.M., and Tijoriwala, S.A. (1996), "Perceived Legitimacy and Unilateral Contract Change: It Takes a Good Reason to Change a Psychological Contract," symposium at the SIOP meetings, San Diego, CA.

Rousseau, D.M., and Tijoriwala, S.A. (1998), "Examining Psychological Contracts: Issues, Alternatives, and Measures," *Journal of Organizational Behaviour*, 19, 679–695.

Rowley, C., Benson, J., and Warner, M. (2004), "Towards an Asian Model of Human Resource Management? A Comparative Analysis of China, Japan, and South Korea," *The International Journal of Human Resource Management*, 15, 4, 917–933.

Rusbult, C.E., Farrell, D., Rogers, G., and Mainouss, A.G. (1988), "Impact of Exchange Variables on Exit, Voice, Loyalty, and Neglect: An Integrative Model of Responses to Declining Job Satisfaction," *Academy of Management Journal*, 31, 599–627.

Schein, E.H. (1965), *Organizational Psychology*, Englewood Cliffs, NJ: Prentice Hall.

Si, S. (1990), *People's Relations in the Chinese Enterprises*, Shanghai: Shanghai Press of Science and Technology Literatures.

Si, S., Ahlstrom, D., and Huo, P. (2001), "A Study of Organizational Learning in Sino–American International Joint Ventures," *International Journal of Business, Economics, and Social Policy (Global Focus)*, 13, 2.

Si, S., and Bruton, B. (1999), "Knowledge Transfer in International Joint Ventures in Transitional Economies: The China Experience," *Academy of Management Executive*, 13, 1, 83–90.

Si, S., and Bruton, B. (2003), "Beyond National Boundaries: International Joint Ventures and Considering the View from Both Sides of the Table," *Organizational Dynamics*, 32, 4, 384–395.

Si, S., and Cullen, J. (1998), "Rating Scales and Cultural Bias: A Test of Neutral Response Tendency between Two International Samples," *International Journal of Organization Analysis*, 6, 3, 218–230.

Si, S., and Hitt, M. (2004), "A Study of Organizational Image Resulting from International Joint Ventures in Transitional Economies," *Journal of Business Research*, 57, 1370–1377.

Sturges, J., and Guest, D. (2004), "Working to Live or Living to Work? Work/life Balance Early in the Career," *Human Resource Management Journal*, 14, 4, 5–20.

Taylor, S., Knox, N., Napier, N., and Mayrhofer, W. (2002), "Women in Global Business: Introduction," *International Journal of Human Resource Management*, 13, 5, 739–742.

Tsui, A.S., Pearce, J.L., Porter, L.W., and Tripoli, A.M. (1997), "Alternative Approaches to the Employee–organization Relationship: Does Investment in Employees Pay Off?," *Academy of Management Journal*, 40, 1089–1121.

Turnley, W.H., and Feldman, D.C. (1998), "Psychological Contract Violations during Organizational Restructuring," *Human Resource Management*, 37, 71–83.

Turnley, W.H., and Feldman, D.C. (1999), "The Impact of Psychological Contract Violations on Exit, Voice, Loyalty, and Neglect," *Human Relations*, 52, 895–922.

Turnley, W.H., and Feldman, D.C. (2000), "Re-examining the Effects of Psychological contract Violations: Unmet Expectations and Job Dissatisfaction as Mediators," *Journal of Organizational Behaviour*, 21, 25–42.

Modelling regional HRM strategies in China: An entrepreneurship perspective

Zhong-Ming Wang and Sheng Wang

Introduction

The rapid economic growth since economic reforms were launched and the 'open door' policy initiated in 1978 in China has increasingly attracted the attention of academic researchers (e.g., Luo 1995; Child 1999; Warner 1999; Law, Tse and Zhou 2003; Atuahene-Gima and Li 2004; Zhou, Wu and Luo 2007). With the entry of China into the WTO and the implementation of various regional development policies and entrepreneurship, it is timely to understand how firms in China may enhance performance and gain competitive advantage across domestic regions and in this more globalized and increasingly competitive market. Among recent developments in China, entrepreneurship, as one of the major approaches to business development, has been emphasized and in the meantime, human resource management (HRM) practices are particularly important in supporting such an approach (Wang and Zang 2005). Indeed, human resources have been identified as a critical source of sustainable competitive advantage (Wright, McMahan and McWilliams 1994; Wright and Barney 1998). Despite much research on entrepreneurship in Western countries (e.g., Zahra, Jenning and Kuratko 1999; Daily, McDougall, Covin and Dalton 2002; Covin, Green and Slevin 2006), research in China, the largest emerging economy, has been active but still lagging behind (Liu, Luo and Shi 2003; Luo, Zhou and Liu 2005). More and more studies focus on regional policies and HRM practices (Wang and Zang 2005). In coping with the challenges of the economic reform and rapid organizational changes, HRM research in China has shifted its focus from more functional HRM practices to more integrated HRM development and strategic HRM practices (Wang 2006). It is important, given recent HRM studies conducted under the context of organizational reform and innovation, that we introduce a *strategic entrepreneurship* perspective and more *regional* considerations into studies in this field.

Moreover, because of the different pace of economic reform, various regions in China offer different external environments in which firms operate (Liu, Luo and Shi 1999). Although there has been some research that shows the regional differences in the adoption of HRM practices (e.g., Ding, Goodall and Warner 2000), the question still remains as to how the relationship between HRM practices and organizational performance is contingent upon regional policies and how strategic entrepreneurship might affect this relationship.

In this study, to address the questions and issues raised, we identify two important HRM practices in the Chinese context, career development and performance management, and the dimensions of strategic entrepreneurship in China, and then examine their influences on organizational performance. Additionally, we investigate the moderating role of regional differences on the relationships between the two HRM practices and organizational performance.

In the following sections, we first review literature related to HRM practices, strategic entrepreneurship and regional differences to develop our hypotheses. Then we present the empirical analysis of our research. Finally, we discuss the results and conclude with the implications of our findings, study limitations and potential for future research.

Literature review

In the past 15 years, more and more firms have been conducting business across regions in China and are preparing themselves for going global. One of the key strategies has been adopting effective HRM practices. This includes two aspects: (1) building up regional models of effective HRM approaches along with organizational characteristics; (2) understanding challenges in HRM practices in working with regional development and entrepreneurship strategies. In the area of entrepreneurship, cross-regional mergers, acquisitions, joint ventures and business alliances were among the popular business strategies for developing larger and stronger firms (Siu and Liu 2005). However, in many Chinese cases of mergers, HRM has been a bottleneck (Wang and Mobley 1999). Therefore, more specific HRM strategies were urgently needed for supporting organizational change, technological innovation and entrepreneurial development (Wang 2006). Among most Chinese firms, there was a lack of strategy-level integration of HRM practices with entrepreneurship, and different HRM approaches were often less effective in terms of sustainability (Wang and Mobley 1999).

How do strategic entrepreneurship and HRM practices affect aspects of organizational performance? Johnson and Van de Ven (2002) used the resource-based perspective to develop the framework for entrepreneurial strategy. More recently, Borch and Madsen (2005) studied innovative SMEs and found a relationship between adaptive capability and entrepreneurship strategies. White (2000) demonstrated significant effects of external environment and internal capacities on technology decisions among Chinese state-owned enterprises. The theoretical development has provided basic constructs and thinking for developing a new framework for this study. Some key issues are addressed in relation to previous research on HRM modelling across regions. First, previous studies mentioned regional differences in economic conditions (e.g., Liu et al. 1999; Ding et al. 2000; Ding et al. 2006) but neglected the regional analysis of HRM practices in relation to firm performance. Second, although there were a few studies on comparing HRM practices among ownerships (state, collective, foreign-funded and private sectors) (e.g., Zhu 2005), little research has examined the relationship between strategic entrepreneurship, HRM practices and organizational performance across regions by controlling characteristics such as ownership, size and firm developmental phases. It has been suggested that research in HRM and business strategies should focus more on regional and strategic modelling of effective HRM (Tsui and Lau 2002; Wang 2006). There has been an increasing demand for integrated strategies of HRM practices and strategic entrepreneurship across regions (Wang and Mobley 1999; Wang and Zang 2005; Wang 2006). Figure 1 presents the conceptual model among strategic entrepreneurship, the two HRM practices of interest in the study, and firm performance.

Hypotheses development

According to the resource-based view of the firm (c.f., Barney 1991; Wright et al. 1994), employees are considered human resource capital. If utilized well, this resource will be able to contribute to the competitive advantage of firms (Barney and Wright 1998). That is, how human resources are utilized and treated will likely affect organizational performance. Prior research in the western context has related HRM practices to

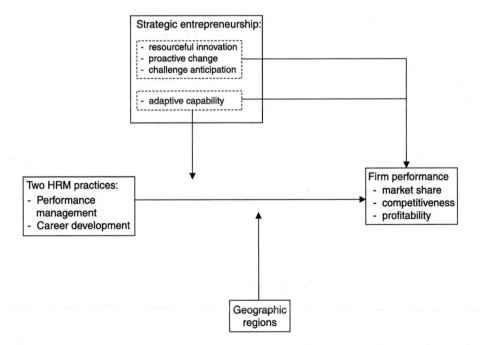

Figure 1.   The relationship between strategic entrepreneurship, HRM practices and firm performance.

firm performance. For example, Huselid and his colleagues (1997) showed that HRM effectiveness was positively related to productivity and market value of firm performance. Delaney and Huselid (1996) found positive associations between HRM practices and perceptual measures of firm performance.

HRM practices have also been the focus of several cross-cultural studies in China (Satow and Wang 1994; Wang and Satow 1994; Verburg, Drenth, Koopman, Van Muijen and Wang 1999). We believe that two HRM practices, performance management and career development, are of particular interest in this study for the following reasons. In the past, especially before the economic reforms of 1978, state-ownership dominated the economy and HRM practices were limited to more functional activities. The evaluation of performance focused more on task accomplishment. Great differentiation among employees was not desirable largely because of the Chinese tradition of 'harmony' (Chow 2004). There was no tight connection between performance and pay and performance appraisals were not conducted in a systematic and periodic fashion. Career opportunities were largely based on seniority rather than performance. Under the system of the 'iron rice bowl' and with the virtue of harmony, there was not enough motivation for employees to pursue more developmental opportunities either. Due to 'institutional continuity' (Warner 1999), it is difficult for many organizations to completely change such practices in a very short time.

Both performance management and career development, which diverge from traditional HRM practices, may play a strategic role in organizations. Performance management involving organizational components links employees' goals and behaviour with the organization's strategic goals. When on-going feedback is provided to the employees, they understand where their efforts should be directed to help achieve organizational goals. It helps improve processes within the organization and can affect business outcomes (Rummler and Brache 1990; Schuler, Fulkerson and Dowling 1991). McDonald and Smith (1995) provided some evidence that linked performance management to organizational performance. Using family-owned SMEs, Carlson and colleagues (2006) also found a positive relationship between the use of performance appraisals and sales growth. Career development, on the other hand, provides the opportunity for employees to grow and excel within the organization. This also allows employees to develop skills, acquire knowledge, and improve their competencies that may contribute to the organization in the long run. Moreover, this sends a signal of organizations' commitment to their employees, which in turn leads to higher employee motivation and morale. Indeed, it has been argued that employee development is a key driver to organizational growth and adds value to organizations (Mayo 2000). Therefore, we expect the extent to which performance management and career development are used will contribute to organizational performance.

Hypothesis 1: Performance management will have a positive influence on organizational performance.

Hypothesis 2: Career development will have a positive influence on organizational performance.

Research has suggested that firm strategies can have a direct impact on its performance in certain contexts (e.g., Chow and Liu 2007; Menguc, Auh and Shi 2007; Sun, Aryee and Law 2007). It has also been argued that entrepreneurship can contribute to firm performance and revitalization. *Corporate entrepreneurship* focuses on creating new business, innovation and growth (Zahra 1991) and is also characterized by seeking and seizing opportunities (McCline, Bhat and Baj 2000; Peng 2001). Some research has shown that entrepreneurship is likely to be associated with financial performance of organizations (e.g., Zahra 1991; Zahra and Covin 1995; Antoncic 2006). In emerging economies in particular, strategic entrepreneurship has increasingly been recognized as a stimulus for wealth creation (Peng 2001). For example, Bruton and Rubanik (2002) found that the more innovative the companies were the more likely they would grow effectively in a transition economy.

In developing a construct and dimensional model of strategic entrepreneurship, Ireland et al. (2003) suggested that strategic entrepreneurship involves simultaneous opportunity-seeking and advantage-seeking behaviour that result in superior firm performance and that strategic entrepreneurship has four dimensions: entrepreneurial mind-set; entrepreneurial culture and entrepreneurial leadership; strategic management of resources; and applying creativity to develop innovations. Yang (2002) argued for an analytic framework for double entrepreneurship in China's economic reforms. That is, on the one hand, an entrepreneur has to be innovative and to be able to identify promising new possibilities but on the other hand, it is also important to be adaptable and able to make adjustments and to take advantage of rules and regulations. In a review of adaptive capabilities, Wang and Ahmed (2007) identified three components for dynamic capabilities: adaptive capability; absorptive capability; and innovative capability. Among the Chinese firms, adaptive capability is more closely related to coordinating efforts and adjusting structures or systems. Innovative capability is more related to acquiring resources for innovation and adopting resources to motivate innovative activities. Zahra et al. (2005) also identify change actions and challenge coping as key strategies for entrepreneurship. Based on previous theoretical developments and Chinese regional entrepreneurial development and organizational change, in this study, we define strategic entrepreneurship as a four-factor concept: adaptive capability; resourceful innovation; proactive change; and risk anticipation. Adaptive capability represents ability in coordinating, facilitating, adjusting, leading and adapting organizational resources for entrepreneurial and business development; resourceful innovation is the strategic management of resources that encourages new ideas and develops innovative projects through mobilizing effective resources and establishing systems for entrepreneurship and creativity; proactive change focuses on strategic change actions and active organization development, whereas risk anticipation represents the ability to recognize current difficulties and challenges and build up the readiness for entrepreneurial actions. We expect these four dimensions of strategic entrepreneurship to be positively related to organizational performance. Moreover, the nature of adaptive capability suggests that it may serve as a moderator, as this capability facilitates the use of resources. A high level of adaptive capability will help a firm to better align their internal resources with encountered demands (Rindova and Kotha 2001). In the meantime, human resources are among the most important resources that may be coordinated and adapted for achieving organizational goals. Thus, we expect a moderating effect of adaptive capability such that the relationship between HRM practices and organizational performance would be stronger with a higher level of adaptive capability.

Hypothesis 3a: Adaptive capability will positively affect organizational performance.
Hypothesis 3b: Resourceful innovation will positively affect organizational performance.
Hypothesis 3c: Proactive change will positively affect organizational performance.
Hypothesis 3d: Risk anticipation will positively affect organizational performance.
Hypothesis 3e: Adaptive capability will moderate the relationship between HRM practices and organizational performance

Several regional strategic actions need to be mentioned in order to fully understand the dynamics of HRM, entrepreneurship and firm performance. First, the western-China development strategy was launched during mid-1990s in order to attract more talented people and promote economic development in the region. The challenge is that talented people traditionally move to the eastern coast areas. It becomes more difficult to attract the best people in the central and western regions. Second, during late 1990s, the northern-China revitalization development strategy was implemented in a region of heavy industry with a large number of downsized labour forces. More recently a comprehensive mid-China development strategy was announced in order to cope with the lack of vital HRM. In the meantime, the Yangtze River Delta area has been seen as the most active entrepreneurship region, with active technological innovation and global entrepreneurship. These regional development policies have greatly promoted HRM strategic modelling strategic entrepreneurship in China.

Despite the economic reform period in China, the eastern coast region has enjoyed much higher economy growth rate compared to the central and western regions which are located in inland China. Along the coastal region, special economic zones and open coastal cities have been created as an open platform for economic development. This region also offers favourable policies to foreign and local enterprises such as preferential tax incentives, organizational autonomy in recruitment and compensation, and support from the government. The region has attracted much foreign direct investment (FDI) which brings with it high technology, modern equipment, advanced practices and high levels of skills (see Caves 1996). As a result, the area is relatively more developed than the western and central regions of China. With a high concentration of FDI on the eastern coast and fast economic growth, this region provides better access to specialized, experienced and well-educated employees (see Porter 1998). Multinational enterprises (MNEs) also help improve the skill and knowledge levels of the labour market indirectly as their employees move to local firms (Blomstrom and Kokko 1998; Buckley, Clegg and Wang 2002). Moreover, Ding and his colleagues (2000) found that the average wages were significantly higher in firms located in coastal China than inland China. The high economy growth rate, which signals more job opportunities, and the high compensation level attract talented individuals from other locations to the eastern coast cities and provinces.

With a larger pool of talents, firms in the eastern regions are more likely to gain higher levels of human capital. However, in the western and central regions, it is relatively difficult to attract, hire and retain individuals with best skills and knowledge. Therefore, we hypothesize the following:

Hypothesis 4: The relationship between performance management and organizational performance is stronger for firms located in the eastern region compared to those in the western and central regions.

Hypothesis 5: The relationship between career development and organizational performance is stronger for firms located in the eastern region compared to those in the western and central regions

Methodology

Participants

The study involved 103 firms from 11 different cities and provinces. They were from Shanghai, Zhejiang (Hangzhou, Wenzhou, Ningbo), Shandong (Qingdao), Hubei (Wuhan), Hunan (Changsha), Guangxi (Guilin), Shanxi (Xian), Guizhou (Guiyang) and Yunnan

(Kunming). Altogether, 606 employees participated in the study. In each company, an in-depth interview was conducted and three surveys about HRM, strategic entrepreneurship and organizational performance were distributed among two HR managers, two–three executives, and two–three top management members, respectively. About 34 bureau officials also participated in the study, serving as external raters of organizational performance. The HRM practices survey was completed by 180 HR managers. The strategic entrepreneurship survey was conducted among 173 executives and the organizational performance survey was completed by 219 top managers and 34 bureau officials. We randomly selected 20 companies from the economic and technology development zone in each city (220 in total). To be included in the sample, the firms also needed to have been created within 10 years of our data collection in 2006. Among the final 150 companies we physically approached, distributed surveys and conducted interviews, 130 survey packages were returned (86.7%) and 103 of all returned parts of the surveys were usable. Out of the initial contact, the final response rate was 47% (103/220). No significant differences were found between these firms and non-responding firms with regard to size and age.

Measures

Performance management and *career development* were each measured with four items adapted from Verburg et al. (1999) and Wang and Zang (2005). A five-point Likert scale was used to measure the degree of practices. A sample item for performance management was 'periodic performance appraisal activity' and an item for career development was 'periodic internal employee position transfer'. The Cronbach alphas were .90 and .84 for performance management and career development, respectively.

A four-factor measurement of *strategic entrepreneurship* was designed on the basis of previous literature (e.g., Ireland, Hitt and Simon 2003), in-depth interviews, and prior research adapted to the Chinese situation (Wang and Zang 2005). A five-point Likert scale was used (1 = very uncharacteristic and 5 = very characteristic). These four factors were: adaptive capability; resourceful innovation; proactive change; and risk anticipation. These four factors were first tested among 10 companies through in-depth interviews and pilot surveys and the Cronbach alphas in the pilot test were .84, .80, .84, and .75, respectively.

In the main study, we conducted an exploratory factor analysis with principal axis factoring using oblique rotation (Direct Oblimin) on the 18-item strategic entrepreneurship scale. Oblique rotation allows intercorrelations among factors. The results revealed four factors. These factors had eigenvalues greater than 1.0 and explained 67.58% of the total variance. Table 1 presents the rotated factor loadings for this four-factor structure. The Cronbach alphas were .90, .90, .86, and .75 for adaptive capability, resourceful innovation, proactive change and risk anticipation, respectively.

In the strategic entrepreneurship survey, respondents were asked to identify in which city their firms were located, i.e. in which *region* they were situated. We coded participating firms into three groups (i.e., eastern, western, and central regions). Two dummy variables with the reference of eastern region were then created based on the location of the city to represent China's western and central regions.

A survey of *organizational performance* was adapted from Wang and Satow (1994) and measured the following three indicators using five-point Likert scale:

- *Market share*: How much market share is held by the company compared with other companies in its industrial sector? (1 = getting smaller, 2 = expanding little, 3 = expanding relatively little, 4 = expanding fast, 5 = expanding very fast)

Table 1. Strategic entrepreneurship factor analysis and factor loadings (oblique rotation).

	Resourceful innovation	Risk anticipation	Adaptive capability	Proactive change
1. The firm sets up rewards for entrepreneurship and creative invention.	**.86**	.12	.05	-.09
2. The firm establishes relevant systems to obtain innovative ideas from employees.	**.77**	-.07	.28	.07
3. The firm sets up procedures to evaluate innovative ideas.	**.76**	-.10	.23	.01
4. The firm sets up formal honorary titles for creative, excellent employees.	**.74**	.07	-.04	-.15
5. The firm provides effective resources to test new projects.	**.58**	-.09	.13	-.19
6. The firm anticipates challenges and risks in raising funds.	.09	**.88**	-.10	.12
7. The firm anticipates high risk in expanding its market.	-.05	**.80**	.05	-.13
8. The firm facilitates new entrepreneurial activities through increasing autonomy of the departments.	.04	-.11	**.82**	-.04
9. The firm flexibly adjusts organizational structure in order to strengthen entrepreneurial capability.	-.01	-.11	**.82**	-.11
10. The firm coordinates departments to enhance entrepreneurial capability.	.19	.09	**.81**	.14
11. The firm adopts various approaches to change into new values, learn new knowledge and technology.	.11	.07	**.74**	-.04
12. The firm organizes and adjusts new departments to enhance innovation and business development	.26	.04	**.63**	-.13
13. The firm adopts strategic change according to competitive environment.	.21	.04	-.13	**.76**
14. The firm plays a change leadership role rather than follower role.	.19	-.12	-.18	**.72**
15. The firm actively expands and takes risks in business.	.09	.06	.13	**.67**
16. The firm adopts proactive strategy in market competition.	-.08	-.08	.36	**.61**
17. The firm tries to adopt new strategies to cope with competitors.	.18	.04	.22	**.59**
18. The firm demonstrates technology change leading roles.	-.22	.18	.21	**.49**
Eigenvalues (variance explained)	7.68 (42.66%)	1.84 (10.22%)	1.47 (8.16%)	1.18 (6.55%)

- *Profitability*: How profitable is this company in comparison with other companies in its industrial sector? (1 = deficit, 2 = small profit, 3 = middle level, 4 = relatively profitable, 5 = very profitable)
- *Competitiveness*: How competitive is this company in comparison with other companies in its industrial sector? (1 = very weak, 2 = relatively weak, 3 = middle level, 4 = relatively strong, 5 = very strong).

Recognizing the limitations of one-item scales, we took the following steps. The indicators of organizational performance were rated by members of top management. For each indicator, we used the average of their ratings in each company based on the acceptable level of intraclass correlation (ICC) coefficients. To check reliability and validity, these indicators were also independently rated by industrial bureau officials. These ratings and the average ratings by top management team members were highly correlated, with an average correlation of .86, suggesting high reliability of the ratings.

Control variables

We included controls for several variables that may affect organizational performance. All these control variables were measured in the strategic entrepreneurship survey. First, we controlled for firm size as measured by the number of full-time employees because larger firms tend to have superior resources compared to smaller firms (Collins and Clark 2003). Specifically, we used five categories (<50 scored 1; $50-100$ scored 2; $100-500$ scored 3; $500-1000$ scored 4; and >1000 scored 5). Second, ownership has been found to be related to firm performance in China (e.g., Peng and Luo 2000; Xu, Pan, Wu and Yim 2006). This variable was measured as state-owned firms (scored 1), privately-owned firms (scored 2), and foreign-invested firms (scored 3). Third, because firms with different developmental phases face fundamentally different problems and have different strategic focuses/goals which may affect their strategies and performance at the time (e.g., Kazanjian, 1988; Randolph, Sapienza and Watson1991), we also controlled for organizational phase. It was measured by (1) start-up phase, (2) growth phase, (3) maturity phase and (4) transformation phase.

Analysis strategy

Hierarchical Ordinary Least Square (OLS) regression was used to test our hypotheses. Control variables were entered in the first step followed by the two HRM practices (performance management and career development), dimensions of strategic entrepreneurship and the regions. In the last step, we included the interaction terms to test moderation effects. The variables, performance management, career development, and adaptive capabilities were entered before product terms were created (Cohen, Cohen, Western and Aiken 2003). Due to the relative small sample size and multicollinearity concern, we included one set of interaction terms at a time.

Results

Table 2 presents descriptive statistics and correlations for all variables used in the study. An average firm in our sample had between 500 to 1000 employees. Table 3 reports the results of hierarchical regression analyses used to examine the effect of strategic entrepreneurship, HRM practices, and regions on organizational performance.

HRM practices

Hypotheses 1 and 2 predicted that performance management and career development would be positively related to organizational performance. Regression results showed that performance management had significant positive effects on all three indicators of organizational performance, competitiveness ($\beta = .35$, $p < .01$), profitability ($\beta = .28$, $p < .01$), and market share ($\beta = .24$, $p < .05$), providing support for Hypothesis 1. Contrary to our hypothesis, career development was negatively related to competitiveness at a marginally significant level ($\beta = -.21$, $p < .10$). No significant effect was found for career development with regard to profitability and market share. Therefore, Hypothesis 2 was not supported.

Strategic entrepreneurship

Hypotheses 3a to 3d predicted positive relationships between dimensions of strategic entrepreneurship and organizational performance. As shown in Table 3, proactive change and risk anticipation had significant effects on all three performance indicators including competitiveness, profitability, and market share while adaptive capability and resourceful innovation were not significantly related to any of these performance indicators. Specifically, firms with higher levels of proactive change focus had higher competitiveness ($\beta = .51$, $p < .01$), profitability ($\beta = .24$, $p < .05$), and market share ($\beta = .40$, $p < .01$). On the other hand, unexpectedly, firms which anticipated greater risk had lower competitiveness ($\beta = -.25$, $p < .01$) and profitability ($\beta = -.37$, $p < .01$). Therefore, Hypothesis 3c was supported while Hypothesis 3a, 3b and 3d were not.

Hypothesis 3e predicted a moderating effect of adaptive capability on the HRM practices–performance relationship. The results showed a significant positive moderation effect ($\beta = .22$, $p < .05$) of performance management on the adaptive capability–competitiveness relationship and a negative moderation effect ($\beta = -.25$, $p < .01$) of career management on the adaptive capability–competitiveness relationship. No moderation effects were found for profitability and market share. The pattern indicated in Figure 2 was consistent with our prediction. That is, the relationship between performance management and competitiveness was stronger, with a higher level of adaptive capability. However, the pattern in Figure 3 was the opposite of our prediction, suggesting the career development–competitiveness relationship was stronger with a low level of adaptive capability. Therefore, Hypothesis 3e was partially supported.

Regions

Hypothesis 4 and 5 predicted the moderating effects of regions on the relationship between performance management and firm performance and between career development and firm performance, respectively. The results showed an interaction effect between performance management and western region ($\beta = -.31$, $p < .01$) on competitiveness, and between performance management and central region on both competitiveness ($\beta = -.43$, $p < .01$) and profitability ($\beta = -.27$, $p < .01$). A post-hoc analysis showed no difference between firms in the central region versus those in the western region with regard to performance management–competitiveness relationship and performance management–profitability relationship. The patterns indicated in Figure 4 and 5 were consistent with those hypothesized. That is, there was a stronger relationship between performance management and competitiveness for firms located in the eastern region than those in the western and central regions; there was a stronger relationship between

Table 2. Descriptive statistics and correlations for all variables.

Variables	M	SD	1	2	3	4	5	6	7	8	9	10	11	12	13
1. Phase	2.52	.79													
2. Ownership	1.67	.71	-.07												
3. Firm size	3.55	1.35	-.02	-.22											
4. Eastern region	.45	.50	-.15	.11	.15										
5. Western region	.21	.41	-.06	-.07	-.13	-.47									
6. Adaptive capability	3.69	.65	.05	-.06	.22	.13	-.09								
7. Resourceful innovation	3.22	.85	.10	-.06	.46	.18	-.19	.63							
8. Proactive change	3.69	.61	-.03	-.03	.40	.18	-.18	.60	.62						
9. Risk anticipation	3.03	.74	.13	-.09	-.13	-.18	.06	-.03	-.10	.06					
10. Performance management	3.59	.88	.09	.15	-.06	.11	.03	.05	.19	.10	.12				
11. Career development	3.06	.77	-.07	.19	-.14	.30	-.12	.32	.29	.24	-.14	.54			
12. Competitiveness	3.63	.71	-.16	.11	.22	.21	-.18	.28	.34	.50	-.26	.31	.19		
13. Profitability	3.16	1.05	-.05	-.07	.26	.14	-.11	.20	.27	.29	-.39	.32	.24	.63	
14. Market share	3.51	.87	-.16	-.21	.38	.29	-.20	.27	.35	.48	-.18	.25	.23	.59	.63

Note: Correlations with absolute values greater than .20, $p < .05$; correlations with absolute values greater than .25, $p < .01$; two-tailed test. Regions were dummy-coded with middle region as reference. Phase: start-up phase (1), growth phase (2), maturity phase (3), transformation phase (4); ownership: state-owned (1), privately owned (2), foreign-invested (3); firm size: <50 (1), 50–100 (2), 100–500 (3), 500–1000 (4), >1000 (5).

Table 3. Hierarchical regression analyses for organizational performance.

Independent variables	Competitiveness			Profitability			Market Share		
	β	Adj.R²	ΔR²	β	Adj.R²	ΔR²	β	Adj.R²	ΔR²
Step 1		.06	.09*		.05	.08*		.18	.21**
Phase	−.14			−.06			−.17†		
Ownership	.13			−.10			−.21*		
Firm size	.25*			.23*			.32**		
Step 2		.38	.36**		.29	.29**		.40	.26**
Performance management (PM)	.35**			.28**			.24*		
Career development (CD)	−.21†			.05			.05		
Adaptive capability	.04			.02			−.02		
Resourceful innovation	−.03			−.07			−.07		
Proactive change	.51**			.24*			.40**		
Risk anticipation	−.25**			−.37**			−.13		
Western region	−.13			−.03			−.17†		
Central region	−.03			.06			−.09		
Step 3		.43	.06**		.28	.01		.39	.00
PM * Adaptive capability	.22*			.06			.06		
CD * Adaptive capability	−.25**			−.07			.02		
Step 3		.47	.09**		.31	.03†		.39	.00
PM * Western	−.31**			−.05			.02		
PM * Central	−.43**			−.27*			−.05		
Step3		.37	.00		.27	.00		.40	.01
CD *Western	−.01			−.03			.05		
CD * Central	−.11			−.08			.18		

Note: Standardized coefficients are reported. The interactions terms were included in the regression one set at a time in the last step of each equation. Adj.R² = Adjusted R². †p < .10,
*p < .05, **p < .01, two-tailed test. Regions were dummy-coded with the Eastern region as the reference. N = 103.

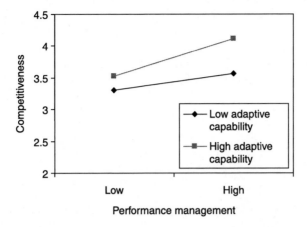

Figure 2.   The moderating effect of adaptive capability on the relationship between performance management and competitiveness.

performance management and profitability for firms located in the eastern regions than those in the central region. No moderating effects of regions were found for the career development–performance relationship. Therefore, Hypothesis 4 was partially supported while Hypothesis 5 was not supported.

Discussion

This study examined the influences of two important HRM practices and strategic entrepreneurship on firm performance and the moderating role of regions. The results revealed some interesting findings. In the research, we used multiple informants from the same firm to complete different surveys. The main predictors' measures in the study were conducted separately, including HRM survey among HR managers, strategic entrepreneurship survey among firm executives and performance survey among top managers. Therefore, the results of this study were less affected by biases such as common-method variance and individual bias.

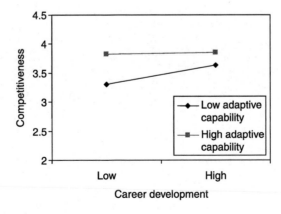

Figure 3.   The moderating effect of adaptive capability on the relationship between career development and competitiveness.

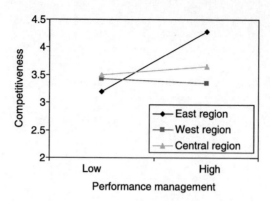

Figure 4.   The moderating effect of regions on the relationship between performance management and competitiveness.

Consistent with prior research (e.g., Zahra and Covin 1995; Peng 2001), our results showed pursuing strategic entrepreneurship can lead to better organizational performance for newly established firms in economic and technological development zones in China. Specifically, the results revealed four dimensions of strategic entrepreneurship: resourceful innovation; proactive change; risk anticipation; and adaptive capability. Among them, proactive change seems to be an influential dimension that had a positive direct effect on organizational performance indicators while risk anticipation, unexpectedly, showed a negative effect on performance indicators. It seems the anticipation of risk and challenge becomes an obstacle for organizations to overcome the risks and pursue their goals. This suggests that entrepreneurial firms may sometimes benefit from not spending too much time anticipating all possible risks and difficulties that might lie ahead, but rather, they need to take some risks and focus on seizing opportunities and putting ideas into action, which is consistent with the concept of entrepreneurship (Ireland et al. 2003). Future research is needed to further examine this dimension. Although adaptive capability and resourceful innovation did not show direct effects on organizational performance, adaptive capability showed its potential as an important moderator as it influenced the HRM practices–performance relationships. It is also likely

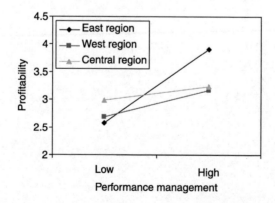

Figure 5.   The moderating effect of regions on the relationship between performance management and profitability.

that these strategic entrepreneurship dimensions may also interact with other resources and contextual factors to affect firm performance.

Consistent with prior research that emphasizes the importance of HRM (e.g., Wright et al. 1994; Delaney and Huselid 1996; Huselid, Jackson and Schuler 1997; Law et al. 2003), performance management was found to be positively related to organizational performance. The unique history of the Chinese labour and personnel management systems leads us to argue that performance management is one of the most important changes that need to be made as it contributes directly to firm performance in the Chinese context. However, we are by no means suggesting that other aspects of HRM are neglectable or not important but because of the Chinese tradition of *harmony* and the *egalitarian* mentality, the adoption of performance management may be a particular challenge for Chinese firms.

It seems that while performance management has been a strategic HRM practice influencing significantly organizational performance and might be better integrated with strategic entrepreneurship at this stage, career development might rquire a longer time period in order to demonstrate its impact on performance. Further, rather unexpectedly, we found a negative relationship between career development and competitiveness at a marginally significant level. One possible explanation is that career development might have resulted in high performers leaving for better external opportunities as they are better equipped to take the opportunities available. Indeed, Chow and Liu (2007) suggested that relatively high turnover rate could significantly undermine the benefits/value of employee development. More research is needed on this issue and a replication of this finding is desirable.

It has been argued that the influence of globalization is uneven on HRM across Asia-Pacific regions (Warner 2002). Due to location differences, firms in different regions in China may affect the adoption of HRM practices (e.g., Ding et al. 2000; Wei and Lau 2005). Our findings showed that with the same level of HRM practices, their influences on firm performance could vary depending on the different labour markets and policies across regions. Prior research tends to compare the coastal region against inland China but our findings suggest that finer categorizations of regions may shed more insights. For example, the performance management–profitability relationship was not significantly different between firms in the eastern and western region but a difference was found comparing those in the eastern and central region. This may indicate that through years of developmental strategies, the gap between the eastern and western regions is getting smaller while the central region was still left behind. Rather than looking at location differences, it might be more fruitful in the future to examine specific relevant issues that are different across regions, such as access to labour, concentration of foreign firms (Li 2004), and labour mobility rates (Schonberg 2007).

Implications and limitations

The results of this study have several important implications for modelling HRM strategies in different regions in China. First, performance management and career development are among the most important HRM practices in linking with strategic entrepreneurship to affect organizational performance in China. Our findings suggest that performance management is critical to firms and by building adaptive capability, firms can better utilize and coordinate human resources to enhance their competitiveness. Second, strategic entrepreneurship including proactive change and risk anticipation should receive special attention as they showed direct relationship with firm performance. However, at the same time, some specific practices related to human resources may provide additional needed support to achieving the goals. Third, regional models of HRM strategies need to be built in order to better understand and develop more strategic HRM approaches to fit with local contingencies such as regional policies, labour markets and entrepreneurship. This has important implications for entrepreneurs who are interested in starting or continuing businesses in the different areas.

There were some limitations that need to be mentioned. First, we adopted the methodology of using independent surveys to collect data from different sources, which alleviated the common method bias. However, in order to build more comprehensive regional models, more sites and regions need be taken into account and as a result, the sample size was relatively small. Second, cross-sectional design was used and this prevented us from making causality conclusions. Although we argued the impact of strategic entrepreneurship and HRM practices on performance, we cannot rule out the possibility that organizational performance might influence choices of strategies and practices. Future research should be carried out using a longitudinal approach in order to test the causal relationship. Finally, we used perceptual measures of organizational performance and adopted external validation rating because we were not able to obtain objective measures. Although prior research has found positive relationship between objective and perceptual measures of performance (Dess and Robinson, 1984; Geringer and Hebert 1991), future research using objective measures is needed to provide more insights.

Conclusions

The main objective of this study was to test the effects of strategic entrepreneurship and HRM practices on organizational performance. Our results showed that among the four dimensions of strategic entrepreneurship, proactive change was critical in determining organizational performance while adaptive capability interacted with performance management and career development to affect performance. Risk anticipation was negatively related to performance. While performance management is crucial for firms, the performance management and performance relationship vary across regions.

Acknowledgement

The research work was supported by the NSF China Key Project (Grant No. 70732001) and the Ministry of Education China doctoral programme funds. We wish to thank the editor of this Volume, Malcolm Warner, as well as the anonymous reviewers for their helpful comments.

References

Antoncic, B. (2006), "Impacts of Diversification and Corporate Entrepreneurship Strategy Making on Growth and Profitability: A Normative Model," *Journal of Enterprising Culture*, 14, 1, 49–63.
Atuahene-Gima, K., and Li, H. (2004), "Strategic Decision Comprehensiveness and New Product Development Outcomes in New Technology Ventures," *Academy of Management Journal*, 47, 4, 583–597.
Barney, J. (1991), "Firm Resources and Sustained Competitive Advantage," *Journal of Management*, 17, 99–120.
Barney, J.B., and Wright, P.M. (1998), "On Becoming a Strategic Partner: The Role of Human Resources in Gaining Competitive Advantage," *Human Resource Management*, 37, 1, 31–46.
Blomstrom, M., and Kokko, A. (1998), "Multinational Corporations and Spillovers," *Journal of Economic Surveys*, 12, 2, 1–31.
Borch, O.-J., and Madsen, E. (2005), "Adaptive Capability and Strategic Entrepreneurship: An Empirical Study of Innovative SMEs," in *Frontiers of Entrepreneurship Research*, eds. S.A. Zahra, C.G. Brush, P. Davidsson, J.O. Fiet, P.G. Greene, R.T. Harrison, M. Lerner, C. Mason, D. Shepherd, J. Sohl, J. Wiklund and M. Wright Braintree, MA: Babson, p. 225.

Bruton, G.D., and Rubanik, Y. (2002), "Resources of the Firm, Russian High-technology Startups, and Firm Growth," *Journal of Business Venturing*, 17, 6, 553–576.

Buckley, P.J., Clegg, J., and Wang, C. (2002), "The Impact of Inward FDI on the Performance of Chinese Manufacturing Firms," *Journal of International Business Studies*, 33, 4, 637–655.

Carlson, D.S., Upton, N., and Seaman, S. (2006), "The Impact of Human Resource Practices and Compensation Design on Performance: An Analysis of Family-owned SMEs," *Journal of Small Business Management*, 44, 4, 531–543.

Caves, R.E. (1996), *Multinational Enterprise and Economic Analysis*, New York: Cambridge University Press.

Child, J. (1999), *Management and Organizations in China: Key Trends and Issues*, Hong Kong: Chinese Management Centre, University of Hong Kong.

Chow, I.H. (2004), "The Impact of Institutional Context on Human Resource Management in Three Chinese Societies," *Employee Relations*, 26, 6, 626–642.

Chow, I.H.-S., and Liu, S.S. (2007), "Business Strategy, Organizational Culture, and Performance Outcomes in China's Technology Industry," *Human Resource Planning*, 30, 2, 47–55.

Cohen, J., Cohen, P., Western, S.G., and Aiken, L.S. (2003), *Applied Multiple Regression/Correlation Analysis for the Behavioral Sciences* (3rd ed.), Mahwah, NJ: Lawrence Erlbaum Association.

Collins, C.J., and Clark, K.D. (2003), "Strategic Human Resource Practices, Top Management Team Social Networks, and Firm Performance: The Role of Human Resource Practices in Creating Organizational Competitive Advantage," *Academy of Management Journal*, 46, 740–751.

Covin, J.G., Green, K.M., and Slevin, D.P. (2006), "Strategic Process Effects on the Entrepreneurial Orientation–Sales Growth Rate Relationship," *Entrepreneurship: Theory & Practice*, 30, 1, 57–81.

Daily, C., McDougall, P., Covin, J.G., and Dalton, D. (2002), "Governance and Strategic Leadership in Entrepreneurial Firms," *Journal of Management*, 28, 387–412.

Delaney, J.T., and Huselid, M.A. (1996), "The Impact of Human Resource Management Practices on Perceptions of Organizational Performance," *Academy of Management Journal*, 39, 949–969.

Dess, G., and Robinson, D. (1984), "Measuring Organizational Performance in the Absence of Objective Measures: The Case of the Privately Held Firm and Conglomerate Business Unit," *Strategic Management Journal*, 5, 265–273.

Ding, D.Z., Akhtar, S., and Ge, G.L. (2006), "Organizational Differences in Managerial Compensation and Benefits in Chinese Firms," *International Journal of Human Resource Management*, 17, 4, 693–715.

Ding, D.Z., Goodall, K., and Warner, M. (2000), "The End of the 'Iron Rice-bowl': Whither Chinese Human Resource Management?" *International Journal of Human Resource Management*, 11, 2, 217–236.

Geringer, M.J., and Hebert, L. (1991), "Measuring Performance of International Joint Ventures," *Journal of International Business Studies*, 22, 249–263.

Huselid, M.A., Jackson, S.E., and Schuler, R.S. (1997), "Technical and Strategic Human Resource Management Effectiveness as Determinants of Firm Performance," *Academy of Management Journal*, 40, 171–188.

Ireland, R.D., Hitt, M.A., and Sirmon, D.G. (2003), "A Model of Strategic Entrepreneurship: The Construct and its Dimensions," *Journal of Management*, 29, 6, 963–989.

Johnson, S., and Van de Ven, A.H. (2002), "A Framework for Entrepreneurial Strategy," in *Strategic Entrepreneurship: Creating a New Mindset*, eds. M.A. Hitt, R.D. Ireland, S.M. Camp and D.L. Sexton, Oxford, UK: Blackwell, pp. 66–86.

Kazanjian, R.K. (1988), "The Relation of Dominant Problems to Stage of Growth in Technology-based New Ventures," *Academy of Management Journal*, 31, 257–279.

Law, K.S., Tse, D.K., and Zhou, N. (2003), "Does Human Resource Management Matter in a Transitional Economy? China as an Example," *Journal of International Business Studies*, 34, 3, 255–265.

Li, S. (2004), "Location and Performance of Foreign Firms in China," *Management International Review*, 44, 2, 151–169.

Liu, A.Y., Li, S., and Gao, Y. (1999), "Location, Location, Location," *The China Business Review,* March–April, 20–25.

Liu, S.S., Luo, X., and Shi, Y.-Z. (2003), "Market-oriented Organizations in an Emerging Economy," *Journal of Business Research*, 56, 6, 481–491.

Luo, Y. (1995), "Business Strategy, Market Structure, and Performance of International Joint Ventures: The Case of China," *Management International Review*, 35, 242–264.

Luo, X., Zhou, L., and Liu, S.S. (2005), "Entrepreneurial Firms in the Context of China's Transition Economy: An Integrative Framework and Empirical Examination," *Journal of Business Research*, 58, 3, 277–284.

Mayo, A. (2000), "The Role of Employee Development in the Growth of Intellectual Capital," *Personnel Review*, 29, 4, 521–533.

McCline, R.L., Bhat, S., and Baj, P. (2000), "Opportunity Recognition: An Exploratory Investigation of a Component of the Entrepreneurial Process in the Context of the Health Care Industry," *Entrepreneurship Theory and Practice*, 25, 2, 81–94.

McDonald, D., and Smith, A. (1995), "A Proven Connection: Performance Management and Business Results," *Compensation and Benefits Review*, 27, 1, 59–62.

Menguc, B., Auh, S., and Shih, E. (2007), "Transformational Leadership and Market Orientation: Implications for the Implementation of Competitive Strategies and Business Unit Performance," *Journal of Business Research*, 60, 4, 314–321.

Peng, M.W. (2001), "How Entrepreneurs Create Wealth in Transition Economies," *Academy of Management Executive*, 15, 1, 95–108.

Peng, M.W., and Luo, Y. (2000), "Managerial Ties and Firm Performance in a Transition Economy: The Nature of a Micro–macro Link," *Academy of Management Journal*, 43, 486–501.

Porter, M.E. (1998), "Clusters and the New Economics of Competition," *Harvard Business Review*, November–December, 77–90.

Randolph, W.A., Sapienza, H.J., and Watson, M.A. (1991), "Technology-structure Fit and Performance in Small Business: An Examination of the Moderating Effects of Organizational States," *Entrepreneurship: Theory & Practice*, 16, 1, 27–41.

Rindova, V.P., and Kotha, S. (2001), "Continuous 'Morphing': Competing through Dynamic Capabilities, Forms, and Functions," *Academy of Management Journal*, 44, 1263–1280.

Rummler, G.A., and Brache, A.P. (1990), *Improving Performance*, San Francisco, CA: Jossey-Bass.

Satow, T., and Wang, Z.M. (1994), "Cultural and Organizational Factors in Human Resource Management in China and Japan: A Cross-cultural Socio-economic Perspective," *Journal of Managerial Psychology*, 9, 4, 3–11.

Schonberg, U. (2007), "Wage Growth Due to Human Capital Accumulation and Job Search: A Comparison between the United States and Germany," *Industrial & Labour Relations Review*, 60, 4, 562–586.

Schuler, R.S., Fulkerson, J.R., and Dowling, P.J. (1991), "Strategic Performance Measurement and Management in Multinational Corporations," *Human Resource Management*, 30, 3, 365–392.

Siu, W.-S., and Liu, Z.-C. (2005), "Marketing in Chinese Small and Medium enterprises (SMEs), The State of the Art in a Chinese Socialist Economy," *Small Business Economics*, 25, 333–346.

Sun, L.-Y., Aryee, S., and Law, K.S. (2007), "High-performance Human Resource Practices, Citizenship Behavior, and Organizational Performance: A Relational Perspective," *Academy of Management Journal*, 50, 3, 558–577.

Tsui, A., and Lau, C.M. (2002), *The Management of Enterprises in the People's Republic of China*, Boston, MA: Kluwer Academic Publishers.

Verburg, R.M., Drenth, P.J.D., Koopman, P.L., Van Muijen, J.J., and Wang, Z.M. (1999), "Managing Human Resources across Cultures: A Comparative Analysis of Practices in Industrial Enterprises in China and The Netherlands," *The International Journal of Human Resource Management*, 10, 3, 391–410.

Wang, C.L., and Ahmed, P.K. (2007), "Dynamic Capabilities: A Review and Research Agenda," *International Journal of Management Reviews*, 9, 1, 31–52.

Wang, Z.M. (2006), "Leadership Competency and Implicit Assessment Modeling," address at Congress Proceedings: XVIII International Congress of Psychology, Beijing 2004. Hove & New York: Psychology Press.

Wang, Z.M., and Mobley, W. (1999), "Strategic Human Resource Management for Twenty-first-century China," in *Research in Personnel and Human Resources Management*, eds. P.M. Wright, L.D. Dyer, J.W. Boudreau and G.T. Milkovich, London: JAI Press Inc, pp. 353–366.

Wang, Z.M., and Satow, T. (1994), "Leadership Styles and Organizational Effectiveness in Chinese–Japanese Joint Ventures," *Journal of Managerial Psychology*, 9, 4, 31–36.

Wang, Z.M., and Zang, Z. (2005), "Strategic Human Resources, Innovation and Entrepreneurship Fit: A Cross-regional Comparative Model," *International Journal of Manpower*, 26, 6, 544–559.

Warner, M. (1999), "Human Resources and Management in China's 'Hi-tech' Revolution: A Study of Selected Computer Hardware, Software and Related Firms in the PRC," *International Journal of Human Resource Management*, 10, 1, 1–20.

Warner, M. (2002), "Globalization, Labour Market and Human Resources in Asia-Pacific Economics: An Overview," *International Journal of Human Resource Management*, 13, 384–398.

Wei, L.-Q., and Lau, C.-M. (2005), "Market Orientation, HRM Importance and Competency: Determinants of Strategic HRM in Chinese Firms," *International Journal of Human Resource Management*, 16, 1901–1918.

White, S. (2000), "Competition, Capabilities, and the Make, Buy, or Ally Decisions of Chinese State-owned Forms," *Academy of Management Journal*, 43, 324–341.

Wright, P.M., and Barney, J. (1998), "On Becoming a Strategic Partner: The Role of Human Resources in Gaining Competitive Advantage," *Human Resource Management*, 37, 1, 31–46.

Wright, P.M., McMahan, G.C., and McWilliams, A. (1994), "Human Resources and Sustained Competitive Advantage: A Resource-based Perspective," *International Journal of Human Resource Management*, 5, 301–326.

Xu, D., Pan, Y., Wu, C., and Yim, B. (2006), "Performance of Domestic and Foreign-Invested Enterprises in China," *Journal of World Business*, 41, 3, 261–274.

Yang, K.M. (2002), "Double Entrepreneurship in China's Economic Reform: An Analytic Framework," *Journal of Political and Military Sociology*, 30, 1, 134–147.

Zahra, S.A. (1991), "Predictors and Financial Outcomes of Corporate Entrepreneurship: An Exploratory Study," *Journal of Business Venturing*, 6, 4, 259–285.

Zahra, S.A., Brush, C.G., Davidsson, P., Fiet, J.O., Greene, P.G., Harrison, R.T, Lerner, M., Mason, C., Shepherd, D., Sohl, J., Wiklund, J., and Wright, M. (2005), *Frontiers of Entrepreneurship Research 2005*, Braintree, MA: Babson.

Zahra, S.A., and Covin, J.G. (1995), "Contextual Influences on the Corporate Entrepreneurship–performance Relationship: A Longitudinal Analysis," *Journal of Business Venturing*, 10, 43–58.

Zahra, S.A., Jennings, D.F., and Kuratko, D.F. (1999), "The Antecedents and Consequences of Firm-level Entrepreneurship: The State of the Field," *Entrepreneurship: Theory & Practice*, 5, 45–65.

Zhou, L., Wu, W.-P., and Luo, X. (2007), "Internationalization and the Performance of Born-global SMEs: The Mediating Role of Social Networks," *Journal of International Business Studies*, 38, 4, 673–690.

Zhu, C.J. (2005), *Human Resource Management in China: Past, Current and Future HR Practices in the Industrial Sector*, London: Routledge.

Human resource management in foreign-owned subsidiaries: China versus India

Ingmar Björkman, Pawan Budhwar, Adam Smale and Jennie Sumelius

Introduction

A distinction often made in the literature is between comparative and international human resource management (HRM). While the former examines differences in HRM across countries and geographical regions the focus of the latter is on HRM in multinational corporations (MNCs) (e.g., Brewster, Sparrow and Vernon 2007). The aim here is to make a contribution at the intersection between these two strands of the literature: what characterizes HRM in Western MNC subsidiaries in China and India respectively and how can the observed features be explained? Two separate issues will be examined: first, to what extent do subsidiary practices resemble those found (i) in the foreign parent organizations ('MNC standardization') and (ii) in local firms ('localization'); and second, what role is played by the HR function in the MNC subsidiaries? Although a considerable amount of research has been carried out on HRM in foreign corporations in China and India and is gaining increasing scholarly attention, to the best of our knowledge this is the first comparative study of HRM in MNC units located in these two major emerging markets.

A number of studies have examined the HRM practices found in foreign-owned subsidiaries of MNCs (e.g., Rosenzweig and Nohria 1994; Hannon, Huang and Jaw 1995; Bae, Chen and Lawler 1998; Gunnigle, Murphy, Cleveland, Heraty and Morley 2002; Gooderham, Nordhaug and Ringdal 2006). Some work has also been published on this issue in the Chinese context, though mostly with a focus on Chinese-foreign joint ventures (e.g., Child 1994; Goodall and Warner 1997; Björkman and Lu 2001; Braun and Warner 2002; Gamble 2003; Yan 2003; Cooke 2004; Farley, Hoenig and Yang 2004; Walsh and Zhu 2007). We seem to have fewer insights about this issue in relation to Western MNCs in India, though some work has helped rectify this situation (e.g., As-Saber, Dowling and Liesch 1998). In this study, we examine the degree to which the HRM practices in MNC units in China and India are standardized and localized, and analyse factors hypothesized to influence subsidiary practices. Our research is on HRM practices concerning local managers and professionals, while rank-and-file employees are excluded. Issues that are predominately determined by local legislation – such as hours of work, annual paid time off work, and forms of job contract (Ferner 1997) – are also left outside the study. Instead, rather similar to previous studies on international HRM (e.g., Hannon, Huang and Jaw 1995), the following classical HRM practices are analyzed: recruitment, training, financial compensation and performance appraisal.

Compared to the considerable number of studies conducted on foreign subsidiary HRM practices, we have scant knowledge of the roles played by HR departments in MNC units overseas. This study will analyze the degree to which the HR departments play a strategic role (Ulrich 1997), and efforts will be made to identify determinants of the strength of this role in MNC subsidiaries in China and India.

The study is structured in the following way. We first review the literature to develop hypotheses concerning factors associated with subsidiary HRM practices and the role played by the HR department. The subsequent methods section describes the Chinese sample consisting of 87 subsidiaries and the Indian sample containing 83 units. The data were collected through personal interviews with HR and/or general managers in each subsidiary and qualitative data from the interviews help shed light on the findings from the statistical analyses reported in the following section. The study closes with a discussion of the implications of this study for HR professionals and researchers.

Literature review

Global standardization and local adaptation of HRM practices

Researchers interested in HRM practices in MNCs have typically examined subsidiary HRM practices in terms of their degree of global 'integration' or MNC 'standardization' versus local 'responsiveness' or 'local adaptation' (Prahalad and Doz 1987; see also Rosenzweig 2006), although it has also been argued that an MNC sometimes may blend global standardization with local responsiveness (Hannon et al. 1995; Taylor, Beechler and Napier 1996). In empirical studies, subsidiary managers have usually been asked to estimate the extent to which the HRM practices resemble those of local firms and the MNC parent organization, respectively. Studies of foreign-owned subsidiaries in the United States (Rosenzweig and Nohria 1994) and Taiwan (Hannon et al. 1995) showed that the HRM practices of MNCs overall were more localized than globally standardized, indicating stronger local than international institutional pressures. On the other hand, a study of Chinese-Western joint ventures revealed that the HRM practices were more similar to those of the MNC parent company than to those of local firms (Björkman and Lu 2001), perhaps in part because the study focused on professionals and managers rather than rank-and-file employees. In this study we will draw on this body of research as well as attempt to theorize about the HRM practices found in foreign-owned units when we develop hypotheses concerning factors explaining variances across subsidiaries in their degree of MNC standardization and local adaptation of HRM practices.

Institutional theory has been used to shed light on a wide variety of organizational phenomena (Scott 2001), including the HRM practices found across countries (Budhwar and Sparrow 2002) and in foreign subsidiaries and joint ventures (e.g., Rosenzweig and Nohria 1994; Ferner and Quantanilla 1998; Björkman and Lu 2001; Ferner, Almond and Colling 2005). Foreign-owned subsidiaries can be seen as being influenced both by institutional factors in the local environment and by international isomorphic processes, including pressures from the MNC parent company (Westney 1993). In the local context, the labor laws and regulations restrict the range of possible HRM practices, local managers have taken-for-granted views about good management practices that influence the policies and practices that they suggest for the subsidiary, strong local professional norms may exist concerning what constitutes appropriate corporate practices, and processes of institutionalization might also take place among MNCs in the focal country. Hence, cultural-cognitive and normative institutional processes (Scott 2001) enfolding in the local context may play important roles in explaining the HRM practices found in situations of uncertainty (DiMaggio and Powell 1983; Levitt and March 1988). At the same time, there may be coercive pressures from the MNC parent organization and taken-for-granted practices may be diffused through organizational actors to foreign subsidiaries (Westney 1993). Below, we will draw on institutional theory in our hypotheses development.

Establishment mode

There is ample evidence that foreign affiliates which have been established through greenfield operations are more isomorphic with their parents' operations than those of the operations of acquired units. A foreign owner is more likely to mould the operational characteristics of a new unit compared to changing ongoing operations. In the latter case, there may be considerable resistance to efforts at changing practices which over time may have become taken for granted as 'the way things are done' in the focal unit. These results are consistent with the view of institutionalization as a process entailing the creation of reality (Scott 1987). This has also been found to be the case for HRM practices in foreign subsidiaries (Rosenzweig and Nohria 1994) and joint ventures (Björkman and Lu 2001). Units established to continue existing locally-owned business operations, through outright acquisitions or through joint ventures with a local partner, are therefore likely to differ from units partly continuing existing activities (for example, only taking over some employees from the local partner) or, even more, wholly greenfield investments. Conversely, the localization of practices is likely to be strongest in MNC units that have been established based on existing operations.

Hypothesis 1a: Units that are established to continue ongoing local operations will have HRM practices that less closely resemble those of the MNC parent organization than units that do not continue ongoing operations.

Hypothesis 1b: Units that are established to continue ongoing local operations will have HRM practices that more closely resemble those of local corporations than units that do not continue ongoing operations.

Joint venture

Joint ventures have at least two parent organizations that may have divergent notions about what constitutes appropriate HRM practices. There may thus be pressure on the joint venture from both parents that in different ways may influence its operations (Shenkar and Zeira 1987). Central to the issue of localization and MNC standardization of HRM practices, the local parent company of the joint venture may play an important role as a conduit of the institutional pressures in the local environment (Rosenzweig and Nohria 1994). Local parent company managers may be under stronger coercive pressure from authorities, be more influenced by the practices in successful local firms that they would like to emulate, and be more intimately involved in local professional bodies where notions of appropriate (local) practices are likely to dominate. Therefore, compared with wholly-owned foreign subsidiaries we can expect joint ventures to exhibit a lower degree of MNC standardization and a higher degree of localization of practices. The results of a study of Chinese-Western joint ventures conducted in 1996 revealed a positive relationship between the percentage of equity held by the foreign parent company and the degree of MNC standardization of HRM practices (Björkman and Lu 2001) are consistent with this reasoning. Further, Braun and Warner (2002) reported that the HRM practices in China-based units where the MNC held a minority share were more locally adapted than those in foreign wholly-owned and majority-owned units and Farley, Hoenig and Yang (2004) found several significant differences in HRM practices between foreign subsidiaries and joint ventures. For these reasons we hypothesize as follows:

Hypothesis 2a: Joint ventures will have HRM practices that less closely resemble those of the MNC parent organization than will wholly-owned subsidiaries.

Hypothesis 2b: Joint ventures will have HRM practices that more closely resemble those of local corporations than will wholly-owned subsidiaries.

Background of the HR manager

The background of key managers is likely to influence the effects of isomorphic pulls from institutional actors on corporate practices. Managers who through their background are already embedded in a certain organizational field may serve as conduits of HRM practices viewed as appropriate in the focal field. For instance, managers recruited from local organizations are more likely to perceive local companies as referents and to take their practices for granted and/or value them as ends in themselves. They also tend to have been exposed to such HRM practices in their previous work life. Therefore, appointing the HR manager from a local corporation is likely to impact on the kind of practices suggested and implemented in the unit (Shenkar and Zeira 1987; Björkman and Lu 2001). Both coercive and mimetic pressures may come into play in this kind of situation, and we would expect such units to have HRM practices that are more similar to those of local organizations and more unlikely to introduce the foreign parent company's HRM practices. One of the cases discussed by Braun and Warner (2002) render some support to this conjecture in the context of foreign-owned units in China. The following hypotheses are therefore forwarded:

Hypothesis 3a: Units in which the HR manager has been recruited from a local organization will have HRM practices that less closely resemble those of the MNC parent organization than will units where the person has been recruited from an MNC.

Hypothesis 3b: Units in which the HR manager has been recruited from a local organization will have HRM practices that more closely resemble those of local corporations than will units where the person has been recruited from an MNC.

The number of expatriates

Expatriate managers also tend to have taken-for-granted views of the kind of HRM practices that are efficient. As a consequence, they may attempt to introduce patterns from their home organizations when functioning in overseas settings as they feel uncertain about what constitutes efficient practices in the new environment. Several studies have shown how home-and third-country expatriates often act as 'cultural carriers' in MNCs (Edström and Galbraith 1977). Therefore, as shown by Rosenzweig and Nohria (1994) in the context of MNC subsidiaries in the US, Myloni, Harzing and Mirza (2007) in a study on European and US MNCs in Greece, and Björkman and Lu (2001) in the context of Chinese-Western joint ventures, if a significant number of managers are expatriates from the MNC organization the unit is more likely to have HRM practices similar to that of the MNC's parent organization. Based on similar arguments we expect there to be an inverse relationship between the number of expatriates and the degree of localization.

Hypothesis 4a: Units with a higher number of expatriates will have HRM practices that more closely resemble those of the MNC parent organization than will units with few expatriates.

Hypothesis 4b: Units with a higher number of expatriates will have HRM practices that less closely resemble those of local corporations than will units with few expatriates.

MNC country HR manager

Western MNCs have already for some time viewed China and India as key for their global expansions, and these countries have been recipients of very considerable inward foreign direct investments. Partly as an outcome of the size of the markets and the considerable geographical distances, many MNCs have established multiple units in each of these countries. In China in particular, a considerable number of corporations have established China headquarters or 'centres' to manage their portfolios of subsidiaries, joint ventures and other activities in the country. The country headquarters tend among others to have senior managers in charge of particular functions for the country in question, including HRM (see Björkman and Lu 1999 for an analysis of their role in China). The existence of a country HR manager is likely also to influence HRM practices in each of the units found in the country. Country HR managers are more likely to be expatriates than are subsidiary HR managers, and even if they are not, then they are more likely to be in close contact with MNC headquarters and the global HR functions than are subsidiaries HR professionals with a more geographically restricted area of responsibility. Based on the arguments presented in conjunction with Hypotheses 3 and 4, we expect the existence of a country HR manager to have the following effects:

Hypothesis 5a: Units belonging to an MNC where there exists a country HR manager will have HRM practices that more closely resemble those of the MNC parent organization than will units where no such manager exists.

Hypothesis 5b: Units belonging to an MNC where there exists a country HR manager will have HRM practices that less closely resemble those of local corporations than will units where no such manager exists.

Host country

Based on theoretical reasoning and some albeit relatively limited empirical research (see Bae, Chen and Lawler 1998; Gooderham, Nordhaug and Ringdal 2006) we can expect there to be differences across host countries in the HRM practices found in MNC subsidiaries. Countries differ institutionally, among others in terms of labor laws and their implementation as well as in the extent to which there exist clear notions about what constitutes appropriate HRM practices. Theoretically we might expect there to be a negative relationship between the institutional distance between the MNC home country/region and the host country and the extent to which MNC practices are transferred to the country in question (cf. Kostova 1999). In other words, we might expect MNC units to have a higher level of MNC standardization in host countries that are close to the MNC home country. Using the same logic, the degree of resemblance of HRM practices in MNC units and in local corporations can be expected to be higher in host countries that are closer to the MNC home country than those that are distant.

Comparing India and China in terms of institutional distance, India would appear to be closer to the Western home countries of the MNCs included in our study. India has an institutional legacy as a British colony, has not been as secluded from Western influences as China was for much of the period after World War II, and English remains an official language in India (Budhwar 2001). Therefore, and although we are not aware of any empirical studies attempting to compare the institutional distances between Western countries and China and India, respectively, neither in general nor concerning HRM in particular, we will test the following hypotheses:

Hypothesis 6a: Units located in India will have HRM practices that more closely resemble those of the MNC parent organization than will units located in China.

Hypothesis 6b: Units located in India will have HRM practices that more closely resemble those of local corporations than will units located in China.

The role played by the HR department

Scholars have suggested various ways to classify the different roles played by the HR function in large firms (Tyson and Fell 1992; Ulrich 1997; Evans, Pucik and Barsoux 2002). Central to many of these models is a concern with the extent to which the department is involved in activities that are of strategic, long-term importance to the corporation. There is some indication that the HR function in some companies is becoming more strategically oriented than before (e.g., Hope-Hailey, Gratton, McGovern, Stiles and Truss 1997). Nonetheless, the available empirical evidence suggests that most HR functions still play a predominately tactical role (Truss, Gratton, Hope-Hailey, Stiles and Zaleska 2002) and that HR professionals have low status and influence in many companies (Berglund 2002). To what extent do subsidiary HR managers play a strategic role and which factors help explain differences across MNC units? As little empirical research has been conducted to date, we will mainly build on theoretical reasoning in the development of hypotheses below.

The hypotheses will be based on a crucial assumption, namely that the role played by the HR department on average is more strategic in Western corporations than in Chinese and Indian firms. This assumption is based on extensive research in China (e.g., Child 1994; Cooke 2004) indicating that Chinese firms in general do not have strategically oriented HR departments. On the other hand, a recent investigation about the nature of HRM systems in Indian-based business outsourcing organizations highlighted a strategic role played by their HR departments (for details see Budhwar, Luthar and Bhatnagar 2006). We would therefore expect MNC units that are under more institutional pressure from MNC headquarters located in a Western country to have HR departments with more important strategic roles than subsidiaries that are less so. From this line of argumentation, several hypotheses can be developed.

First, as argued earlier, units that have been established through greenfield operations are likely to be more isomorphic with their parents' operations than those of the operations of acquired units. Second, joint ventures are likely to be more similar to local corporations in their operations than are wholly foreign-owned subsidiaries. Third, HR managers who have been recruited from an MNC rather than from a local organization are more likely to try to play a strategic role personally and gain a strategic role for the department as a whole. Furthermore, HR managers with MNC experience may have a higher level of credibility with line managers when it comes to enacting such a role. Fourth, we would expect that expatriates are more likely to expect and accept an HR function that actively engages in activities of a strategic nature. Fifth, based on the argument that the institutional distance between India and Western countries is shorter than that between the latter and China we find reasons to believe that subsidiaries located in India would play more significant strategic roles than units located in China.

Therefore, we propose the following hypotheses:

Hypothesis 7: Units that are established to continue ongoing local operations will have HR departments playing a less strategic role than units that do not continue ongoing operations.

Hypothesis 8: Joint ventures will have HR departments playing a less strategic role than will wholly-owned subsidiaries.

Hypothesis 9: Units in which the HR manager has been recruited from a local organization will have HR departments playing a less strategic role than units in which the HR manager has been recruited from an MNC.

Hypothesis 10: Units with a higher number of expatriates will have HR departments playing a more strategic role than units with a smaller number of expatriates.

Hypothesis 11: Units located in China will have HR departments playing a less strategic role than units located in India.

Methods

Sample

A mixed methodology comprising a questionnaire survey as well as in-depth interviews was used to conduct this research in foreign firms operating in both China and India. The data were collected from 87 European-owned units in China during 2005 and 2006 and from 83 Western-owned subsidiaries in India during 2002 and 2003. Access to the foreign investment units was based first on lists of Western-owned units obtained from embassies and business councils, subsequent to which they were contacted and/or secured through the researchers' previous research undertakings and other contacts, and with snowballing techniques that utilized contacts of contacts. In China, the majority of the MNC units were located in the Shanghai and Beijing areas, whereas they were located in several locations in India, but with a majority in north India (Delhi and surrounding areas). While the Chinese data set only consisted of European-owned units, the observations from India also contained US firms. However, as there was no significant difference between the European and US sub-samples in India on the independent and dependent variables, the sub-samples were combined in the analyses reported below.

Data for the hypotheses testing were obtained through questionnaires completed during a personal visit to the focal company. During the visits, the respondents also provided qualitative data on the firm's HRM practices and elaborated on their experiences with these practices. The interviews lasted between forty-five minutes and more than two hours. The most senior HR specialist of the unit or someone who had good understanding of the HRM practices and the HR department provided data for the study. The most commonly used job designations of the respondents were HR manager/director and general manager/president. In 76 of the 87 units of the Chinese sample we obtained data from both the general managers/president and the HR/personnel manager whereby the average of their responses was used in the data analysis. As the same person provided data on all variables, following Podsakoff and Organ (1986) we used Harman's one-factor test to examine whether the data suffered from common method bias. The emergence of multiple factors (Podsakoff and Organ 1986) indicates that common method bias was not a serious problem in this study.[1]

Measures

Independent variables

During the interviews the respondents were asked whether their unit: (i) continued on-going operations undertaken by a local firm, (ii) partly continued on-going operations, (iii) started from scratch. Based on these answers a three-point scale for *Establishment mode* was created.

Data were collected on whether or not the HR/personnel manager had been transferred or recruited directly from the Chinese parent organization or from another Chinese organization to establish *HR manager from a local organization*.

The total *number of expatriates* was solicited.

We measured the *joint venture* variable by including a dummy variable where joint ventures were assigned the value 1 and non-joint ventures the value 0. Following Makino and Beamish (1998), we used an 80% equity share on the part of the MNC as a cut-off point between wholly-owned units and joint ventures.

The respondents were asked to indicate whether the MNC had a *country HR manager* (assigned the value 1) or not.

Dependent variables

MNC HRM standardization and local adaptation

During the interviews, the respondents were asked to answer the following questions concerning the degree to which the unit's HRM practices resembled those of the foreign parent organization: 'Compared to the MNC's home country operations, the [unit's HRM practices] are very similar (1) to very different (7)'. The same question was asked concerning the degree of similarity with the operations of local companies. The questions are similar to those used in previous studies (Rosenzweig and Nohria 1994; Hannon et al. 1995). The same question was asked for:

1. The methods and the criteria used when recruiting new local managers and professionals;
2. The amount and the content of management and professional training;
3. The methods and the criteria used to appraise managers' and professionals' performance; and

4. The methods and the criteria used to determine performance-based pay for managers and professionals.

We ran factor analyses of the MNC standardization and local adaptation items. Whereas all eight MNC standardization items loaded on the same factor, we had to omit two of the local adaptation items (both dealing with performance appraisal) before arriving at two-factor structure without cross-loadings amounting to 0.45 or above. For the statistical analyses, overall measures of the unit's MNC standardization and local adaptation were computed as the average of the respondents' estimate of the different HRM practices. In other words, the dependent variables were measured with multiple items, seven-point scales from 1 (very similar) to 7 (very different). The reliability measures for the constructs were .84 for MNC standardization and .79 for local adaptation.

HR department role

The construct consisted of the following three items adapted from Becker and Huselid (1998): To what extent does your company make an explicit (conscious) effort to align business and HR/personnel strategies? To what extent is the HR/personnel department involved in strategic planning processes? To what extent are HR/personnel managers viewed by those outside the function as partners in the management of business and agents for change? Cronbach's alpha for this scale was .83.

Control variables

We controlled for *subsidiary size* in the OLS regression analyses used to test the hypotheses. It is conventional in management studies to control for size, and Gupta and Govindarajan (2000) maintain that larger subsidiaries have a greater pool of resources dedicated to the creation of new knowledge. This means that the size of the subsidiary could positively influence the development of subsidiary HRM capabilities to play a strategic role. We measured subsidiary size by taking the natural logarithm of the number of employees in the subsidiary in order to dampen the high variation in size and achieve a more normal distribution for the variable.

A correlation matrix which also contains the means and standard deviations of the variables (Table 1) indicates no risk of multicollinearity.

Analyses and results

Table 2 shows the results of OLS regression analyses of the hypothesized models (Models 1-4).

Model 1 examines factors hypothesized to explain the variance in degree of MNC standardization of HRM practices. The model is significant at $p < .01$. Several of the hypotheses were supported, albeit the statistical significance levels varied. The number of expatriates was by far the strongest predictor of MNC standardization ($p < .001$, one-tailed test), supporting hypothesis 4a. The existence of a country HR manager was also significantly associated with a higher level of MNC standardization (at $p < .05$, one-tailed test), thus providing support for Hypothesis 5a. One of the hypotheses received only marginal support as the practices in foreign-owned units located in India (Hypothesis 6a) were found to be marginally more MNC standardized than those in China-based subsidiaries (both at $p < .1$, one-tailed tests). Hypotheses 1a, 2a and 3a must be rejected as neither the establishment mode nor the status as a joint venture seemed to have any impact

Table 1. Correlation matrix.

	Mean	STD	1	2	3	4	5	6	7	8	9	10
1. MNC HRM standardization	4.83	1.05	1									
2. Local HRM adaptation	3.97	0.94	-.09	1								
3. HR dept. role	3.74	0.80	.21**	.07	1							
4. Mode of establishment	2.49	0.77	.06	.02	.01	1						
5. Joint venture	0.27	0.45	.06	.08	.02	-.28**	1					
6. HR manager from local org.	0.35	0.48	.10	.09	-.08	-.02	.07	1				
7. Number of expatriates	7.48	22.3	.24**	-.05	.06	.04	.06	-.10	1			
8. Country HR manager	0.87	0.34	.15#	-.03	.11	-.10	.08	-.09	.10	1		
9. Host country (China = 1)	0.51	0.50	-.02	-.19*	-.37**	.03	-.15*	-.22**	.25**	-.03	1	
10. Subsidiary size (log.)	5.69	1.62	-.02	.10	.32**	-.04	.24**	.04	.22**	.25**	-.35**	1

Significance in two-tailed tests: # $p <= 0.10$; * $p <= 0.05$; ** $p <= 0.01$.

on the extent to which the MNCs had transferred their parent company practices to their units overseas. HR managers recruited from local organizations (Hypothesis 3a) were found to be marginally (at $p < .1$) related with a higher (rather than lower, as hypothesized) degree of MNC standardization. Finally, there seemed to be some tendency for larger subsidiaries to have a lower degree of MNC standardization.

Models 2 and 3 show two different OLS analyses with the level of resemblance of subsidiary HRM practices with those found in local corporations as the dependent variable. Model 2 contains all the independent variables and the control variable. However, as this model turned out to be non-significant we went through a process of backward selection of variables until we arrived at a statistically significant model (Model 3). In Model 3, only one variable was statistically significant: the host country location, with units located in India exhibiting a higher level of local adaptation of their HRM practices (at $p < .05$, single-tailed test).

Model 4, with HR department role as the dependent variable, was highly statistically significant. The strongest predictor of the level of strategic role played by the HR function was subsidiary location – MNC units in India were clearly viewed as playing more strategic roles than were the corresponding units in China, rendering support for Hypothesis 11. Consistent with Hypothesis 9, the background of the HR manager was strongly associated with the strength of the strategic partner role on the part of the HR department. The number of expatriates (Hypothesis 10) was marginally related with the HR department role (at $p < .0$, one-tailed test). Neither the establishment mode nor the ownership structure of the unit was found to be related with the perceived role of the HR department. There was a positive relationship between the size of the subsidiary and the extent to which the HR department played a strategic role.

Discussion

In this study of 170 Western-owned subsidiaries located in China and India, we have analyzed the extent to which the HRM practices associated with the local professionals and managerial-level employees resembled those of local firms versus those of the (main)

Table 2. Regressions on HRM practices (Models 1–3) and HR department role (Model 4).

	Model 1	Model 2	Model 3	Model 4
Independent variables	MNC Stand.	Localization	Localization	HR Dept. Strat. Role
Mode of establishment	.04	.04		− .00
Joint venture	− .07	.07	.05	− .08
HR manager from local org.	.13#	.04		− .15*
Number of expatriates	.28***	− .03		.10#
Country HR manager	.18*	− .04		
Host country (China = 1)	− .12#	− .14	− .18*	− .37***
Subsidiary size (log.)	− .15*	.05		.19**
R^2	.11	.04	.04	.21
Adjusted R^2	.07	.00	.03	.18
F	2.93**	1.06	3.23*	7.35***

Standardized regression coefficients are shown. Significance in one-tailed tests: # $p < = 0.10$; * $p < = 0.05$; ** $p < = 0.01$; *** $p < = 0.001$.

Western parent organization, and examined the degree to which the unit's HR department was perceived to play a strategic role.

Probably the most striking result of our study is the importance of the location. Western-owned units located in India tended to be perceived to be playing a considerably stronger strategic role than were China-based subsidiaries. Further, the HRM practices were more locally adapted (i.e. more similar to those of local corporations) and marginally less similar to those of the MNC parent corporation. These differences are consistent with the institutional theory arguments presented here. India has an institutional legacy as a British colony, has not been as secluded from Western influences as China was for much of the period after World War II, and English remains an important language in education and business (Budhwar 2001). These factors may at least partly facilitate the transfer of organizational practices from the parent corporation (cf. Kostova 1999; Kostova and Roth 2002) and tend to strengthen processes of convergence of HRM practices (Rowley, Benson and Warner 2004). It should be noted that an analysis of the changes in the degree of MNC standardization and local adaptation of HRM practices in Western subsidiaries in China during 1996–2006 revealed that both had increased significantly over this time period (Björkman, Smale, Sumelius, Suutari and Lu 2008). Thus, as the Indian data for this study were collected some three years before the Chinese data, it is likely that the 'real' differences between MNC subsidiaries in the two locations might be even more significant than reported here.

Two other factors helped explain a significant part of the variance in the HRM practices and the HR department role. First, the background of the HR manager seems to matter for the role played by the HR department. At least two explanations are possible. Viewed from an institutional theory perspective, HR managers are likely to enact what they have been exposed to in their past and refrain from supporting unfamiliar practices and roles – thus, persons recruited from local organizations are less likely to adopt HR department roles from the MNC parent company. However, it is also conceivable that the roles played by the HR function are contingent on the expectations held by top and line managers – key actors in the role set (Katz and Kahn 1978) of the HR organization – towards the department. Such expectations may at least partly be an outcome of the perceived competency of the HR managers, with managers being recruited from other units of the focal MNC or other (leading) MNCs being perceived as more competent and thus in a better position to enact a strategic role. Some of the comments made by both HR managers and general managers support this interpretation.

Second, the higher the number of expatriates, the more similar the HRM practices were to those of the MNC parent companies. This finding is consistent with those obtained in previous research on foreign subsidiaries in the US (Rosenzweig and Nohria 1994) and Chinese-Western joint ventures (Björkman and Lu 2001), and corroborate general observations in the literature concerning the crucial role played by expatriates in the transfer of practices and (embedded) knowledge in MNCs. The amount of expatriates was also (marginally) positively related with the perceived role of the HR department. It is conceivable that the expatriates had higher expectations vis-à-vis the strategic contribution of the HR function, and that these expectations were reflected both in the competencies of the people working in the HR department and in the tasks that they were undertaking.

Implications

Our research suggests that staffing decisions are of crucial importance for foreign subsidiary HRM practices and the roles played by its HR department. The choice of HR manager seems both to influence the strategic role played by the HR department in foreign-owned subsidiaries and the kind of HRM practices that are enacted in the unit; HR managers recruited from an MNC are more likely to be associated with a more strategic role on the part of the HR department and (albeit marginally) a higher degree of standardized HRM practices. This study also indicates that the extensive use of expatriates often leads to the use of HRM practices from MNC headquarters (though marginally) and the HR department playing a more strategic role.

When considering the results of the study, some limitations of the present research should be noted which at the same time suggest possible avenues for future research. First, while the sample from India consisted of both European and US units the Chinese sample contained only European subsidiaries. Second, in accordance with the technique used in many previous studies (Rosenzweig and Nohria 1994; Hannon et al. 1995), the dependent variables MNC standardization and local adaptation were operationalized in a relatively simplistic manner using perceptual data. Indications of actual practices in the subsidiaries and in the MNC parent organization and in local corporations would arguably give better measures of the degree of resemblance of HRM practices. Third, data were in roughly half of the sampled units collected from one respondent. The systematic use of multiple respondents would have further increased the validity of the data. Fourth, the study did not examine the effects of MNC home country nationality on subsidiary HRM. Fifth, we built our research on institutional theory only, leaving out, among others, cultural factors (see e.g., Aycan 2005; Brewster, Sparrow and Vernon 2007) and possible explanations related to the resource-based view and resource dependency theory (cf. Myloni, Harzing and Mirza 2007) as they were outside the scope of the study. Finally, there tend to be differences in the degree to which MNCs standardize different HRM practices in their foreign units (cf., Rosenzweig and Nohria 1994). The present study, like most previous research on HRM practices in foreign-owned units, has concentrated on HRM practices as a whole.

An interesting topic for future research would be to analyse managers' perceptions of efficient HRM practices and how these perceptions change over time. On the one hand, in a situation where few foreign managers were certain about the kind of practices that would be efficient in China and India, it appears that many looked to their own parent organizations for models of HRM practices that they could implement in their Chinese operations. Hence, extensive efforts at transferring Western home-country HRM practices were found in many companies. Research is needed on the effectiveness of the different HRM practices, including detailed analyses of different ways to implement a certain practice in the Chinese and Indian settings. The present study has provided a snap-shot of factors that in a cross-sectional analysis appear to be associated with the HR department playing a strategic role in their units. Additional research is warranted on the processes through which subsidiary HR departments may enhance the strategic roles that they are playing.

Conclusions

To summarize, the aim of this research was to shed light on HRM in foreign-owned units located in China and India. The results indicate clear differences between HRM practices and the role played by HR departments in Western-owned units in China and India, and suggest that the use of expatriates and the background of the HR managers are important determinants of subsidiary HRM.

Note

1. Although we made sure that the respondent was the firm's most knowledgeable about its HRM practices and most of the firms were small-to medium-sized, and a recent study using single respondents reported acceptable degrees of rating agreements in their sample firms with multiple responses (Datta, Guthrie and Wright 2005), the use of one respondent per firm may still be associated with measurement errors (Wright, Gardner, Moynihan and Park 2001). Conducting longitudinal research and/or gathering data from multiple informants (as we did in some 5% of the companies) would help researchers avoid this common method bias problem; the former would also corroborate the direction of causality which always is a problematic issue in cross-sectional studies.

References

As-Saber, S.N., Dowling, P.J., and Liesch, P.W. (1998), "The Role of Human Resource Management in International Joint Ventures: A Study of Australian-Indian Joint Ventures," *International Journal of Human Resource Management*, 9, 751–766.

Aycan, Z. (2005), "The Interplay between Cultural and Institutional/structural Contingencies in Human Resource Management Practices," *International Journal of Human Resource Management*, 16, 1083–1119.

Bae, J., Chen, S.-J., and Lawler, J.J. (1998), "Variations in Human Resource Management in Asian Countries: MNC Home-country and Host-country Effects," *International Journal of Human Resource Management*, 9, 653–670.

Becker, B.E., and Huselid, M.A. (1998), "High Performance Work Systems and Firm Performance: A Synthesis of Research and Managerial Implications," *Research in Personnel and Human Resources Journal*, 16, 1, 53–101.

Berglund, J. (2002), "De otillräckliga: En studie av personalspecialisternas kamp för erkännande och status," unpublished doctoral thesis, EFI, Stockholm School of Economics.

Björkman, I., and Lu, Y. (1999), "A Corporate Perspective on the Management of Human Resources in China," *Journal of World Business*, 34, 16–25.

Björkman, I., and Lu, Y. (2001), "Institutionalization and Bargaining Power Explanations of HRM Practices in International Joint Ventures: The Case of Chinese–Western Joint Ventures," *Organization Studies*, 22, 491–512.

Björkman, I., Smale, A., Sumelius, J., Suutari, V., and Lu, Y. (2008), "Changes in Institutional Context and MNC Operations in China: Subsidiary HRM Practices in 1996 versus 2006," *International Business Review*, forthcoming.

Braun, W., and Warner, M. (2002), "Strategic Human Resource Management in Western Multinationals in China: The Differentiation of Practices across Different Ownership Forms," *Personnel Review*, 31, 553–579.

Brewster, B., Sparrow, P., and Vernon, G. (2007), *International Human Resource Management*, London: CIPD.

Budhwar, P. (2001), "Doing Business in India," *Thunderbird International Business Review*, 43, 549–568.

Budhwar, P., and Sparrow, P. (2002), "An Integrative Framework for Determining Cross-national Human Resource Management Practices," *Human Resource Management Review*, 12, 377–403.

Budhwar, P., Luthar, H., and Bhatnagar, J. (2006), "Dynamics of HRM Systems in BPOs Operating in India," *Journal of Labour Research*, 27, 339–360.

Child, J. (1994), *Management in China during the Age of Reform*, Cambridge: Cambridge University Press.

Cooke, F.L. (2004), "Foreign Firms in China: Modelling HRM in a Toy Manufacturing Corporation," *Human Resource Management Journal*, 14, 3, 31–52.

Datta, D.K., Guthrie, J.P., and Wright, P.M. (2005), "Human Resource Management and Labour Productivity: Does Industry Matter?," *Academy of Management Journal*, 48, 135–145.

DiMaggio, P., and Powell, W. (1983), "The Iron Cage Revisited: Institutional Isomorphism and Collective Rationality in Organizational Fields," *American Sociological Review*, 48, 147–160.

Edström, A., and Galbraith, J. (1977), "Transfers of Managers as a Coordination and Control Strategy in Multinational Organizations," *Administrative Science Quarterly*, 22, 248–263.

Evans, P., Pucik, V., and Barsoux, J.-L. (2002), *The Global Challenge: Frameworks for International Human Resource Management*, Boston, MA: McGraw-Hill.

Farley, J.U., Hoenig, S., and Yang, J.Z. (2004), "Key Factors Influencing HRM Practices of Overseas Subsidiaries in China's Transition Economy," *International Journal of Human Resource Management*, 15, 688–704.

Ferner, A. (1997), "Country of Origin Effects and HRM in Multinational Companies," *Human Resource Management Journal*, 7, 1, 19–37.

Ferner, A., Almond, P., and Colling, T. (2005), "Institutional Theory and the Cross-national Transfer Of Employment Policy: The Case of 'Workforce Diversity' in US Multinationals," *Journal of International Business Studies*, 36, 304–321.

Ferner, A., and Quantanilla, J. (1998), "Multinationals, National Business Systems and HRM: the Enduring Influence of National Identity or a Process of 'Anglo-Saxonization'," *International Journal of Human Resource Management*, 9, 710–731.

Gamble, J. (2003), "Transferring Human Resource Practices from the UK to China: The Limits and Potential for Convergence," *International Journal of Human Resource Management*, 14, 369–387.

Goodall, K., and Warner, M. (1997), "Human Resources in Sino-foreign Joint Ventures," *International Journal of Human Resource Management*, 8, 569–594.

Gooderham, P., Nordhaug, O., and Ringdal, K. (2006), "National Embeddedness and Calculative Human Resource Management in US Subsidiaries in Europe and Australia," *Human Relations*, 59, 1491–1513.

Gunnigle, P., Murphy, K., Cleveland, J.N., Heraty, N., and Morley, M. (2002), "Localization in Human Resource Management: Comparing American and European Multinational Corporations," *Advances in International Management*, 14, 259–284.

Gupta, A.K., and Govindarajan, V. (2000), "Knowledge Flows within Multinational Corporations," *Strategic Management Journal*, 21, 473–496.

Hannon, J., Huang, I.-C., and Jaw, B.-S. (1995), "International Human Resource Strategy and its Determinants: The Case of Subsidiaries in Taiwan," *Journal of International Business Studies*, 26, 531–554.

Hope-Hailey, V., Gratton, L., McGovern, P., Stiles, P., and Truss, C. (1997), "A Chameleon Function? HRM in the 1990s," *Human Resource Management Journal*, 7, 3, 5–18.

Katz, D., and Kahn, R.L. (1978), *The Social Psychology of Organizations* (2nd ed.), New York: John Wiley.

Kostova, T. (1999), "Transnational Transfer of Strategic Organizational Practices: A Contextual Perspective," *Academy of Management Review*, 24, 308–324.

Kostova, T., and Roth, K. (2002), "Adoption of an Organizational Practice by Subsidiaries of Multinational Corporations: Institutional and Relational Effects," *Academy of Management Journal*, 45, 215–233.

Levitt, B., and March, J.G. (1988), "Organizational Learning," *Annual Review of Sociology*, 14, 319–440.

Makino, S., and Beamish, P.W. (1998), "Performance and Survival of Joint Ventures with Non-conventional Ownership Structures," *Journal of International Business Studies*, 29, 797–818.

Myloni, B., Harzing, A.-W., and Mirza, H. (2007), "The Effect of Corporate-level Organizational Factors on the Transfer of Human Resource Management Practices: European and US MNCs and their Greek Subsidiaries," *International Journal of Human Resource Management*, 18, 2057–2074.

Podsakoff, P.M., and Organ, D. (1986), "Self-reports in Organizational Research: Problems and Prospects," *Journal of Management*, 12, 531–544.

Prahalad, C.K., and Doz, Y. (1987), *The Multinational Mission: Balancing Global Demands and Global Vision*, New York: Free Press.

Rosenzweig, P.M. (2006), "The Dual Logic Behind International Human Resource Management: Pressures for Global Integration and Local Responsiveness," in *Handbook of Research in International Resource Management*, eds. G. Stahl and I. Björkman, Cheltenham: Edward Elgar, pp. 36–48.

Rosenzweig, P.M., and Nohria, N. (1994), "Influences on Human Resource Management Practices in Multinational Corporations," *Journal of International Business Studies*, 25, 229–251.

Rowley, C., Benson, J., and Warner, M. (2004), "Towards an Asian Model of Human Resource Management? A Comparative Analysis of China, Japan and South Korea," *International Journal of Human Resource Management*, 15, 917–933.

Scott, R. (1987), "The Adolescence of Institutional Theory," *Administrative Science Quarterly*, 32, 493–511.

Scott, W.R. (2001), *Institutions and Organizations* (2nd ed.), Thousand Oaks, CA: Sage.

Shenkar, O., and Zeira, Y. (1987), "Human Resource Management in International Joint Ventures: Directions for Research," *Academy of Management Review*, 12, 546–557.

Taylor, S., Beechler, S., and Napier, M. (1996), "Toward an Integrative Model of Strategic International Human Resource Management," *Academy of Management Review*, 21, 959–985.

Truss, C., Gratton, L., Hope-Hailey, V., Stiles, P., and Zaleska, J. (2002), "Paying the Piper: Choice and Constraint in Change of HR Functional Roles," *Human Resource Management Journal*, 12, 39–63.

Tyson, S., and Fell, A. (1992), *Evaluating the Personnel Function* (2nd ed.), Cheltenham Nelson Thornes.

Ulrich, D. (1997), *Human Resource Champions: The Next Agenda for Adding Value and Delivering Results*, Boston, MA: Harvard Business School Press.

Walsh, J., and Zhu, Y. (2007), "Local Complexities and Global Uncertainties: A Study of Foreign Ownership and Human Resource Management in China," *International Journal of Human Resource Management*, 18, 249–267.

Westney, E. (1993), "Institutionalization Theory and the Multinational Corporation," in *Organization Theory and the Multinational Corporation*, eds. S. Ghoshal and E. Westney, New York: St. Martin's Press, pp. 53–76.

Wright, P.M., Gardner, T.M., Moynihan, L.M., and Park, H.J. (2001), "Measurement Error in Research on Human Resources and Firm Performance: Additional Data and Suggestions for Future Research," *Personnel Psychology*, 54, 875–901.

Yan, Y. (2003), "A Comparative Study of Human Resource Management Practices in International Joint Ventures: The Impact of National Origin," *International Journal of Human Resource Management*, 14, 487–510.

INDEX